101 Best Resumes
to Sell Yourself

101 Best Resumes to Sell Yourself

JAY A. BLOCK, IJCTC, CPRW

McGraw-Hill

New York   Chicago   San Francisco   Washington, D.C.   Auckland   Bogotá
Caracas   Lisbon   London   Madrid   Mexico City   Milan
Montreal   New Delhi   San Juan   Singapore
Sydney   Tokyo   Toronto

McGraw-Hill

*A Division of The **McGraw·Hill** Companies*

Gen Fund 1/04 - $13⁰⁰

1 2 3 4 5 6 7 8 9 0   QPD/QPD   0 9 8 7 6 5 4 3 2

ISBN 0-07-138552-5

Printed and bound by Quebecor / Dubuque.

McGraw-Hill books are available at special quantity discounts to use as premiums and sales promotions, or for use in corporate training sessions. For more information, please write to the Director of Special Sales, Professional Publishing, McGraw-Hill, Two Penn Plaza, New York, NY 10121-2298. Or contact your local bookstore.

This book is printed on recycled, acid-free paper containing a minimum of 50% recycled, de-inked fiber.

To Ellen: My eternal soul mate.

Contents

Foreword

I have had the good fortune to know Jay Block, and the honor to call him my friend, since 1989. Through the years, I have had the privilege of watching him take his place as one of the career industry's most innovative thinkers and contributors. He is always challenging traditional and accepted ways of thinking to develop new concepts and approaches to inspire other people to achieve career success. It is little wonder, then, that he is a leading international author and speaker in this field.

The book you now hold is unlike any other. Jay's "Organizational Message Chart" (OMC) and "Showcase Format" for presenting a resume have already been acclaimed by professional resume writers and career coaches throughout North America. In a series of certification workshops Jay has presented since 2000, veteran colleagues in the career field have heralded this groundbreaking information and now use this new approach with their own clients.

And here's a little secret: The "Presidential Message" that Jay explains in developing the Organizational Message Chart isn't limited to just a resume or job search. I now find myself looking for the "presidential" core message in all facets of my business and personal life...both in the messages that I need to communicate, and also in evaluating the information presented to me by others.

In short, this is a book that you will use...and that will provide an ongoing benefit long after you've dog-eared the pages and loaned it to friends, colleagues, and family members. One last suggestion: Be sure to read the text—as many people purchase these books simply to replicate a sample resume. The text will change how you think about resumes and the job search process itself!

Frank Fox
Founder & Executive Director
Professional Association of
Resume Writers & Career Coaches
St. Petersburg, Florida

Acknowledgments

I have been in the employment and career industry since 1986 and have met so many wonderful, loving, and supporting people who have helped me climb the ladder of success. Certainly my family has been behind me all the way, including my two sons Ian and Ryco. I also want to thank my editors Susan Clarey, Michelle Howry, and Sally Glover, who worked hard to make this book possible.

And to all my friends and colleagues in the career coaching field who, over the years, have been pillars for me to lean on—I say, "thank you." You have all challenged me to grow and to constantly expand my thinking. At the risk of leaving some out, I want to especially thank Walt Schuette, John Suarez, Alesia Benedict, Wendy Enelow, Jerry Bills, Debra O'Reilly, Don Orlando, Makini Siwatu, Wayne Gonyea, Louise Kursmark, Mark Berkowitz, Martin Buckland, and all the dedicated PARWCC members who contributed their fine work to my past books.

A special thanks goes out to my dear friend Frank Fox, who had the foresight and determination to start PARWCC some 12 years ago and created a forum for resume and career coaches to share ideas and further the ideals of the employment industry. I also want to thank Michael Betrus, who has coauthored four books with me, in addition to two more titles that we are currently working on. The journey has been thrilling and highly rewarding.

Finally, I want to thank the thousands of clients I have worked with over the years who have shared their feedback and have allowed me to improve my skills in the art of strategic resume development and career coaching.

Introduction

Some years back, I made the conscious decision that the best way I could help people improve the quality of their lives would be by writing resumes and becoming a job coach. I could integrate my marketing and writing skills with my passion to be a force for positive change in people's lives. By helping people market and maximize their skills, abilities, qualifications, and desires, I came to approach the resume business much like a Madison Avenue marketing professional approached hers. In my case, I help package and promote the best product on the planet: people! It didn't take long for the resume style and format I developed to catch on. Not only did hundreds and hundreds of my clients secure the jobs they sought at the salary they wanted, but other notable resume professionals and authors began to emulate this new style. A whole new industry was evolving.

I was the contributing cofounder of the Professional Association of Resume Writers and Career Coaches, launched in 1990. I chaired the Resume Certification Committee that developed the first international certification standards for resume writing professionals. I began speaking to various groups and associations on resume and job search issues around the country and was the Keynote Speaker at the 1994 Annual Convention of the Professional Association of Resume Writers and Career Coaches in Las Vegas. I started writing books and CD ROM programs—all this to call attention to what's wrong with the way we are taught to write resumes and secure gainful, meaningful employment. All too often, we conform to ambiguous standards, dumb rules, and humiliating, sometimes fear-inducing job search tactics that have proven—decade after decade—not to work.

> *Too often, we conform to ambiguous standards, dumb rules, and humiliating, often fear-inducing job search tactics that have proven, decade after decade, not to work.*

Consider this: We work hard to get good grades in school in order to distinguish ourselves from others and to see how high we can climb the ladder of achievement. Why then, when it comes to the resume writing process—a process that offers us the opportunity to distinguish ourselves from others and to see how high we can climb the ladder of career achievement—do we "blend?" If Pepsi looked like Coke, if Dell looked like Gateway, and if Bayer looked like Anacin—how would the public differentiate between competing brands? If our resumes and our job search strategies are identical to everyone else's, how can we possibly differentiate ourselves from the pack? The answer is that we can't and we don't—and as a result, up to 87 percent of all working Americans are uninspired with their jobs and careers.

YOUR MARKETING STRATEGY IS EVERYTHING

No matter how good a product is, you will consistently get poor and disappointing results if you use a flawed marketing strategy to sell it. If Coca Cola used rap music as a strategy to sell its products to senior citizens, it wouldn't work. It would be a poor strategy, and the results would be disappointing at best! If you used the same marketing strategy to sell a product in New York City as you used to sell it in Nashville, it wouldn't work either. You need separate strategies for different and distinct markets. Yet, if you ask most job seekers what their marketing strategies are for developing their resumes and promoting themselves to prospective employers, guess how they'd answer? You're right: They'd ask, "What strategy?"

TAKE CONTROL OVER YOUR CAREER

The purpose of this book is to give you permission and groundbreaking strategies to take back power and control over your resume and your career. You will learn to package, market, and promote—in a word, *sell*—yourself in your resume and job search campaign. I will provide you with the most up-to-date, cutting-edge ideas, trade secrets, intelligence information, and winning philosophies of resume writing and job seeking to enhance the quality of your career and the quality of your life.

Most athletes love their careers, and so can you. Most entertainers get a thrill out of their vocation, and so can you. Most educators and social service professionals derive deep, inner satisfaction from their work and so can you. Success, happiness, and career fulfillment are not reserved for a fortunate few. Success, happiness, and career fulfillment is a process that must be pursued—but most people haven't been introduced to the process.

YOUR RESUME: THE CENTERPIECE OF YOUR JOB SEARCH CAMPAIGN

In this book, I will introduce you to the process of developing highly effective resumes that support your overall career design and job search campaign. Your resume must work in concert with all other job search components. For instance, if you are using executive recruiters or employment agencies as your primary marketing strategy, your resume will look completely different than if your principal strategy is to conduct an Internet job search, posting your resume on the Web. Your resume, job search strategy, references, and job interview must all dance to the same music. Your references and reference letters must support and "bear witness" to the information you provide on your resume. You must be able to comfortably and compellingly defend the resume in an interview setting. What you will soon discover—and what most people fail to understand—is that when produced properly, the resume is the centerpiece of the entire job search campaign.

Thank you for investing in this book, but more importantly, thanks for investing in you. Turn the pages, and let it change your life!

—Jay A. Block

101 Best Resumes
to Sell Yourself

Part I

HOW TO USE A RESUME TO SELL YOURSELF

1

Writing Resumes That Sell Your Value to Employers

This is a resume book that can change your life. How is that possible? Because this book introduces two groundbreaking ways to create resumes that set the stage so you can land the job you've prepared so hard to get—at the salary you deserve. They are:

1. The Organizational Message Chart: a breakthrough tool for preparing resumes
2. The Showcase Format: an exciting way to promote your value to prospective employers

When you put these powerful concepts to work, you'll find that securing top jobs at top pay will become the norm, not the exception. And when you're working at a job that has purpose, meaning, and financial rewards, the satisfaction you get from work can change your whole life!

A BETTER WAY TO THINK ABOUT RESUMES

Over the past decade, the career/employment industry has significantly expanded and matured. Well-respected journalists, authors, resume-writing professionals, career coaches, and other industry experts have offered new and evolving information on resume development. We are slowly getting away from the old, antiquated notions of chronological versus functional resumes, or the one-page rule versus the two-page rule. Today, career coaches and writers are talking about achievement-focused resumes, keyword resumes, and executive portfolios. This transformation has been important and refreshing. However, with all the progress we've made in the area of resume development as a career design and job search tool, most people continue to distribute resumes that "undersell" their true worth, and accept jobs below their abilities and earning potentials. With all the advancement we've made, however, there remained a critical component missing from the resume-writing process that continued to hinder the job search process, leaving most of us frustrated in our careers.

THE ORGANIZATIONAL MESSAGE CHART

That missing component is The Organizational Message Chart®. The Organizational Message Chart (OMC) is a model that changes the way we write resumes and prepare for interviews. Some of the world's best-known resume and employment professionals agree that it is an innovative and powerfully effective tool to prepare candidates for the job search process with confidence. The Professional Association of Resume Writers and Career Coaches offers a certification program with the Organizational Message Chart as its nucleus. Most importantly, hundreds and hundreds of people have achieved career success they never dreamed possible using this powerful tool.

> *The Organizational Message Chart is a powerful tool that changes the way to write resumes and prepare for interviews.*

The Organizational Message Chart offers a whole new way to market and sell yourself to prospective employers. It differs from standard resume models in several important ways. The traditional chronological format simply indicates employment history and basic responsibilities in chronological order beginning with the most recent job and working backwards. It simply communicates a work biography and is often of very little value to the reader. The functional format—highlighting skills and achievements first, followed by a mere listing of employment—all too often turns out to be a functional disaster. Survey after survey shows that most hiring professionals dislike this format because it is disjointed and includes even fewer value messages than the chronological format. A combination format is just that—a hybrid between the chronological and functional formats that simply communicates skills, employment, and employment responsibilities. And the curriculum vitae format is a unique format that lists information—without any commentary such as responsibilities or achievements. The Organizational Message Chart approach, on the other hand, is a methodology for identifying *one's value* to a prospective employer and developing powerful messages that, based on that value, tell prospective employers how you can benefit them and why they should hire you.

HOW RESUMES THAT EMPHASIZE YOUR VALUE HELP YOU "SELL" YOURSELF TO EMPLOYERS

A powerful and effective resume communicates value. The resume must cry out to prospective employers and declare how you can contribute to them, how you can solve their problems, and how you can meet their organizational needs. In short, the resume is your marketing tool of first resort, because it "packages" your skills, abilities, and experience and sells them to prospective employers.

A resume that communicates your value—I call it the *value-based resume*—is benefits oriented, just as a good marketing campaign zeroes in on the benefits of a product or service to a prospective purchaser. A value-based resume communicates how you will benefit a company when hired. Unlike a traditional resume, it answers the question, "Why should I hire you?" Sure, hiring managers care about your skills, abilities, talents, employment history, and education. But what they care about first and foremost is, "What overall value do you represent to me and my company?"

Today's employers are interested in and pay only for value. You don't get paid for bringing your *need* for a job to the marketplace, and you don't get paid for the hours you work. You get paid for bringing your *value* to the marketplace and for the value that you add to the company during the hours you spend there. The guy who earns $100 an hour is ten times more valuable to the marketplace than the guy who makes $10 an hour.

This book shows how to communicate your value to an employer in your resume and, by extension, your job interview. Your value-based resume matches your talents, skills, qualifications, and abilities with prospective employers who have a need for your *labor assets*.

Throw Out the Old Rules

There aren't any set-in-stone, ironclad rules for writing value-based resumes—except that the resume must effectively communicate value. Rules mean conformity. How can you distinguish yourself from everyone else if you look like everyone else? To attract outstanding opportunities, you must present yourself as an outstanding candidate—and in order to do that effectively, you must *stand out* on your resume! How you do that is determined by strategic thought and creative implementation, not by following the rules that everyone else is following.

21 Guidelines for Creating Value-Based Resumes

While there are no ironclad rules in writing value-based resumes, there are a number of guidelines to follow. Chief among them, however, is this: You must powerfully promote and communicate your value to a prospective employer. How you effectively achieve that is ultimately up to you. To assist you, I have provided 21 guidelines below, a selection of time-tested, proven tips that have worked time and time again. In the final analysis, however, you'll need to decide which guidelines best serve your resume and job-search strategy.

Guideline #1: Make sure your resume is free of all spelling, grammatical, or typographical errors.

Guideline #2:	Keep the resume as brief as possible without compromising your value messages. 1–2 pages is preferable, but there are exceptions.
Guideline #3	Think bottom line. How can you improve a company's economics?
Guideline #4:	Think goals. What can you do to further the achievement of organizational goals?
Guideline #5:	Think about ways to *exceed expectations*, such as noting that you made more sales than you were projected to make or serviced more customers than required.
Guideline #6:	Choose your words with care. Make them powerful and compelling, and include keywords—that is, accepted language in your industry.
Guideline #7	Remember that your resume is a sales tool. Don't write an autobiography or memoir.
Guideline #8:	Use strategy, not gimmicks, like hiding dates or leaving them out completely.
Guideline #9:	Test-market your resume before using it. Ask for feedback from people whose opinions you respect.
Guideline #10:	Make the format "reader friendly." Key points should be easy to find, easy to read, and readily accessible.
Guideline #11:	Show your human side. Capture the emotion behind your background and accomplishments.
Guideline #12:	Don't be afraid to blow your own horn. Remember, your competition will!
Guideline #13:	Don't use long paragraphs, as they are difficult to read. Use short paragraphs and bullets.
Guideline #14:	Don't include salary or other information not relevant to your career objective.
Guideline #15:	Separate responsibilities from achievements in the employment section. For instance, responsibilities can be outlined within paragraphs but achievements can be bulleted to stand out. In most cases, it's not what you did but how well you did it that determines hireability.
Guideline #16:	Don't shortchange yourself when describing your past achievements and bottom-line results. Achievements determine hireability.
Guideline #17:	Know your audience before writing your resume, and target your resume to your audience.
Guideline #18:	Avoid fluff. *Fluff* means general information that almost everyone uses. For example, a people person, good communication skills, or able to work with people at all levels. Many times, fluff is contained in the resume as character traits (hard-working, energetic, and results-oriented). Fluff does not distinguish you from other candidates.

Guideline #19: Put yourself in the shoes of the person who is hiring you. What would he or she want to see on your resume?

Guideline #20: Identify and clearly document your signature talents, such as saving money, adding to sales, improving productivity, or enhancing efficiency. These have high-impact value.

Guideline #21: Wear your resume with pride, confidence, and certainty. When you do, you'll interview well.

The Six "Ps" for Creating the Value-based Resume

Apart from these 21 general guidelines, there are six key principles to keep in mind when creating a value-based resume. These six Ps take their cue from the principles that underlie sales and marketing campaigns.

1. Purpose
2. Packaging
3. Positioning
4. Punch
5. Personality
6. Professionalism

Purpose

The first principle in creating a value-based resume is to understand clearly and to articulate its purpose. All too often, a job candidate isn't getting the results she wants because what she wants is not personally meaningful, inspiring, exciting, or even well defined. If you don't know where you're going on vacation, how will you ever know what to pack in the suitcase? Likewise, if you don't know specifically what you want to do or where you are heading in your job search, how do you know what to put on the resume?

One of the greatest gifts we have ever been given is the gift of free will—the freedom to choose, the freedom to aspire! If you're unsure of your career direction, you should embark on a crusade to find out. It's time to begin the process of self-exploration. You can use the wisdom of a career counselor, the skill of a career coach, or take advantage of any number of books, audiocassette programs, and videos. Purpose creates urgency, and if there is little purpose or desire behind your career objective, you won't get far.

A strong resume begins with purpose and a career destination that moves you to want to act in a big way. We must know what we want and want what we know, for if we don't know what we want, we'll be destined to settle for what we get.

> "When a man does not know what harbor he is making for, no wind is the right wind."
> —Seneca

Packaging

Toilet paper is better packaged and promoted than 99 percent of the resumes circulating out there. They change the name to bathroom tissue and get a salesman to try to stop people from "Squeezing the Charmin." While companies spend countless hours and dollars to package and sell their products, job seekers continue to send out resumes promoting themselves on white paper with black ink, all saying about the same thing using the same format.

What's wrong with this picture? A recent survey from Burke Marketing, hired by Robert Half International, one of the largest personnel placement organizations in the United States, estimated that if we placed every resume in circulation today end-to-end, they would circle the equator 26 times! That's 650,000 miles of resumes, all of them out in the job market competing for attention.

Packaging is critical to any marketing endeavor. Conformity is a recipe for disaster, and uniqueness and individuality are the ingredients for success. An outstanding resume packages and presents your credentials in a way that makes you stand out from the crowd. Choosing paper stock, graphics, desktop publishing, type fonts, and creative presentations are part of the resume packaging process. I don't suggest bright pink paper, bells, whistles, and resumes that play music (unless such features match your career objective perfectly). Instead, choose a packaging scheme that is tastefully and professionally distinctive. High-quality paper, clear and legible typeface, and even a logo or appropriate graphic would help distinguish your resume from all others.

Good packaging also means high quality and attention to detail. No matter how good the product, you probably wouldn't buy it if the package were damaged or broken. By the same token, no matter how strong your employment credentials, they are useless if your resume is sloppy, disorganized, and cumbersome to read. Prospective employers throw away poorly presented resumes.

Positioning

Good positioning of information means organizing your resume so that the format and the flow is "reader friendly" and emphasizes your value. Hiring professionals spend, on average, between 15 and 20 seconds reviewing a resume to determine if they want to keep on reading. That means you have only 15–20 seconds to make an initial positive impact on a prospective employer.

Hiring professionals spend, on average, between 15 and 20 seconds reviewing a resume to determine if they want to keep on reading.

The *showcase format* is a high-impact way to do just that. It's a powerful tool to *showcase your value quickly and clearly to prospective employers.* This book shows how to create a special showcase section on your resume to control the reader's eyes and convey the critical information that leads to an interview.

Punch

This "P" is crucial. When you deliver punch, you are communicating core messages about yourself that prospective employers want to see. In marketing terms, these core messages are called *hot buttons.* Punch—or power information—gives readers of our resumes just what they are looking for by hitting them hard with our skills, abilities, qualifications, credentials, and value that meet their needs.

Here is where strategy plays a crucial role. The challenge is to address the concerns of the hiring managers, to get inside their heads and determine what they are thinking. What do they want to see in a job candidate? What information are they searching for? What can you communicate that will create immediate interest and enthusiasm?

Personality

Hiring managers want to hire people with pleasing personalities. Your resume should have a personality of its own, mirroring yours. Your packaging should convey your unique attributes as a person, along with your value message. Words are powerful tools, and carefully chosen, they can speak volumes about you as an individual. By using a sumptuous vocabulary, you can turn a dull statement into a lavish and opulent one. Change the word *increased* to *ignited*. Replace the term *top producer* with *peak performer*. Instead of *being responsible for something*, show that you were *a catalyst for major improvements in....* Lighten up and let your resume dance a bit, sing a little, and entertain the reader—in a subtle and professional way. By displaying personality, you're displaying emotion—and emotion sells!

Professionalism

Let's assume you've followed the first five "Ps." Now, consider the following options:

____ Send the resume out without a cover letter	OR	____ Enclose a personal cover letter addressed specifically to a targeted individual on matching stationary.
____ Fold the resume into thirds and stuff it in a business envelope	OR	____ Send the resume out in an attractive flat envelope without folding the resume at all.
____ Send the resume regular mail	OR	____ Send it overnight or 2-day priority to make a more powerful entry into the organization.
____ Expect the prospective employer to call you after mailing the resume, taking passive responsibility	OR	____ Make it clear that you will telephone the prospect shortly after distributing the resume to try to arrange an interview, taking proactive responsibility.

Managers know that the way people present themselves, professionally on paper and in person in the interviews, predicts how professionally they will represent the companies and approach their jobs. Think about it: you buy expensive clothing, practice good hygiene, and make sure you look your best when going to an interview because you want to make a lasting and professional first impression. Your resume and the way you deliver it need to do the same.

Review the options offered above. Which seem more professional to you? Hiring authorities agree that among job seekers, professionalism is in short supply. Embrace this "P" and you'll be invited to more interviews leading to multiple job offers!

CHOOSING TARGETED VERSUS INVENTORY RESUMES

There are only two effective types of resumes: the targeted resume and the inventory resume. We are either clear on what we want to do or we are not. If you have a clearly focused career objective, then you would use the targeted resume. If you don't have a clear career objective, or you decide not to narrow the focus of your job search, then you would use the inventory resume.

Targeted Resume

A *targeted resume* is a resume aimed toward a specific environment and/or activity. Because you know the target audience, you can clearly and accurately determine the specific criteria for hire. Once you have defined your target, you can create a document emphasizing your value, including skills, abilities, qualifications, and credentials—what I call *labor assets*—that match the criteria for hire. For example, association directors would want to show that they have skills in recruiting new members, retaining existing ones, and developing training programs to help members grow and prosper—all skills that an association would find highly valuable for its continued growth and financial well being.

Inventory Resume

If you don't have a specific target, or if you don't want to narrow the scope of the resume to a specific job or industry, a targeted resume won't work. To keep your resume more generalized, use an inventory resume. What is an inventory resume? Well, think of your resume as a store filled with shelves of merchandise for many customers. On these shelves are skills, qualifications, and labor assets that you are merchandising. Once you've defined the value you are selling (skills, qualifications, and labor assets), you can write your resume around them with clarity and precision.

Regardless of the resume type you choose, you should incorporate only pertinent information applicable to a prospective employer. Remember, you have only about 20 seconds to communicate your value in your resume.

Selecting the Correct Type

Type:	Use When:
Targeted	■ You know the position and/or industry in which you want to work. ■ You can identify a job title, industry, or both. ■ All information included is targeted toward your specific goals.
Inventory	■ You are open to options. ■ You cannot clearly identify what you want to do. ■ You can identify your value—marketable skills, qualifications, intangible assets.

HOW TO STRUCTURE A VALUE-BASED RESUME

Once again, there are only guidelines, not rules, for writing value-based resumes because each of us needs to stand out from the others. The only way to do that is to express our value freely, in a way that gets us noticed! The form your resume takes will also depend on your field of employment. For instance, resumes tend to be longer in the social services sector, where they can range from 2 to 10 pages or more. On the other hand, many executive recruiters prefer one-page resumes. Tailor your resume to your job strategy and objective.

Regardless of the type of resume you choose, targeted or inventory, there are only *three principal sections* that make up a successful value-based resume. They are:

1. Heading
2. Showcase
3. Evidence

The Heading

JENNIFER ROGERS
1252 Dodge Drive
Corvallis, Oregon 97335
Phone: (503) 555-1212/Cell: (503) 555-1313
Swiniters@email.email.com

The heading provides basic contact information, including name, address, and phone numbers. Cell phones may be included if you can answer the portable phone call professionally. You may also include fax numbers and even a personalized Web site if you have one.

JENNIFER ROGERS
1252 Dodge Drive
Corvallis, Oregon 97335
Phone: (503) 555-1212
Cell: (503) 555-1313
Swiniters@email.email.com

Your name: A resume is not a formal, legal document, so it is perfectly acceptable to use the name by which you are popularly called. If your name is Charles but you answer to Chip, use Chip. However, make sure your choice of name suits your marketing strategy and the position you're seeking. For some jobs, your formal name may be the better choice. For instance, if your formal name is Eugene, your nickname is Genie, and you are entering the highly conservative world of banking, consider using Eugene.

Your address: Use care when your address is a PO box. In some parts of the country (Florida and Southern California in particular), PO boxes can be construed as, "I don't live in the area, but I'd like to someday." In some highly transient areas, many employers won't even consider interviewing a candidate with a PO box, for several reasons: first, because candidates are not around to interview readily; second, because employers know that candidates will often ultimately decide not to relocate; and finally, relocation is costly to employers and the subsequent "life adjustment" for employees might not go smoothly once the move has taken place.

If you use a PO box for mailing purposes because you have trouble getting mail, include your physical address on your resume as well (see below). If you are living out of the area and seeking to relocate, use a physical address (Mail Boxes Etc., a friend or relative). If relocation is your objective, use your real address and discuss relocation strategies in the cover letter.

JENNIFER ROGERS

Physical Address	**Mailing Address**
1252 Dodge Drive	PO Box 55555
Corvallis, Oregon 97335	Corvallis, Oregon 97334
Phone: (503) 555-1212/Cell: (503) 555-1313	Email@email.email.com

The Showcase

The showcase format provides a hard-hitting, impactful format that immediately sells your value to a prospective employer. All of the sample resumes use the showcase format, but I have provided a sample below:

TOP-PRODUCING REAL-ESTATE SALES PROFESSIONAL
Multimillion Dollar Producer

Lead Generation & Networking Specialist/Relationship Building
High-Impact Presentation & Closing Skills

A dynamic, highly motivated, and results-oriented real-estate sales professional with nine years of success in the South Florida market—supported by credible references. Additional skills include:

Contract negotiation & administration	Administration & organization
Time management—deadline sensitive	Customer relations
Professional demeanor	High ethical standards

The showcase is, of course, the crucial section of the resume. It answers the all-important question, "Why should you hire me?" We will discuss this in much detail in the following chapters, but it's important here to understand that *this section is the section that clearly defines your market value*. The showcase section, in a reader-friendly manner, communicates to prospective employers how you can best contribute to their organizations or influence and enhance their companies' goals and objectives. The showcase ignites interest and entices a prospective employer to read the rest of the resume and invite you in for an interview.

The Evidence

The evidence section consists of numerous subsections: employment, education, military, affiliations, and so on. These subsections are typically included in traditional resumes, but they take on a new importance in a value-based resume because they support, defend, and provide evidence of the value highlighted in the showcase section. If you state that you have outstanding training and development skills in the showcase, you must provide evidence of where you trained, how well you trained, and how your contributions impacted the bottom line.

If you're a teacher, for example, and you state in your showcase section that you're able to raise student test scores, your evidence section must include specific examples about where, when, and to what extent you have raised scores in the past. If you're a recent college graduate and have no hard evidence to support your claims, you can demonstrate that you have the potential based on prior experiences. Let's say, for example, that you're a recent grad and your showcase section highlights your knowledge of quantitative statistical analysis. Your evidence section should demonstrate how you learned and used this knowledge—perhaps in a thesis or an intern assignment—and the impact it had on your school or organization.

Evidence can come in many forms. Below is a listing of some of the more popular subsections that make up the evidence section.

1. Professional employment and work experience section
2. Education and continuing education
3. Self-improvement and personal development (seminars, workshops, etc.)
4. Licenses and certifications
5. Awards and recognitions
6. Military service
7. Internships
8. Professional affiliations
9. Community service and contribution
10. Volunteer work
11. Activities
12. Teaching and writing assignments—patents owned

Consolidating your evidence: A resume is like a book report. The reader doesn't need or want to know the whole scenario—only the important stuff! If you're trying to keep your resume to one or two pages and have limited space, you can combine subsections. You can consolidate education and military service into one subsection, for example, or combine volunteer work with professional affiliations and even personal information and activities, if appropriate.

WHAT TO LEAVE OUT OF YOUR RESUME

Personal Information

Unless there is a strategic reason to include it, superfluous and "ego-driven" information with no direct link to your core value messages should be left off your resume. The same holds true for personal information, including social security number, age, marital status, and number of children and pets.

What you include will depend on your circumstances. If you are developing a resume for a position with the federal government, and you're asked for a social security number, you should, of course, furnish it. If you are seeking a sales position, you play golf, and you determine that many sales deals are closed on the links, you may want to include golf on your resume, if space permits. On the other hand, you would probably leave off the fact that you enjoy cooking, gardening, and working for the Republican Party if there is no direct or indirect value to including it.

Religious and Political Issues

Leave all information relating to religious, political, and any other volatile subjects off your resume unless you have a good, strategic reason to include it. It doesn't pay to take a chance with these no-win issues.

Salary Requirements and Salary History on Resumes

Salary history is usually not included on a resume and is best left for face-to-face discussions, preferably following a job offer. Your goal is to establish value and compatibility first and then seek compensation equaling your value. Why is it best to discuss salary following a job offer? Because when it comes to salary negotiations, your strongest leverage as a job candidate is to negotiate salary *after* the offer but *before* you actually accept the job. If you put off the subject of compensation until a job offer has been made, you will strengthen your negotiating position.

Should You Hide Information?

I have seen many imaginative efforts to hide weaknesses and problems on a resume. For the most part, they fail to fool anyone. The best way to overcome a weakness is to identify a corresponding strength. Let's say, for example, you have an associate's degree and you are applying for a position in which a bachelor of arts degree is required. Don't omit your degree, or worse, falsify your credentials. Instead, pinpoint areas of past experience where you have excelled and emphasize your achievements and contributions. Write with high energy and enthusiasm, and demonstrate your commitment to giving 150 percent to the position. If appropriate, suggest on your resume or in your cover letter that you are planning to enroll in school part time to earn a bachelor's degree.

> *The best way to overcome a weakness is to identify a corresponding strength.*

STRATEGY EQUALS SUCCESS

Strategy and tactical planning and execution are so important that an entire book could be written on the subject. Here's why strategy is so crucial. If you plan to conduct your job-search campaign targeting executive recruiters, your resume will look different than if your strategy is to post your resume to the Internet using an ASCII text file. If you're a recent college graduate, your resume will look distinctively different than if you're a seasoned CEO earning $300,000 a year. If you're an artist, your job strategy—and your resume—will be different from the strategy employed by a financial planner. A strategy for a national job-search campaign will be different from an international one.

If you've been downsized but given a generous 12-month severance package, you'll design your resume and job-search campaign in a completely different manner than you would if you'd been terminated with no notice and no severance package. A person distributing her resume in Boise, Idaho will produce a resume that looks somewhat different from someone seeking a similar job in Philadelphia.

Strategy is crucial to the resume-writing and job-search process. Often, differences in strategy are subtle and small but deliver *big* results. In the same way, not making even the smallest of changes can lead to monumental and painful mistakes. Take a cue from advertising: The same commercial for Chevy trucks is used in Boston and New Orleans, with one important difference. A Boston accent sells more trucks in Beantown, and a southern accent sells more trucks down South.

The message is this: A well-thought-out strategy based on common sense, intelligence gathering, brainstorming, and commitment is usually the difference between a highly successful resume and career design campaign and a mediocre resume and long, disappointing job search.

2

Groundwork for a Great Resume: The Organizational Message Chart

The Organizational Message Chart is a way to approach resume writing that will change the way you think about resumes and the strategies you use to develop them. It will make a *huge* difference in the results you get from your resume!

The goal of a resume is to get an interview. The goal of an interview is to get a job offer. So if you can determine what information you'd need to communicate in an interview to get a job offer, why not communicate it on the resume?

Resume ⇒ Interview ⇒ Job Offer

The Mission: To develop resumes that will secure job
interviews that lead to job offers.

In the end, successful candidates—the ones who get hired—do two things better than anyone else, both on their resumes and in the interviews!

1. They are able to sell and deliver the right messages (value). You can sell and communicate your value by showing you have specific skills and abilities that have value to a prospective employer. You can also sell and deliver the right messages by showing you have key quali-

fications and/or credentials that indicate your value. You can also outline your experience, track record, achievements, and recognitions that provide proof that you can benefit a potential employer. You can demonstrate that you have intangible value, meaning other sources that provide evidence of value, that demonstrate your worth to a potential company or organization.

2. Present the messages well to build rapport. In many instances, if not most, it's not what we say, but how we say it. A resume must be presented with confidence, with professionalism, with intelligence, and with class. You want to connect with the readers of the resume—to get them to want to read the resume and invite you in for an interview.

MAKE SURE YOUR RESUME HAS THE RIGHT INFORMATION

What is the right information? That's what the Organizational Message Chart is all about. The right information is the information that best addresses the question, "Why should I hire you?"

> *The right information answers the questions, "Why should I hire you, and how can you best contribute to our goals and objectives?"*

It is crucial to communicate messages that employers want to see on a resume. Employees are paid for value, so prospective employers are looking for messages that represent value—that is, messages that clearly express benefits to them. In other words, what can you do for them? Realistically, employers don't care first and foremost about what *we* want. They care about what *they* want. Employers don't care about *our* job objectives; they care about *their* corporate or organizational objectives. If hiring us can help solve their problems, we're in the running for the job. If a prospectitve employer doesn't think we can be of much help, it doesn't matter what we bring to the table. We won't get hired.

When crafting a resume, begin by asking yourself the questions an employer will ask you: Why should I hire you? What do you bring to our company that will benefit us? How can you contribute to our goals and objectives?

Below are types of information employers are looking for:

- I can be a contributing team member in increasing sales and market share.
- I can help collect outstanding money, improving cash flow.
- I can improve efficiency and productivity.
- I can integrate high technology with more traditional methodologies.
- I can improve student test scores and enhance academic curricula.
- I can improve customer relations and increase retention service levels.
- I can better train taxi drivers, thereby reducing accidents and liability premiums.
- I can purchase supplies for lower costs without compromising quality.
- I can complete commercial construction projects on time and on budget, avoiding cost overruns.

- I can improve equipment productivity by maintaining equipment and eliminating downtime.
- I can clean homes as if they were my own.

Here's the exciting part about identifying the right messages: If you are confident that you have the right messages, you will be confident in your delivery and presentation style at an interview. Like a good sales professional, the more confident you are in your product (yourself), the more you believe in the product (yourself), and the more you are passionate about promoting the product (yourself), the more successful you will be in presenting the product—*you*—and closing the deal.

The goal of the Organizational Message Chart is to provide a system for determining what the "right" messages are and prioritizing those messages in order of importance. Once you've identified the messages that answer the all-important question, "Why should I hire you?," you can build a resume around these messages.

> *Once you have identified the value messages that answer the all-important question, "Why should I hire you?," you can build a resume around these messages.*

Two Formulas for Identifying the Right Messages

The 6–8/90 Formula

For most resumes and interviewing situations, there's a powerful and accurate formula that makes it easy to identify the right messages. The 6–8/90 formula says that there are usually about six to eight messages that make 90 percent of the difference in getting an interview and a job offer. To repeat, there are about six to eight *core* messages that make 90 percent of the difference in getting hired. The good news is that you don't need to communicate a hundred things on a resume to get attention—just six to eight key messages. Depending on individual circumstances, it's not always six to eight , and it's not always 90 percent. But the lesson here is clear: Determine those few significant *core* messages that, when communicated on a resume and supported by evidence (experience, education, volunteer work and, so on), will trigger action—an interview opportunity.

> *There are about 6–8 core messages that make 90 percent of the difference in getting hired!*

Curly's "One-Thing" Formula

In the movie *City Slickers*, the tough cowboy and "rough-around-the-edges" trail boss ferries well-to-do city-folk going through midlife crisis on a cattle drive. In a pivitol and hilarious scene, Curly, the trail boss (played by Jack Palance) has a talk with Mitch (played by Billy Crystal), who is going through a midlife crisis of his own. Mitch, says Curly, is just like all the other city slickers who escape to the ranch: He's trying to make sense of life. But the real meaning to life, according to Curly, all comes down to just *one thing*.

"What's that one thing, Curly?" Mitch asks as they're riding side-by-side back towards their campsite.

"You have to figure that out for yourself," Curly responded. "It's different for everyone."

Curly's "one thing" formula applies to writing resumes and preparing for interviews. One message (and that message is different for everyone) reigns supreme. I call this "one thing" the *presidential message*. Just as the president presides at the top of every organizational chart, so the "presidential message" presents a single, overriding theme for a resume and job search. What is the single most important message you can convey that makes the most difference? Your first step before writing a resume is to identify your one presidential message to employers. That done, the next step is to invoke the 6–8/90 formula: Identify the six to eight key supporting messages that give credence to the main message. Then, you can build a resume around these messages.

WHAT IS THE ORGANIZATIONAL MESSAGE CHART?

The Organizational Message Chart is a tool for identifying that *one core message* and the six to eight supporting messages that define the critical value required for getting interviewed and eventually hired. The process is fun, thought-provoking, and enlightening. The term "organizational message chart" is derived from the organizational chart of a typical company, with a president at its head (the "presidential message") and a supporting team of vice presidents, who report to the president ("vice presidential messages"). The purpose of the Organizational Message Chart is to assist you in defining your value to prospective employers.

Defining Your Value

In most cases, you will be hired for a position based upon your value to the company or organization. Value is made up of three components:

1. Skills
2. Qualifications
3. Intangible value

Skills

Skills are specific talents and capabilities you have that are valuable to a prospective employer. They are the benefits you offer and the ways in which you can contribute to a prospective employer's goals and objectives.

Sample Skills

Teaching and empowering	Team building/team leadership	Management/supervision	Purchasing
Bookkeeping/ budgeting	Accounts payable and receivable	Maintenance and repair	Inventory control
Public speaking	Curriculum development	Technical troubleshooting	Problem solving
Start-up management	New product introduction	Classroom management	Meeting planning
Computer programming	Expense/cost control	Regulatory compliance	Customer service

Qualifications

Qualifications encompass specific training and preparation, including academic achievement, credentialing, certifications, licenses, and so on. Don't overlook informal qualifications such as sales seminars, specialized computer or other skills training, and customer service workshops.

Sample Qualifications

Bachelor of arts degree	Master's degree	Licenses	Certifications
Specific qualifications	Honorariums	Special training	Other credentials

Intangibles

Intangible value is neither a skill nor a qualification, but it represents value just the same. A salesperson with a book of clients that can be transferred from one company to another brings what we call an *intangible value*. An attractive person who wants to become a model brings "good looks" as an intangible value. If you have a good reputation in your field, that represents an intangible value that would interest a prospective employer. (Celebrities who sponsor products and services offer their reputations as intangible values.)

While in many instances, employers are looking for specific skills and academic credentials, it's often the intangible value that makes the difference between getting an offer and losing out to another candidate.

Sample Intangibles

15 years' experience in...	A network of global contacts	Best-selling author	A reputation
Professional demeanor	Proven track record	Awards & recognitions	Achievements

HOW TO CREATE YOUR VALUE MESSAGES USING THE ORGANIZATIONAL MESSAGE CHART

Let's start by taking a look at a typical company organizational chart and modifying it to become an Organizational Message Chart. A typical organizational chart lists the president on top, the vice presidents below, managers below that, and support staff below managers. It looks like a pyramid. Here's an example:

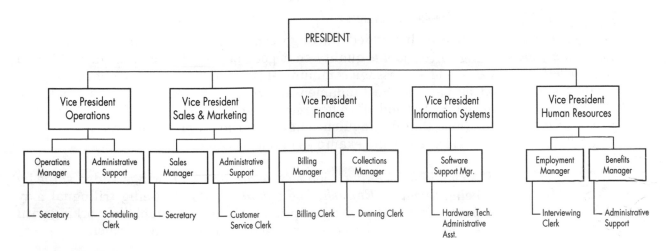

The most important position on the chart, in terms of economic value, is the president. After the president, come the vice presidents and then the rest of the gang. Turning this organizational chart into a powerful tool for identifying the core messages produces a new, parallel chart that looks like this:

Messages that Communicate *Value*

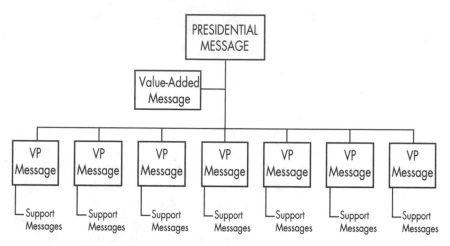

The Hierarchy of Messages

Just as an organizational chart depicts a hierarchy of employees, so the Organizational Message Chart depicts a hierarchy of messages.

1. Presidential message
2. Value-added message
3. Vice presidential messages
4. Support messages

The Presidential Message

The presidential message is the single most important message you can convey on a resume. It answers this all-important question, "Why should I hire you?" All other messages support, defend, and complement the presidential message.

Value-Added Messages

When a candidate brings added value to her resume, she brings something valuable to the table that distinguishes her from other candidates.

The value-added message communicates added value that you bring to the job, a quality that goes beyond the call of duty. While a value-added message communicates value, it is *not* necessarily expected as part of the fundamental job requirements. When a candidate brings "value added" to her resume, she brings something important to the table that distinguishes her from the other candidates.

Here are some examples of added value:

- A candidate seeking a job as a *retail manager* brings added value by being *fluent in English, Spanish, and French*. Being trilingual may not be part of the job description but can be valuable in working with employees and customers who speak Spanish and French.

- A candidate seeking a job as an *elementary school teacher* brings added value by being an *expert in computers and computer programming*. These skills may *not* be part of the job description, but they can be valuable not only in a teaching position, but also as a support person to assist other teachers.

- A candidate seeking a job as an *electrician* brings added value by being *skilled in business development techniques*. Having these skills may *not* be part of the job description but can be valuable to companies looking for good employees who can help promote and grow the business in addition to performing their primary responsibilities.

- A candidate seeking a job as an assistant warehouse manager brings added value by being an *expert in automated Just-in-Time inventory control systems*. Having this particular skill may *not* be part of the job description but is extremely valuable, as it can help save thousands of dollars in inventory and carrying costs as the company expands.

- A candidate seeking a job as a *sales associate* brings added value by having *an existing book of businesses in the form of clients from a former job* ready to use to ignite sales in her new job. Having this list may *not* be part of the job expectations, but is extremely valuable to a prospective employer seeking to grow and expand quickly.

Vice Presidential Messages

Vice presidential messages complement and support the presidential message. Like the presidential message, they are important, but less so than the single, compelling presidential message.

Supporting Messages

Supporting messages support the vice presidential messages. Most traditional resumes consist of support messages—but they are insignificant compared to the presidential and vice presidential messages.

CONSTRUCTING ORGANIZATIONAL MESSAGE CHARTS

The best way to show how an Organizational Message Chart is constructed is by example.

Example 1: Retail Sales Clerk

Step 1: Presidential Message. To construct an OMC for a candidate seeking a position as a retail sales clerk, begin by asking, "Why should the company hire me?"

Presidential Message: They should hire me because I can build sales by providing exceptional customer service.

Step 2: Vice Presidential Message. Use the next question to determine vice presidential messages: What skills, abilities, qualifications, and credentials do you offer that would indicate that you could achieve the presidential message?

VP Message #1:   Proven sales skills

VP Message #2:   Excellent communications skills

VP Message #3:   Outstanding merchandising skills

VP Message #4:   Effective employee training skills

VP Message #5:   Tactful problem-solving and conflict-resolution skills

VP Message #6:   Professional, courteous, and polished demeanor

Intangibles: What additional messages show your intangible value and further distinguish you from other candidates? Directly or indirectly, these intangibles should support the presidential message.

VP Message #7:   Four years of successful, progressive experience in retail environments

VP Message #8:   Have highly credible references supporting your value and past accomplishments

Step 3: Value-Added Messages. Use the next question to determine value-added messages: What shows a prospective employer that you bring more to the job than what's expected?

Value Added Message: Recipient of "Nordstrom's Gold Service Award," for customer service excellence

Step 4: Constructing the Chart. Once you've identified the presidential, vice presidential, and value-added messages, you can construct your Organizational Message Chart and fill in the supporting messages as shown below:

OMC 1: Retail Sales Clerk

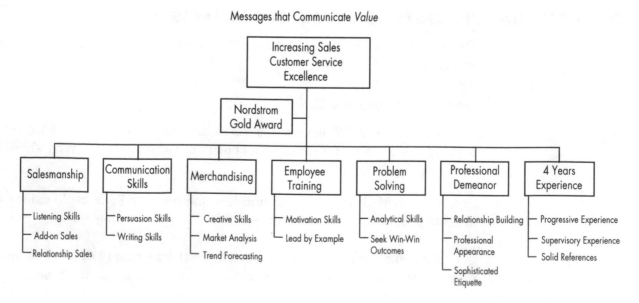

Example 2: Sixth-Grade Elementary Schoolteacher

Step 1: Presidential Message. To construct an OMC for a candidate seeking a position as a sixth-grade elementary schoolteacher, begin by asking, "Why should the company hire me?"

Presidential Message: To significantly enhance the educational experience and to prepare students for a rewarding life.

Step 2: Vice Presidential Messages. The next question determines vice presidential messages: What skills, abilities, qualifications, and credentials, do you offer in order to achieve the presidential message?

VP Message #1:   Improving reading scores
VP Message #2:   Improving math scores
VP Message #3:   Classroom management—discipline
VP Message #4:   Student/parent interface
VP Message #5:   Field trip and "real-life" education coordination
VP Message #6:   Curriculum enhancement

What additional messages show your intangible value and distinguish you from other candidates? These should directly or indirectly support the presidential message.

VP Message #7:   Three-time state delegate to the National Teacher's Conference, Washington, D.C.

Step 3: Value-Added Messages. The next question determines your value-added messages—the messages that distinguish you from others by indicating to a prospective employer that you bring more to the job than what's expected.

Value-Added Message: MBA: Library Science—able to improve library facilities

Step 4: Constructing the Chart.

OMC 2: Sixth-Grade Teacher

Messages that Communicate *Value*

```
                    ┌─────────────────────────┐
                    │   Quality Education      │
                    │ Leading to an Enriched Life│
                    └─────────────────────────┘
                         ┌──────────────┐
                         │     MBA      │
                         │Library Science│
                         └──────────────┘
```

Reading Scores	Math Scores	Classroom Management	Student/ Parent Liaison	Real-Life Educator	Curriculum Enhancement	State Delegate
— One-on-One	— Incentive Teaching	— Discipline	— Communications	— Field Trips	— Research & Analysis	— 1997 to Current
— Group	— One-on-One/Group	— Structure	— Email	— Outside Speakers	— Measurement Analysis	— Secretary 1998– 99
		— Enriching Environment	— Open-Door Policy	— Movies and Films		— Statewide Contacts

Example 3: Company President/CEO

Step 1: Presidential Message. To construct an OMC for a candidate seeking a position as CEO/President, you begin by asking that all-important question, "Why should the company hire me?"

Presidential Message: They should hire me because I can promote global expansion and enhance shareholder value/earnings.

Step 2: Vice Presidential Message. The next question determines vice presidential messages: What skills, abilities, qualifications, and credentials, do you offer in order to achieve the presidential message?

VP Message #1: International corporate leadership
VP Message #2: Re-engineering and corporate restructuring
VP Message #3: Merger and acquisitions management
VP Message #4: Organizational and personnel leadership
VP Message #5: MBA: Oxford

What additional messages can you send that might show your intangible value, to further distinguish you from other candidates, that directly or indirectly support the presidential message?

VP Message #6: Leadership role in building/directing four multimillion-dollar companies
VP Message #7 Highly experienced in raising capital for growth and expansion

Part I: How to Use a Resume to Sell Yourself

Step 3: Value-Added Messages. The next question determines your value-added messages—the messages that distinguish you from others by indicating to a prospective employer that you bring more to the job than what's expected!

Value-Added Message: Key business and political contacts in 23 nations

Step 4: Constructing the Chart.

OMC 3: Company President/CEO

Messages that Communicate *Value*

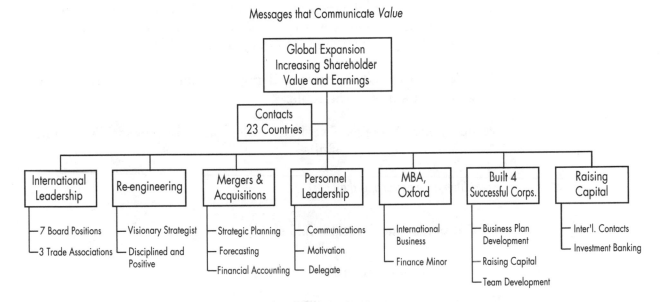

Example 4: Graduating Student—MIS Major

Step 1: Presidential Message. To construct an OMC for a college graduate seeking a position in MIS, we begin by asking, "Why should the company hire me?"

Presidential Message: They should hire me to advance the goals and objectives of the MIS department by utilizing strong programming expertise

Step 2: Vice Presidential Message. The next question determines what the vice presidential messages are: What skills, abilities, qualifications, and credentials, do you offer in order to achieve the presidential message?

VP Message #1:   COBOL, FORTRAN, C, C++, SQL, CICS, JAVA, and Visual Basic
VP Message #2:   Windows NT, Unix, OS/2, DOS, Linux, and Windows 2000

VP Message #3:   Mac and PC literate

VP Message #4:   Speech recognition

VP Message #5:   MS Office, Desktop publishing, Web design, Database management

What additional messages can you send that might show your intangible value, to further distinguish you from other candidates, that directly or indirectly support the presidential message?

VP Message #6:   Vice President, Yale University MIS Club

VP Message #7:   Two successful internships with Fortune 500 companies

The next question determines our value-added messages—the messages that distinguish you from others by indicating to a prospective employer that you bring more to the job than what's expected!

Step 3: Value-Added Messages. Bring excellent sales and business development skills to the table.

Value-Added Message: Excellent sales and business development skills

Step 4: Constructing the Chart.

OMC 4: Graduating Student—MIS Major

Messages that Communicate *Value*

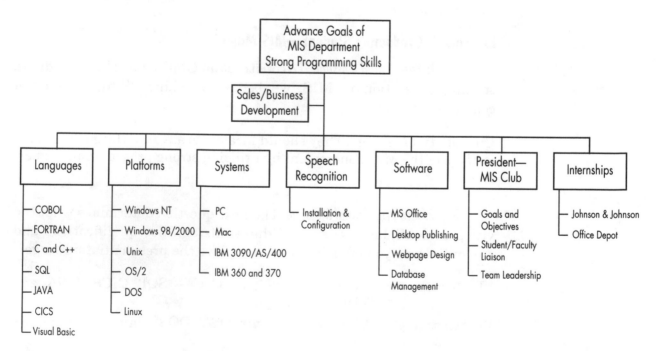

Example 5: Licensed Massage Therapist

Step 1: Presidential Message. To construct an OMC for a Licensed Massage Therapist seeking a position with a rehabilitation or chiropractic center, we, again, ask the question, "Why should the company hire me?"

Presidential Message: They should hire me to provide a therapeutic and safe, healing environment for all clients.

Step 2: Vice Presidential Message. The next question determines what the vice presidential messages are. What skills, abilities, qualifications, and credentials do you offer in order to achieve the presidential message?

VP Message #1:   Relaxation and sports treatments
VP Message #2:   Trigger point work
VP Message #3:   Physical-therapy certified
VP Message #4:   Cross-fiber & longitudinal release

What additional messages can you send that might show your intangible value to further distinguish you from other candidates, that directly or indirectly support the presidential message?

VP Message #5:   Customer service
VP Message #6   New-business development
VP Message #7   Trainer and mentor

Step 3: Value-Added Messages. The next question determines your value-added messages—the messages that distinguish you from others by indicating to a prospective employer that you bring more to the job than what's expected!

Value-Added Message: In addition, I am an expert in nutrition.

Step 4: Constructing the Chart.

OMC 5: Licensed Massage Therapist

Messages that Communicate *Value*

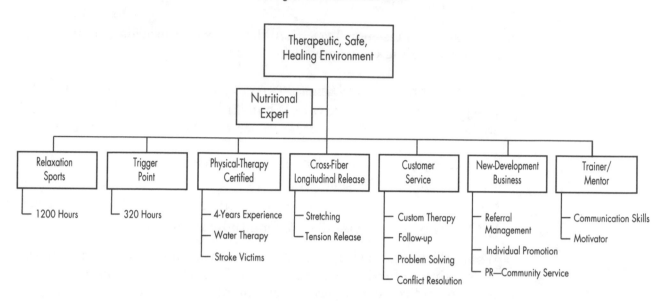

Example 6: Pharmaceutical Sales

Step 1: Presidential Message. To construct an OMC for a Pharmaceutical Sales Representative, you first ask yourself the question, "Why should the company hire me?"

Presidential Message: They should hire me to dramatically increase sales and expand market share.

Step 2: Vice Presidential Message. The next question determines what the vice presidential messages are: What skills, abilities, qualifications, and credentials do you offer in order to achieve the presidential message?

VP Message #1:   Senior-level, high-impact presentation/closing skills
VP Message #2:   New product rollout/launch management
VP Message #3:   Start-up and turnaround management experience
VP Message #4:   Building strategic relationships—power networking
VP Message #5   Brand management

What additional messages can you send that might show your intangible value, to further distinguish you from other candidates, that directly or indirectly support the presidential message?

VP Message #6: Top producer in *all* previous positions held

VP Message #7 Seven consecutive years of uninterrupted growth in sales and profits

Step 3: Value-Added Messages. The next question determines your value-added messages—the messages that distinguish you from others by indicating to a prospective employer that you bring more to the job than what's expected!

Value-Added Message: Liaison for 230 physicians for APPM in South Florida

Step 4: Constructing the Chart

OMC 6: Pharmaceutical Sales

Messages that Communicate *Value*

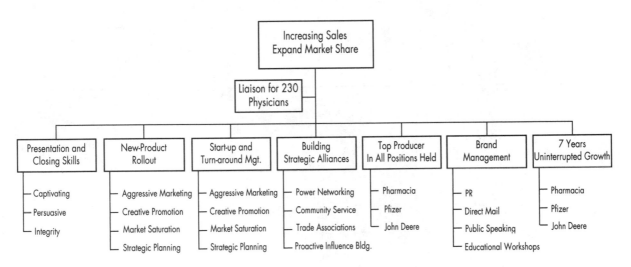

A POWERFUL TOOL

The Organizational Message Chart is a powerful, easy-to-do, confidence-building, and highly effective tool for creating resumes and preparing for interviews. It's well worth the time it takes to identify core values and map out a strategy that matches what prospective employers are looking for in job candidates. When you concentrate on what employers want rather than just jotting down your employment history and education, you can control the messages that your resume communicates. Your reward is the job you want—at the salary you deserve.

3

Creating Showcase Formats
That Get Results

> *The showcase format sells your value to employers and helps you secure top jobs at top dollars.*

This chapter introduces a proven format for creating resumes that get results. Called the showcase format, it sells your value to prospective employers and helps you secure top jobs at top dollars.

TRADITIONAL RESUME FORMATS

Before exploring the showcase format, let's review the four traditional resume presentations: the chronological format; the functional format, the combination format (a combination of the chronological and functional formats); and the curriculum vitae (CV), a resume that is primarily a listing of information without extensive detail. Depending on your circumstances, you may need to adapt some of the features of these traditional formats when creating your own showcase resume.

■ Chronological Format

This format demonstrates continuing upward career growth by emphasizing employment history. A chronological format lists job positions held in a progressive sequence, beginning with the most recent and working back. The distinguishing feature of this format is that with each job listing, you communicate key responsibilities and specific job achievements.

The focal points of the chronological format are time, job continuity, growth, advancement, and accomplishments.

- Functional Format

  The functional format emphasizes skills, abilities, credentials, qualifications, and accomplishments at the beginning of the document, but does not associate these characteristics with a specific employer. Titles, dates of employment, and employment track records are de-emphasized. Many hiring managers feel that this format is used when job candidates have specific problems in their employment histories—they are job-hoppers, older workers, career changers, or they have employment gaps, academic skill-level deficiencies, or limited experience. The general consensus among hiring managers is that the chronological format is preferred, and a functional resume deserves closer scrutiny.

  The focus of the functional format is on your skills and accomplishments, not when or where you accomplished them.

- Combination Format

  The combination format offers a quick synopsis of your key abilities and qualifications (functional format) followed by your employment history (chronological format). This is a well-accepted and effective format; in fact, the showcase format is a specialized version of the combination format. The traditional combination format allows us first to list our skills and achievements and then provide supporting documentation to back them up.

  The focus of the combination format is to combine the best of both the chronological and functional formats.

- Curriculum Vitae (CV)

  A curriculum vitae is used chiefly by professionals (physicians, for example) where a mere listing of credentials or information communicates the value of the candidate.

  The focus of the CV is on credentials or information listing, where these credentials and listed information alone communicate a candidate's value.

THE SHOWCASE FORMAT

> *The showcase resume format sends a powerful, proactive message to employers, answering the question, "Why should I hire you?"*

The showcase format takes the combination format to a whole new strategic level. Rather than spending your time identifying your skills, abilities, keywords, and qualifications and listing them on your resume, the showcase format focuses your efforts on answering the question, "Why should I hire you?" From there, it helps you develop and deliver proactive, powerful messages about your value to prospective employers. Like any good marketing tool, the showcase resume clearly communicates the contributions you can make to a company and the benefits you offer.

Emphasizing Benefits

Most resume formats simply list your skills, experience, education, and training, leaving it to hiring managers to figure what all this "stuff" means to them and how they can benefit from it. The showcase format turns these aspects of your background—your *labor assets*—into targeted messages that communicate your bottom-line value. Here are some examples:

Skills, Abilities, Education, and Training		*Benefit to the Hiring Company*
Good communication skills	=	Improve sales
Collection of accounts receivable	=	Enhance cash flow
Problem-solving and trouble-shooting skills	=	Reduce downtime
Harvard MBA	=	Grow company and profits quickly
Computer skills	=	Improve productivity; reduce payroll costs
Good "people skills"	=	Build strategic alliances to improve sales
Solid network of contacts	=	Make contacts for increasing revenues
Good organization and time-management skills	=	Increase efficiency and production

The showcase format is strategic. It packages the presidential and vice presidential messages you developed in your Organizational Message Chart and telegraphs them straight to prospective employers, answering that all-important question, "Why should I hire you?"

Five Criteria for Creating an Effective Showcase Resume

There are five key criteria for creating a showcase:

1. The showcase must clearly, quickly, and concisely communicate a candidate's *core value*.
2. The showcase must be *reader friendly*—easy and pleasant to read.
3. The showcase must address *the needs of prospective employers* rather than the desires of the candidate.
4. The showcase must incorporate *emotionally charged words* to initiate action—an interview.
5. The showcase must be *supportable and defendable* in all other sections of the resume.

We said in Chapter 2 that there are only three principle sections that make up a successful, value-based resume: heading, showcase, and evidence. It is this showcase section that distinguishes the showcase resume from other formats—and it is the showcase itself that creates the magic and the success behind the resume.

The Showcase: Three Parts

The showcase is divided into three subsections.

1. The "billboard"
2. Short introduction
3. Keyword/career highlights

Writing the Billboard

Developing the showcase section of your resume is like creating your very own billboard. Imagine that a prospective hiring manager is driving down the highway and sees your "employment billboard." What would the message on the billboard have to communicate in a few brief seconds that would be so convincing and compelling he'd want to stop the car and invite you in for an interview?

The billboard answers two key questions: Who you are and why you are here. (For example, I'm a sales professional and I'm here to make you money.) Just as important, it must include your presidential message. At the same time, it may incorporate other messages about you: your profession, the industry you want to work in, your vice presidential messages, even testimonials.

Here's an example:

EXECUTIVE CHEF

4 Years as Assistant Chef in the White House

The billboard can spell out your career objective, provided that it demonstrates value rather than need.

Seeking position as...

Human Resource Assistant

Utilizing Outstanding Organization, Communication, and Interpersonal Skills

Research Experience/Interviewing Skills Proactive—Team-spirited

The billboard is to the resume what a headline is to a news story. It sets the stage for the rest of the resume and gives the reader a reason to want to read more.

Writing the Short Introduction

A short introduction lets you expand upon the core messages communicated by your billboard. It also offers you the chance to introduce a *human element* into the resume. The short introduction should be just that—short. Two or three lines at most.

EXECUTIVE CHEF

4 Years as Assistant Chef in the White House

23 years' five-star experience, four years as Assistant Chef at the White House (1976–80). Strong leadership skills—motivating staff to be the very best!

OR

Seeking position as...

Human Resource Assistant

Utilizing Outstanding Organization, Communication, and Interpersonal Skills

Research Experience/Interviewing Skills
Proactive—Team-spirited

A college graduate with a 3.75 GPA (HR Management Major) seeking entry-level HR position where high energy, disciplined work ethic, and academic skills can contribute to HR department.

Writing Keyword/Career Highlights

This is the last section of the showcase. It contains keywords, vice presidential messages, career highlights, and other supporting messages from the Organizational Message Chart. It should answer the question, "What does the reader want to see that will support the billboard?" Below are two examples, one using Core Professional Strengths (Keywords) and the other Career Highlights

EXECUTIVE CHEF

4 Years as Assistant Chef in the White House

23 Years' five-star experience, four years as Assistant Chef at the White House (1976-80). Strong leadership skills—motivating staff to be the very best!

Core Professional Strengths

- Consistent five-star food preparation and delivery
- Sourcing/purchasing best quality food and ingredients
- Organizational skills; deadline management
- Full-course menu planning—national/international cuisine

- Staff management—training and development
- On-site and off-site (catering) coordination
- Regulatory and health code compliance
- VIP/dignitary food and service management

Seeking position as...

Human Resource Assistant

**Utilizing Outstanding Organization, Communication, and
Interpersonal Skills**

*Research Experience/Interviewing Skills
Proactive—Team-spirited*

A college graduate with a 3.75 GPA (Human Resource Management Major) seeking entry-level HR position where high energy, disciplined work ethic, and academic skills can contribute to HR department.

CAREER HIGHLIGHTS

- Member of the Phi Beta Kappa Honor Society for Academic Achievement
- Supervisor of Volunteers—*Make a Wish Foundation's* Annual Fundraising Auction (22 volunteers)
- Rush Chairperson for Alpha Chi Sorority, responsible for 18 new members per semester
- Philanthropic Assistant Chair for Alpha Chi Sorority, coordinating three charity events per year
- Worked a 20-hour week for four straight years while attending college full time (retail positions)

Following the showcase, the balance of the resume consists of the evidence—sections that support the showcase and give the resume integrity.

Turning Organizational Message Charts into Showcases

Using the OMCs from the examples in Chapter 2, let's develop a resume showcase for each.

Example 1: Retail Sales Clerk

RETAIL SALES CLERK: ORGANIZATIONAL MESSAGE CHART

Messages that Communicate *Value*

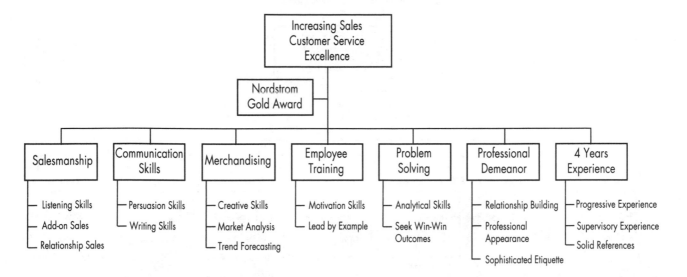

RETAIL SALES CLERK: RESUME SHOWCASE

Seeking position as...

RETAIL SALES CLERK/SUPERVISOR

Utilizing Outstanding Sales, Merchandising, and Customer-Service Skills

***Four-Year Record of Contributing to Departmental Growth
& Success at Nordstrom's***

An imaginative, resourceful, and detail-oriented individual offering more than four years of experience for one of the world's top retailers. A verifiable record of consistently exceeding production expectations.

CORE STRENGTHS

- Sales, promotion, and merchandising
- Organizational/project leadership
- Research and problem solving
- Customer service/quality assurance

- Bookkeeping/record keeping
- Personnel training
- Up-selling and add-on sales
- Professional demeanor

- Computer Skills: Windows, Word, Excel, Proprietary software and Internet applications

Example 2: Sixth-Grade Elementary Schoolteacher

SIXTH-GRADE ELEMENTARY SCHOOLTEACHER: ORGANIZATIONAL MESSAGE CHART

Messages that Communicate *Value*

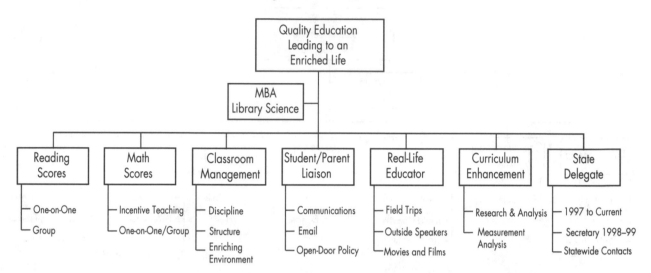

SIXTH GRADE ELEMENTARY SCHOOLTEACHER: RESUME SHOWCASE

CERTIFIED TEACHER (Social Studies/English), Grades 5–9
TAA State Delegate—Colorado

Creating an Inspiring and Empowering Learning Environment
Classroom Management/Meeting Individual Needs—Improving Scores
Integrating Real-Life and Academic Experiences

More than nine years of teaching experience for both public and private institutions. Incorporate real-life experiences with scholastic curriculum utilizing high-tech computer and audio/visual teaching aids.

CORE STRENGTHS

- Communication skills—verbal/written
- Problem-solving/mediation skills
- Community outreach/relations
- Higher-level critical thinking
- Curriculum development
- Cultural diversity awareness

Example 3: President/CEO

PRESIDENT/CEO: ORGANIZATIONAL MESSAGE CHART

Messages that Communicate *Value*

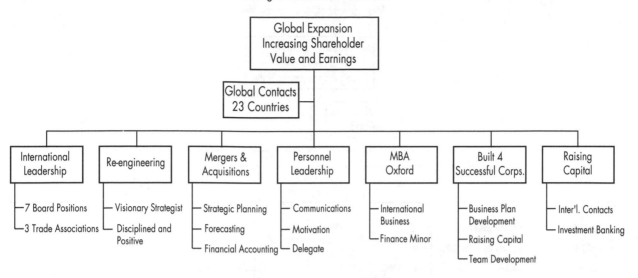

PRESIDENT/CEO: RESUME SHOWCASE

CEO/PRESIDENT

**Leader of Dynamic Growth in Clothing/Fashion Environments
in Global Arena**

*P&L Management—Manufacturing and Production
National and International Experience—Industry Leaders
Fluent in English, Spanish, and Italian*

Twenty years in high-visibility positions in the clothing/fashion industry with emphasis on manufacturing and distribution. Expert at start-up, turn-around, and explosive-growth situations.

CORE STRENGTHS

- Strategic planning/goal setting
- Spearhead acquisitions/mergers
- Negotiation, persuasion, and public-speaking expertise

- International finance
- Business development/sales
- Building global alliance

"A consistent record for improving shareholder value and earnings."

Example 4: Graduating Student

GRADUATING STUDENT: ORGANIZATIONAL MESSAGE CHART

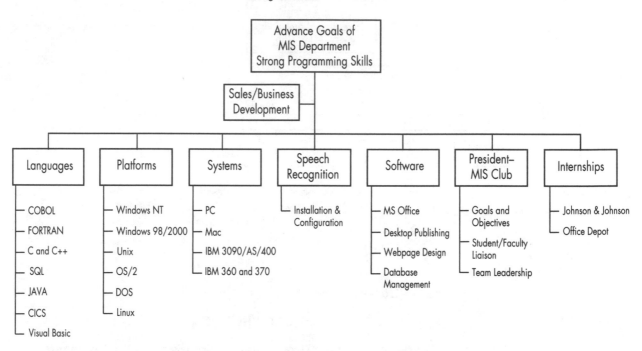

Messages that Communicate *Value*

GRADUATING STUDENT: RESUME SHOWCASE

Graduating Student Seeking...

ENTRY-LEVEL PROGRAMMING/ANALYST POSITION

Advancing the Goals and Objectives of MIS Departments

Languages	Platforms	Systems	Software
COBOL	Windows NT	PC	Office
FORTRAN	Windows 98/2000	Mac	Desktop Publishing
C/C++	UNIX	AS/400	Web Page Design
SQL	OS/2	IBM 3090	Database Management
JAVA	DOS	IBM 360/370	
CICS	LINUX		
Visual Basic			

- Motivated, hard-working, and team-oriented MIS professional
- Highly skilled in troubleshooting, debugging, and problem analysis
- Strong project management experience—team member/leadership role
- Highly effective time manager—deadline and budget focused

Example 5: Licensed Massage Therapist

LICENSED MASSAGE THERAPIST: ORGANIZATIONAL MESSAGE CHART

Messages that Communicate *Value*

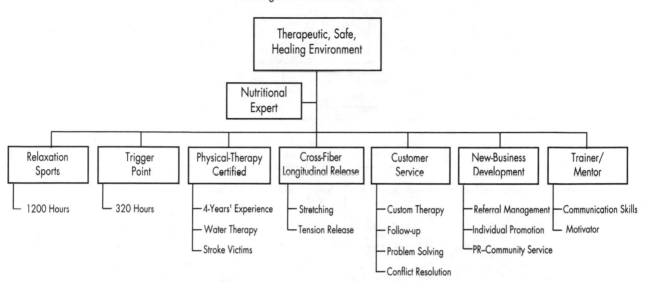

LICENSED MASSAGE THERAPIST: RESUME SHOWCASE

Certified Therapeutic Massage Therapist
Nutrition Expert

An intuitive, reputable, and customer-service-oriented individual offering 18+ years of professional experience in therapeutic, safe, healing environments.

***Specialties*:**

Relaxation	Physical-Therapy Certified
Sports	Cross-Fiber Release
Trigger Point	Herbal Healing Techniques

***Additional Skills*:**

Training Skills	New-Business Development
Customer Service	New-Technology Integration

CAREER HIGHLIGHTS

- Licensed and certified in four states: California, Oregon, Washington, and Arizona
- Lead person for 12-person staff at Costa del Sol Spa
- Business development specialist—integrate sales and marketing with clinical skills
- Recognized therapist for professional athletes—Los Angeles Dodgers and the Lakers

Example 6: Pharmaceutical Sales Representative

PHARMACEUTICAL SALES REPRESENTATIVE: ORGANIZATIONAL MESSAGE CHART

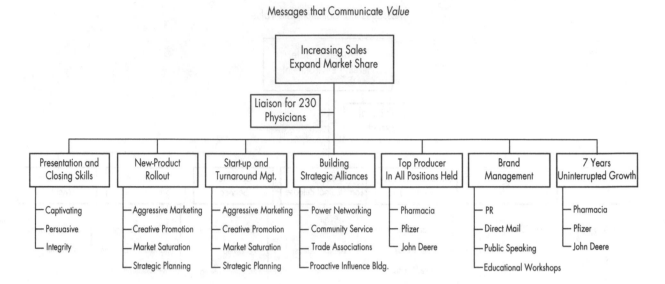

PHARMACEUTICAL SALES REPRESENTATIVE: RESUME SHOWCASE

PHARMACEUTICAL SALES/KEY ACCOUNT MANAGEMENT

Seven Years Experience in Diversified Medical Environments

"Top producer in all positions held"

- Senior-level presentation and closing skills
- Start-up and turnaround management experience
- New-product rollout expertise—brand management
- Team/organizational leadership

A highly competitive, tenacious, and results-oriented professional combining polished interpersonal and rapport-building skills to significantly enhance growth, profits, and return on investment.

CAREER HIGHLIGHTS

- Liaison for more than 230 physicians
- 100% of accounts added new product on formulary
- Promoted to highest performance category—only 12 professionals out of 348 in U.S.
- Achieved 119% of quota with successful launch of Zyvox; achieved 122% increase of Fragmin
- Ignited territorial sales in three years from $556,000 to $2.7 million

4

From Low Profile to High Impact: Five "Before-and-After" Resumes

The following five samples show how resumes can be transformed from mundane to memorable using the showcase format. The "befores" are based on standard formats. The "afters" are value-based resumes that feature showcase sections. Notice not only the format and presentation modifications, but also changes to the content, including numbers, figures, and specific contributions. Notice too how reader friendly the "after" resumes are. As you examine these resumes, you'll see how effectively they sell job candidates and set them apart from the competition. Why? Because they deliver effective messages that answer the question, "Why should I hire you?" and they do it with power and punch!

BEFORE

SUE ANN SZUMIAK
63 Tamiami Trail, #22
Sarasota, Florida 34242
(666) 555-1212/email@email.com

Career Objective:

A position as administrative/executive assistant

Summary of Qualifications:

Over nine years experience using excellent organization, communications, and accounting and bookkeeping skills. Outstanding computer skills, including:

> PC and Mac systems: Windows, Word, WordPerfect, Excel, Lotus, Corel Draw, Publisher, PowerPoint, Access, Photoshop, Peachtree Accounting XL, Quicken, and Internet Applications

Experience:

DRUG ENFORCEMENT ADMINISTRATION, Tampa, Florida   1992 to Present
Office Assistant (1994-Present)
- Provide high level of administrative support for agency tasked with addressing drug-trafficking and abuse issues.
- The Tampa office is the largest office statewide, supporting more than 25 field agents comprising drug-enforcement task forces.
- Directly support Resident-Agent-in-Charge (RAC), managing and coordinating high-volume office/administrative documents.
- Organize all travel arrangements for task force members for national and international travel.

Group Secretary (1992–94)
- Provided secretarial and administrative support for up to ten agents.
- Prepared investigative reports, filed and maintained important records, and produced appropriate correspondences for field personnel.

Education:

TAMPA BAY COMMUNITY COLLEGE, Tampa, Florida
Associate's Degree: Business Administration, 1992

Activities:

Sunday School Teacher
Choir Member
Blood Donor, Reading, Computers, and Aerobics
References Furnished Upon Request

References Furnished Upon Request

AFTER

SUE ANN SZUMIAK
63 Tamiami Trail, #22
Sarasota, Florida 34242
(666) 555-1212/email@email.com

> **ADMINISTRATIVE/EXECUTIVE ASSISTANT**
> *"Enhancing Efficiency and Productivity via Operations & Sales Support"*
>
> **Organizational Leadership/Special-Event & Project Coordination/Problem-Solving**
> **High-Tech Integration—Solid Computer Hardware & Software Expertise**

Highly motivated Administrative Professional recognized for exceeding organizational/administrative goals utilizing solid communication, interpersonal, and team-building skills. Highly credible references.

CORE STRENGTHS

- Bookkeeping and budgeting
- Multiple project management
- Writing skills—reports-presentations
- Time management

- Sales support—customer service management
- Flexible and adaptable to changing environments
- Follow-through/follow-up skills—detail oriented
- Systems improvement—improving efficiency

Computer Skills: PC and Mac systems; Windows, Word, WordPerfect, Excel, Lotus, Corel Draw, Publisher, PowerPoint, Access, Photoshop, Peachtree Accounting XL, Quicken, and Internet Applications

PROFESSIONAL EXPERIENCE

DRUG ENFORCEMENT ADMINISTRATION, Tampa, Florida   1992 to Present
Office Assistant (1994–Present)
Provide high level of administrative support for agency tasked with addressing drug-trafficking and abuse issues. The Tampa office is the largest office statewide, supporting more than 25 field agents comprising drug-enforcement task forces. Directly support Resident-Agent-in-Charge (RAC), managing and coordinating high-volume office/administrative documents.

- Overhauled organizational reporting systems resulting in more timely and accurate reports/data to improve flow of information to field personnel. Field productivity improved 13% in first month alone.
- Slashed travel expenses by 9% ($62,500) by using in-house Internet technology.
- Recipient of six awards for outstanding work performance and customer service excellence.

Group Secretary (1992–94)
Provided secretarial and administrative support for up to ten agents. Prepared investigative reports, filed and maintained important records, and produced appropriate correspondences for field personnel.

- Recipient of the "Rookie of the Year" award for outstanding work performance and customer service excellence.
- Promoted to Office Assistant as a result of consistently exceeding work quality and productivity.

EDUCATION

TAMPA BAY COMMUNITY COLLEGE, Tampa, Florida. Associate's Degree: Business Administration, 1992

ACTIVITIES

Sunday School Teacher, Choir Member, Blood Donor, Reading, Computers, and Aerobics

References Furnished Upon Request

(Note: The box at the top of the resume and the Core Strengths section is inviting and provides a reason to keep reading the resume—the ability to enhance efficiency and productivity.)

BEFORE

JEFF KILPATRICK
143 West Park City Drive • Dallas, Texas 75222
Phone: (214) 555-1212 • Cell: (214) 555-2121 • email@email.com

CAREER OBJECTIVE:

Senior-Level Marketing Director

SUMMARY:

Outstanding marketing professional with more than 12 years experience with Fortune 100 Company—the past nine years as Marketing Director for a $219 million operation of Proctor & Gamble. Recognized for segmentation targeting, financial forecasting, advertising, marketing, and promotions. Highly skilled in brand development and management, lead generation, and high-impact presentations. Skilled at enhancing market-share ratings, new product rollout, and community/public relations management.

PROFESSIONAL EXPERIENCE:

PROCTER & GAMBLE, Cincinnati, Ohio   1988 to Current
Marketing Director—Paper Products Div. (1992–current)
Marketing Director of Paper Products Division—an operation contributing $219 million in revenues operating in the North American markets. Direct a staff of nine in analyzing market trends, long/short-term forecasting, brand development, new-product-rollout management, advertising/marketing-campaign coordination, and internal/external communications. Manage an annual operating budget of $21.4 million.

■ Improved market share after conducting extensive market research and creating high-impact product-launch strategy.
■ Developed new distribution channel for P&G paper-products line, including retail recruitment, rollout schedule, inventory management, and training schedule.
■ Analyzed and initiated shift in "brand image" in targeting "younger buyers"—resulting in improved name recognition.
■ Improved overall brand awareness for individual lines.
■ ESS feedback for the team reached 20% in all of P&G.

Manager Market Development (1988–92)
Assessed market conditions and analyzed consumer buying patterns as team leader in initiating new product for P&G. Emphasis was on reacting quickly to changing market conditions and developing quality products to meet those needs.

■ Team identified niche market for 2 new products.
■ Identified untapped "dealer/distributor" network to accelerate sales in Canadian market.

EDUCATION:

University of Texas—Austin, Texas
MBA, 1985

Vanderbilt University, Nashville Tennessee
Bachelor of Arts: Marketing, 1980

References Furnished Upon Request

AFTER

JEFF KILPATRICK
143 West Park City Drive • Dallas, Texas 75222
Phone: (214) 555-1212 • Cell: (214) 555-2121 • email@email.com

SENIOR-LEVEL MARKETING DIRECTOR
*"Eight Consecutive Years of Solid Growth in Sales &
Revenues For Fortune 100 Company."*

New-Product & Service-Launch/Start-up &Turnaround Leadership/MBA—University of Texas

MARKET VALUE

Segmentation Targeting	Brand Development and Management
Financial Forecasting	Lead Generation, Presentation/Closing Skills
Advertising, Marketing, and Promotions	New-Product Rollout
Total-Communications Strategist—PR Coordination	Market share rating enhancement

Management Experience

PROCTER & GAMBLE, Cincinnati, Ohio   1988 to Current
Marketing Director—Paper Products Div. (1992-current)
Marketing Director of Paper Products Division—an operation contributing $219 million in revenues operating in the North American markets. Direct a staff of nine in analyzing market trends, long/short-term forecasting, brand development, new-product-rollout management, advertising/marketing-campaign coordination, and internal/external communications. Manage an annual operating budget of $21.4 million.

Selected Contributions:

- Captured 32% market share within six months after conducting extensive market research and creating high-impact product-launch strategy.
- Developed new distribution channel for P&G paper products line, including retail recruitment, rollout schedule, inventory management, and training schedule.
- Initiated shift in "brand image" in targeting "younger buyers"—resulting in improved name recognition with that population by 12%. Brand awareness for Individual lines peaked at 93%.
- ESS feedback for the team reached 20% in all of P&G.

Manager, Market Development (1988–92)
Assessed market conditions and analyzed consumer buying patterns as team leader in initiating new product for P&G. Emphasis was on reacting quickly to changing market conditions and developing quality products to meet those needs.

Selected Contributions:

- Team identified niche market for two new products that captured 17% marketshare ($72 million).
- Identified untapped "dealer/distributor" network to accelerate sales in Canada—adding $31 million.

Education

MBA, 1985	University of Texas—Austin, Texas
Bachelor of Arts: Marketing, 1980	Vanderbilt University, Nashville, Tennessee

References Furnished Upon Request

(Note: The box at the top of the resume and the Core Strengths section provide compelling evidence of past achievement that would quickly indicate economic value—in this case, eight years of solid growth for Fortune 500 companies.)

BEFORE

WILLIAM L. SMITH
69 52ND Street
Troy, Illinois 62294
(555) 555-1212/email@email.net

Objective

Seeking Position as VEHICLE MAINTENANCE TECHNICIAN

Summary

Extensive hands-on vehicle-maintenance technician/supervisor specializing in complex military vehicles. Recognized for extraordinary preventative-maintenance management, effectively troubleshooting difficult systems/problems, and for maintaining exemplary levels of work in fast-track, high-stress environments.

Areas of Strength

Customer-service/quality-control management; documentation and record keeping; time management (deadline sensitive); high-volume fleet maintenance; developing/enforcing stringent safety policies/procedures; training; curriculum development; maintaining high, above-industry level "in-commission" rates; and budgetary and expanse control.

Experience

UNITED STATES AIR FORCE   1982 to 2001
Service Manager/Mechanic
Supervised and performed vehicle maintenance and body work, including diagnostics, repair, rebuilds, and preventative maintenance. Provide timely and cost-effective service commensurate with high-quality standards expected in military environments. A skilled training instructor having trained more than 650 technicians over 18-year period.

Conducted comprehensive diagnostic and quality-assurance inspections for fleet totaling 450 vehicles. Attained a 0% repeat-maintenance record exceeding all possible expectations. Developed and established an annual privately owned vehicle-safety program—to identify mechanical/safety defects. Developed and conducted in-shop training workshops.

Eliminated unnecessary expenses by establishing both a mechanical-overhaul program.

Education/Specialized Training

Vehicle Maintenance Management • Honor Graduate, USAF Automotive Training Course • Distinguished Graduate, USAF M.A.N. Vehicle Maintenance Course • HMMWV Organizational Program

ASE Certifications

Engine Repair	Suspension and Steering	Brake Repairs
Electrical/Electronic Systems	Heating and Air Conditioning	Engine Performance

WILLIAM L. SMITH
69 52ND Street
Troy, Illinois 62294
(555) 555-1212/email@email.net

Seeking Position as...

VEHICLE MAINTENANCE TECHNICIAN
**Combining Speed, Quality, and Cost-Effective Vehicle Maintenance Expertise
18 Years Distinguished Service as Air Force Mechanic**

*Troubleshooter for All Repairs—Minor & Major/
Preventative-Maintenance Manager and Skilled Trainer & Team Leader*

ASE Certifications

Engine Repair	Suspension and Steering	Brake Repairs
Electrical/Electronic Systems	Heating and Air Conditioning	Engine Performance

Overview

Extensive hands-on vehicle-maintenance technician/supervisor specializing in complex military vehicles. Recognized for extraordinary preventative-maintenance management, effectively troubleshooting difficult systems/problems, and for maintaining exemplary levels of work in fast-track, high-stress environments.

Areas of Strength

Customer-service/quality-control management	Documentation and record keeping
Time management; deadline sensitive	High-volume fleet maintenance
Developing/enforcing stringent safety policies/procedures	Training; curriculum development
Maintaining high, above-industry-level "in-commission" rates	Budgetary and expanse control

Professional Experience

*UNITED STATES AIR FORCE
1982 to 2001*

Service Manager/Mechanic

Supervised and performed vehicle maintenance and body work, including diagnostics, repair, rebuilds, and preventative maintenance. Provide timely and cost-effective service commensurate with high-quality standards expected in military environments. A skilled training instructor having trained more than 650 technicians over 18-year period.

- Conducted comprehensive diagnostic and quality-assurance inspections for 450 vehicles.
- Attained a 0% repeat-maintenance record exceeding all possible expectations.
- Developed and established an annual privately owned vehicle safety program.
- Developed and conducted in-shop training workshops resulting in
    - Increased productivity and vehicle in-commission rates exceeding 95%.
    - Productivity rates that were 20% above industry standards.
- Eliminated $34,000 in expenses by establishing a mechanical-overhaul program.

Education/Specialized Training

Vehicle Maintenance Management • Honor Graduate, USAF Automotive Training Course • Distinguished Graduate, USAF M.A.N. Vehicle Maintenance Course • HMMWV Organizational Program

(Note: The shaded box at the top of the resume catches the eye and grabs the reader's attention. The information in the box is information that the reader is looking for. The bullets, in the Professional Experience section, assist the reader to quickly see bottom-line results that would show the benefit the candidate possesses that would be of value to the prospective employer.)

EDDIE C. JOHNSTON
888 Village Street
Oakland, California 94602
(510) 555-1212/email@email.com

Career Objective

Seeking an executive position in the media/entertainment field...
utilizing experience, reputation, and contacts

Areas of Expertise

High-level industry contacts—national/international; writing, editing, and presentation/public-speaking skills; building strategic alliance throughout media industry; constant evolution of new concepts/market opportunities; online media growth, development, and expansion; Evaluation, recruiting, and working with top-shelf talent; Establishing and maintaining cutting-edge concepts; delivering high-quality material on limited budgets.

Highlights of Expertise

- Increased growth of national publications by improving weekly circulation
- Positioned publication as one of America's most profitable magazines
- Created niche market resulting in increased earnings over past six years
- Created one of the very first profitable online publications
- Established key, high-level contacts—entertainment, TV, radio, print, and electronic media

Employment History

NATIONAL MEDIA GROUP, INC. San Francisco, California   1981 to Current
Vice President/Media Consultant/Editorial Director

  – Recruited by Founder and CEO Gordon Kilkrist to create a supermarket tabloid

ST. PETERSBURG TIMES/EVENING INDEPENDENT, St. Petersburg, Florida   1972 to 1981
Copy Editor/Reporter/Wire Editor

  – Regular and investigative reporting/writing; never missed a deadline in 9 years with the company

Professional Affiliations/Activities

Selected Keynote Addresses (From more than 30 presentations)

Florida Bar Association
American Society of Magazine Editors
Florida Society of Newspaper Editors
Tiger Bay Political Club of Florida
The Inland Society of Independent Publishers
Ignited growth of national publication by increasing circulation from 200,000 to 1 million+

Education

UCLA Graduate: Entertainment Management/Business, 1997 (B.A. degree)

References Furnished upon Request

EDDIE C. JOHNSTON
888 Village Street • Oakland, California 94602
(510) 555-1212/email@email.com

NATIONAL & INTERNATIONAL MEDIA EXECUTIVE
"The Most Creative Editor in America"

—Entertainment Weekly

Writing/Editing/Program & Concept Development
Increasing Circulation & Audience/Capitalizing on Emerging Opportunities
Familiar with Traditional & Emerging Broadcast Mediums (Online)

Areas of Expertise

High-level industry contacts—national/international
Writing, editing, and presentation/public-speaking skills
Building strategic alliance throughout media industry
Constant evolution of new concepts/market opportunities
Online media growth, development and expansion
Evaluation, recruiting, and working with top-shelf talent
Establishing and maintaining cutting-edge concepts
Delivering high-quality material on limited budgets

Verifiable Highlights of Expertise

- Ignited growth of national publication by increasing circulation from 20,000 to 400,000+

- Positioned publication as one of America's most profitable magazines

- Created niche market resulting in increased earnings of $20 million over past six years

- Created one of the very first profitable online publications

- Established key, high-level contacts—entertainment, TV, radio, print, and electronic media

Professional Achievements

- Subject of 30+ magazine articles, including *Smithsonian*, *Entertainment Weekly*, *Spin Magazine*, and *M Magazine*

- Recognized by the *Boston Globe*, *Washington Post*, *Miami Herald*, and *LA Times* for professional achievement

- Guest appearances on television, including NBC, CNN, and ABC News

- Worked with NBC programming chief Larry Cook in creating 13-episode family television series

- Author of the top-selling book, *Top Dog*, a book of humor columns—a Canterbury publication

(Page 1 of 2)

Employment History

NATIONAL MEDIA GROUP, INC. San Francisco, California   1981 to Current
Vice President/Media Consultant/Editorial Director

- Recruited by Founder and CEO Gordon Kilkrist to create a fresh, innovative supermarket tabloid—*Weekly International Forum News*. Spearhead the project—total circulation exceeding 1 million.
- Editor of the *Weekly International Forum News*, Editorial Director of weekly tabloid and special editions of National Enquirer Publications—West Coast operations.
- Oversaw an editorial staff of 53 journalists, layout artists, and copy editors in publishing weekly magazine. Responsible for budgets and editorial liaison with circulation and distribution.
- Editorial legal liaison for the publications, and in 20 years—did not incur any legal action.
- Never missed a deadline in 19+ years with the company.

St. Petersburg Times/Evening Independent, Florida   1972 to 1981
Copy Editor/Reporter/Wire Editor

- Regular and investigative reporting/writing; never missed a deadline in 9 years with the company.
- Comprehensive portfolio of writing/project assignments available upon request.

Education

UCLA, Los Angeles, California
Bachelor of Arts Degree: Entertainment Management/Business, 1997

Professional Affiliations/Activities

Selected Keynote Addresses (From more than 30 presentations)

Florida Bar Association
American Society of Magazine Editors
Florida Society of Newspaper Editors
Tiger Bay Political Club of Florida
The Inland Society of Independent Publishers

References and Portfolio

Furnished upon request

(Note: The quote, at the top of the resume, is unique and meant to get immediate attention—and credibility. The shaded section titles help the reader to navigate more easily through the resume.)

MICHELLE PHELPS

236 Marlborough Street
Nashville, Tennessee 38495
725-555-1234/email@email.com

CURATORIAL INTERN

A highly motivated, detail-oriented, and personable individual with a passion for the arts seeking to contribute to the growth and success of a museum/arts center. Combining strong academic studies with diversified and successful work experience. A certifiable expert of the work of Henry Dolsen, an important 20th-century visual artist.

Areas of Strength

Experience in dealing with issues of authenticity of art; fundraising/volunteer coordination; research and documentation; art-world savvy (collectors/dealers); provide high-quality levels of customer service; effective grant writing.

Education

UNIVERSITY OF WASHINGTON, Seattle, Washington
Master of Arts Degree: Emphasis on Modern and Contemporary American Art, 2000
Bachelor of Arts: International Political Economy (Emphasis: Russian and European Studies), 1995

Fluent in English, French, Italian, and German

Professional Experience

JACOB LAWRENCE CATALOGUE PROJECT, Seattle, Washington   1995 to Present
Associate Director
Formed a nonprofit organization dedicated to the location, documentation and authentication of all known works of art produced by the artist Jacob Lawrence, for the purpose of publishing these works in both manuscript and digital formats.

Director of Research
Responsible for seeking and pursuing leads for possible locations of works from a variety of archival sources; contacting individual collectors and institutions and gathering information; researching provenance, exhibition, and publication histories. Worked with the Getty Conservation Institute to establish baseline of information about the materials used by artist, in order to provide information to conservators engaged in the preservation of artist's work.

DONALD YOUNG GALLERY, Seattle, Washington   1993 to 1994
Administrative Assistant
Administrative support for contemporary art gallery representing artists such as Jeffery Koons, Robert Ryman, and Gary Hill. Worked with clients providing information about artists. Maintained publicity files for all artists.

OPPENHEIMER & COMPANY, Seattle, Washington   1986 to 1990
Sales Associate
Worked in managerial capacity as a liaison between New York and Seattle offices. Trained and advised financial consultants on products and companies that the New York office wished to promote.

Lectures and Panels

"Autopoeisis: The Art of Jacob Lawrence" (October 10, 2000, University of Washington, Seattle).
"The Complete Jacob Lawrence," hosted panel discussion, the Schomburg Library in Harlem (New York, October 15, 2000).

Professional Associations

Catalogue Raisonné Scholar's Association; College Art Association

References and Supporting Documentation Furnished Upon Request

MICHELLE PHELPS

236 Marlborough Street • Nashville, Tennessee 38495
725-555-1234/email@email.com

Seeking Position as...

CURATORIAL INTERN
In an Academic Museum or Related Environment

Strong Command of Art History and Methodology

**Master of Arts Degree with Emphasis on Modern and Contemporary American Art
Fluent in English, French, Italian, and German**

A highly motivated, detail-oriented, and personable individual with a passion for the arts seeking to contribute to the growth and success of a museum/arts center. Combine strong academic studies with diversified and successful work experience. A certifiable expert of the work of Henry Dolsen, an important 20th-century visual artist.

Core Professional Strengths

Experience in dealing with issues of authenticity of art	Fundraising/volunteer coordination
Comprehensive research and documentation	Art-world savvy (collectors/dealers)
Provide high-quality, sophisticated levels of customer service	Effective grant writing

Education

UNIVERSITY OF WASHINGTON, Seattle, Washington
Master of Arts Degree: Emphasis on Modern and Contemporary American Art, 2000
Bachelor of Arts: International Political Economy (Emphasis, Russian and European Studies), 1995

Professional Experience

JACOB LAWRENCE CATALOGUE PROJECT, Seattle, Washington   1995 to Present
Associate Director
- Formed a nonprofit organization dedicated to the location, documentation, and authentication of all known works of art produced by the artist Jacob Lawrence, for the purpose of publishing these works in both manuscript and digital formats. Raised funds from a variety of sources, including individual donors, corporate donors (including Microsoft Corporation and Ford Motor Company), and granting agencies (including the National Endowment of the Humanities).

Director of Research
- Sought and pursued leads for possible locations of works from a variety of archival sources; contacting individual collectors and institutions and gathering information; researching provenance, exhibition, and publication histories. Worked with the Getty Conservation Institute to establish baseline of information about the materials used by artist, in order to provide information to conservators engaged in the preservation of artist's work. Acted as member of authentication committee; established standardized approach for authenticating all works in artist's oeuvre.

Page 1.

Professional Experience

JACOB LAWRENCE CATALOGUE PROJECT (continued)
- Acted as Managing Editor for *Over the Line: The Art and Life of Jacob Lawrence*—a volume of eight critical essays about the artist and his work. Identified and approached authors about contributing essays. Conducted two all-day writer's conferences to discuss issues of importance to cover in the book. Provided writers with research and maintained constant contact with them to prevent overlap of material.
- Responsible for editing content, coordinating work of editorial and proofreading teams, and assisting curatorial staff at the Philips Collection in Washington D.C. in obtaining artwork for their exhibition based on essays in *Over the Line*. (Exhibition will travel to the Whitney Museum; Museum of Fine Arts, Houston; Los Angeles County Museum of Art; and the Detroit Institute for the Arts.)

DONALD YOUNG GALLERY, Seattle, Washington   1993 to 1994
Administrative Assistant
- Administrative support for contemporary art gallery representing artists such as Jeffery Koons, Robert Ryman, and Gary Hill. Worked with clients providing information about artists. Maintained publicity files for all artists.

OPPENHEIMER & COMPANY, Seattle, Washington   1986 to 1990
Sales Associate
- Worked in managerial capacity as a liaison between New York and Seattle offices. Trained and advised financial consultants on products the New York office wished to promote.
- Publications: *The Complete Jacob Lawrence* (a two-volume publication including a catalogue raisonné and a critical monograph) co-published with the University of Washington Press, Seattle.

Lectures and Panels

"Autopoeisis: The Art of Jacob Lawrence" (October 10, 2000, University of Washington, Seattle).

"The Complete Jacob Lawrence," hosted panel discussion, the Schomburg Library in Harlem (New York, October 15, 2000).

Professional Associations

Catalogue Raisonné Scholar's Association
College Art Association

References and Supporting Documentation Furnished Upon Request

(Note: The box at the top sets off the resume. The shaded section titles help the reader to navigate more easily through the resume making it easier to get key information.)

5

Your Personal Resume Workshop: Create Your Own Blueprint for Success

In this chapter, you'll develop your own showcase resume, from strategy to finished product. This personal resume workshop consists of eight exercises and related worksheets you can follow in sequential order, step-by-step. As your personal resume coach, I will guide you through each exercise and prepare you to write your final resume. Set aside plenty of quality time for each exercise. Remember, you are designing a resume that will help build the future you want for yourself and your family.

Each exercise includes an example you can follow as a model for creating your own resume. Worksheets may be completed on your computer, typewriter, or using pencil and paper. *Don't* limit your responses to the spaces on the worksheets. Use extra space or paper if necessary so that your answers are comprehensive, detailed, and well thought out.

EXERCISE 1: LIST YOUR CONTACT INFORMATION

Name: _____   Professional/Career Objective: _____

Address: _____   City/State/Zip: _____

Daytime Phone: _____   Evening Phone: _____   Fax: _____

Cell Phone: _____   Email: _____   Other: _____

EXAMPLE: ERIC SCOTT'S CONTACT INFORMATION

Name: Eric J. Scott _____   Professional/Career Objective: Operations Manager _____

Address: 123 Diamond Street _____   City/State/Zip: Swampscott, Massachusetts 01907 ___

Daytime Phone: (781) 555-1212 ____   Evening Phone: (Same) _____   Fax: N/A _____

Cell Phone: (781) 555-3232 _____   Email: badgeman@email.com ___   Other: _____

EXERCISE 2: DEFINE YOUR VALUE TO PROSPECTIVE EMPLOYERS

You will typically be hired based upon your value to your prospective employer. Expressed on your resume, value is made up of three components: skills, qualifications, and intangible value.

1. *Skills* are specific talents you offer a prospective employer—that is, your ability to contribute to an employer's goals and objectives.

2. *Qualifications* include specific training and preparation, such as academic credentials, certifications, and licenses. Your qualifications may be formal (a Master's degree or driver's license) or informal (attended training courses or seminars) but relevant to a particular position.

3. *Intangibles* are neither skills nor qualifications, but they are valuable to employers just the same. If a father has a connection at his place of employment that might help his son get a summer job, this connection is an intangible value. If a person has a strong and respected reputation in the community, this reputation would be a valuable asset to a company seeking to improve its image. If you have strategic contacts that would be of value to a prospective employer, they qualify as intangibles.

Spend 10–15 minutes thinking about the job responsibilities you've had in prior positions, and specific ways you've made contributions in those positions. If you're a recent college graduate or you're entering a field in which you've had little or no prior experience, think about how you can best make a contribution if hired. Whatever your employment history, ask yourself what skills you have. What specific qualifications do you possess that would contribute to a prospective employer? What intangible value do you bring to the table that would benefit a hiring entity? Bottom line: How would you respond if asked in an interview, "Why should I hire you? How would you contribute to our company?"

A word of caution: Loyalty, dependability, and hard work are *not* skills. They are character traits. Focus on your concrete skills. Another caution: Avoid "fluff" and ambiguity. Instead of saying, "I have good communication skills," go a step further, be more specific, and say, "I have good writing, negotiating, and public-speaking skills, especially in front of large audiences." Rather than saying, "I have good 'people' skills," go a step further and be more specific, "I have outstanding mediation, conflict resolution, and rapport-building skills."

Worksheet: Identify Your Value Messages

After giving it careful thought, list 10 skills, qualifications, and intangible values that you might bring to a potential employer. Remember, your value messages should answer this all-important question, "Why should I hire you?

1. _____
2. _____
3. _____
4. _____
5. _____
6. _____
7. _____
8. _____
9. _____
10. _____

Examples: Eric Scott's Value Messages

1. Rapid-expansion management/acquisition management
2. Integration of bottom-line operations management with revenue-generating sales leadership
3. Personnel recruitment, training, and empowerment
4. Computer and high-technology integration
5. Product development and improvement
6. National reputation in the law-enforcement uniform industry—start-up and expansion management
7. Key-account/national-account development and management—High-impact marketing
8. Personal contacts with international, industrywide manufacturers
9. High-volume inventory control and inventory turn management
10. P&L management—12 years of consistent, above-industry-standard profit achievement

Worksheet: Identify Your Career Highlights

The next step in this exercise is to identify your career highlights. Identify eight achievements you are most proud of in your career. If you are a college graduate or entering the workforce for the first time, what are your greatest academic, scholastic, community service, civic, or life accomplishments?

1. _____
2. _____
3. _____
4. _____
5. _____
6. _____
7. _____
8. _____

EXAMPLE: ERIC SCOTT'S CAREER HIGHLIGHTS

1. Start-up of uniform company with $1,500 from garage and built into $1.6 million law-enforcement-uniform industry leader
2. Identified three prospective acquisitions, performed due diligence, and negotiated successful purchase—adding $600,000 in sales
3. Created specifications for "brand name" trousers and increased sales of trousers 47% with profit margins improving 75%
4. Developed powerful contacts with manufactures and negotiated exceptional prices and purchasing terms (90 days)
5. Closed and managed 4 national accounts, including IBM, Wackenhut Security, Pinkerton Security, and Raytheon Corp.
6. Awarded "Distributor of the Year" by *Made to Measure Magazine* (industry trade publication)
7. Awarded "Quality Dealer" award by *Made to Measure Magazine* 7 consecutive years (industry trade publication)
8. Positioned company for successful sale—with one-year working contract

Worksheet: Create Your Personal Profile

Write three sentences that powerfully describe who you are and why you deserve to be selected as the successful job candidate:

_____

_____

_____

EXAMPLE: ERIC SCOTT'S PERSONAL HISTORY

I am a team-spirited, growth-oriented, profit-centered operations professional. I have a proven, verifiable record for strategically orchestrating explosive growth and profits in highly competitive, global markets through creative, aggressive, and tactically-designed marketing concepts. Recognized for positioning company as industry leader.

EXERCISE 3: BUILD YOUR OWN ORGANIZATIONAL MESSAGE CHART

Using the information gathered in Exercise 2, you can develop your own presidential message, vice presidential messages, and key supporting messages. Here's a suggestion: Get a large poster board, some colored pencils, and get ready to have fun.

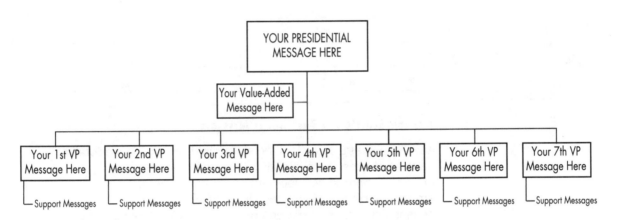

Messages that Communicate *Value*

Worksheet: Writing Your Presidential Message

When developing your presidential message, consider this: What is the single most important message you want to convey to a prospective employer—a message that your employer wants to hear? What is the one thing above all else that sets you apart from other job candidates? It bears repeating. The presidential message answers these questions: "Why should I hire you? What do you bring to our company that would benefit us?"

Put the presidential message in the presidential message box on your poster, preferably in your favorite color. If you are seeking a position as a corporate accountant, for example, your presidential message might be: "As Corporate Accountant, I can *ensure the financial vitality of your company.*" If you're asked in an interview, "Why should we hire you?" your corresponding answer would be, "As Corporate Accountant, I would *ensure the consistent and ongoing financial vitality of your company.*"

Write your own presidential message:

- I can deliver explosive growth and profits while integrating operational leadership with strong sales management skills.

Worksheet: Writing Vice Presidential Messages

Now that you have created your presidential message, you can begin developing your vice presidential messages. Review your listings on the worksheets in Exercise 2. Prioritize them and select the six to eight most important that support the presidential message.

1. _____
2. _____
3. _____
4. _____
5. _____
6. _____
7. _____
8. _____

EXAMPLE: ERIC SCOTT'S VICE PRESIDENTIAL MESSAGES

1. I have strong strategic planning skills/rapid expansion leadership.
2. I have solid experience in acquisition management.
3. I am good at brand development and management.
4. I am very good at national account development.
5. I possess strong organization and personnel-leadership skills.
6. I am proficient at high-technology integration.
7. I strongly believe in customer-service "WOW management—exceeding customer's expectations.

Worksheet: Writing Supporting Messages

Now that you've developed your vice presidential messages, you need to identify key supporting messages. Below, write down each of your vice presidential messages from the previous exercise. Under each vice presidential message are spaces to incorporate two supporting messages. You are not limited to two. If you wish to write down four or five, feel free to do so.

Vice Presidential Message #1: _____

    – Supporting Message #1_____
    – Supporting Message #2_____

Vice Presidential Message #2: _____

    – Supporting Message #1_____
    – Supporting Message #2_____

Vice Presidential Message #3: _____

    – Supporting Message #1_____
    – Supporting Message #2_____

Vice Presidential Message #4: _____

    – Supporting Message #1_____
    – Supporting Message #2_____

Vice Presidential Message #5: _____

    – Supporting Message #1_____
    – Supporting Message #2_____

Vice Presidential Message #6: _____

    – Supporting Message #1_____
    – Supporting Message #2_____

Vice Presidential Message #7: _____

    – Supporting Message #1_____
    – Supporting Message #2_____

Vice Presidential Message #8: _____

    – Supporting Message #1_____
    – Supporting Message #2_____

EXAMPLE: ERIC SCOTT'S SUPPORTING MESSAGES

VP Message #1:	Strategic planning skills/Rapid expansion leadership
Supporting Messages:	Market analysis/Logistical expertise
VP Message #2:	Acquisition management
Supporting Messages:	Competitive intelligence/Financial & profit analysis/Integration management
VP Message #3:	Brand development and management
Supporting Messages:	Product development/Aggressive marketing
VP Message #4:	National account development
Supporting Messages:	Key-contact development/Building market dominance/Referral management
VP Message #5:	Organization and personnel leadership
Supporting Messages:	Team-employee leadership/Lead by example/Management by Objectives (MBO)
VP Message #6:	High-technology integration
Supporting Messages:	Ordering—accounts payable/Collections/Inventory—JIT/Customer communications
VP Message # 7:	Customer-service "WOW"
Supporting Messages:	Telephone/In-store/Mail—email/Special events

Worksheet: Writing Value-Added Messages:

What do you bring to the job that would be unexpected but valuable just the same? The answer is your value-added message. List one to two below.

1. _____

2. _____

EXAMPLE: ERIC SCOTT'S VALUE-ADDED MESSAGES

I have national and international experience.

Worksheet: Building the Organizational Message Chart

Using the information you've gathered above, you can now build your own Organizational Message Chart.

EXAMPLE: ERIC SCOTT'S ORGANIZATIONAL MESSAGE CHART

Messages that Communicate *Value*

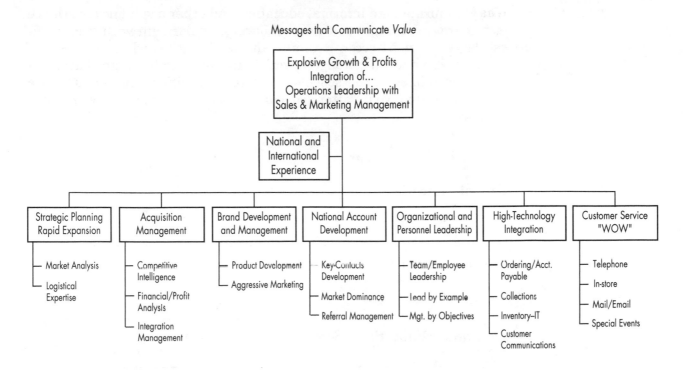

Explosive Growth & Profits Integration of... Operations Leadership with Sales & Marketing Management

National and International Experience

Strategic Planning Rapid Expansion	Acquisition Management	Brand Development and Management	National Account Development	Organizational and Personnel Leadership	High-Technology Integration	Customer Service "WOW"
— Market Analysis — Logistical Expertise	— Competitive Intelligence — Financial/Profit Analysis — Integration Management	— Product Development — Aggressive Marketing	— Key-Contacts Development — Market Dominance — Referral Management	— Team/Employee Leadership — Lead by Example — Mgt. by Objectives	— Ordering/Acct. Payable — Collections — Inventory–IT — Customer Communications	— Telephone — In-store — Mail/Email — Special Events

Messages that Communicate *Value*

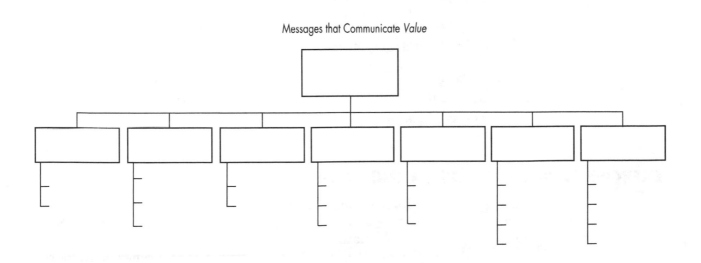

EXERCISE 4: LIST YOUR QUALIFICATIONS

List your formal and informal education and other academic experience (seminars, workshops, self-taught courses, etc.): Begin with your highest degree or most recent training and work backwards chronologically. If you have a college degree, you do not need to list high school. Include the names of the schools you attended, cities and states where they are located, years attended, curricula, and any special awards you received.

Worksheet: Qualifications

Formal Education

_____

_____

Licenses/Certifications

_____

_____

Continuing Education—Seminars/Workshops/Other

_____

_____

Other

_____

Example of Eric Scott's Qualifications:

Bachelor of Arts: Business, UNH, Durham, New Hampshire
Continuing-Education Courses

– Dale Carnegie   – Anthony Robbins
– Tom Hopkins   – Lenore Johnston
– Inventory Management Workshop

EXERCISE 5: PROVIDE SUPPORTING INFORMATION

List supporting information that would add value to your resume in the eyes of a prospective employer. Do not include irrelevant information; your supporting information should bolster your presidential message and be directly relevant to the job you want. Specific types of supporting information are listed below, but these are not all-inclusive. Include additional information if it supports your case.

Worksheet: Supporting Information

Military

_____

_____

Professional Affiliations

_____

_____

Volunteer Work/Civic & Charitable Involvement/Community Service

_____

_____

Special Awards and Recognitions

_____

_____

Special Hobbies

_____

_____

Other

_____

_____

EXAMPLE: ERIC SCOTT'S SUPPORTING INFORMATION

Formal Education—Bachelor of Arts degree: Business, University of New Hampshire, Durham, NH, 1986 (GPA: 3.1)

Licenses/Certifications—N/A

Continuing Education—Seminars—Workshops—Other

Dale Carnegie—Successful Selling, Tom Hopkins Sales Seminar; Anthony Robbins Sales Seminar; Johnston's

Customer-Service Excellence, the Week-long Seminar; High-tech Inventory Management Systems, by Creative Software.

Other   N/A

Military   N/A

Professional Affiliations

American Association of Uniform Retailers (Co-founder); National Uniform Association of America (NUAA); ASIS; Local Chambers

Volunteer Work/Civic & Charitable Involvement/Community Service

Make a Wish Foundation; Special Olympics; Little League Coach; President/member of the Board—POA

Special Awards and Recognitions

(See Career Highlights—Assignment #2C)

Awarded "Distributor of the Year" by *Made to Measure* magazine (industry trade publication)

Awarded "Quality Dealer" award by *Made to Measure* magazine seven consecutive years (industry trade publication)

Recognized for positioning company for successful sale—with one-year working contract

Special Hobbies

Collecting autograph books; Jet ski competitor; Downhill skiing; Public speaking; Gardening

Other   N/A

EXERCISE 6: CREATE YOUR EMPLOYMENT HISTORY

Referring to your Organizational Message Chart, document prior job responsibilities and achievements, providing clear, quantitative or qualitative evidence of the presidential, vice presidential, and supporting messages in the OMC. Your employment history should be presented in a way that reflects your core values.

Fill out a detailed form for *each* position you have held unless it is NOT going on your resume—for example, when it's too far back or it was held for a short time (a month or two), or when it is consolidated with a buyout or merger, etc. Go as far back as necessary to demonstrate your value (10 to 12 years is usually sufficient).

Company/Organization Name

_____

City and State

_____

Dates of Employment

_____

Your Title

_____

Environment (Type of business or organization/annual sales/what they do)

_____

_____

Detailed Job Responsibilities

_____

_____

_____

_____

_____

Specific Accomplishments

* _____

* _____

* _____

* _____

* _____

* _____

EXAMPLE: ERIC SCOTT'S WORK HISTORY

GREAT SCOTT ! Uniform Company, Boston, MA   1992 to Current
General Sales & Operations Manager
(A law-enforcement-uniform company specializing in private/corporate security organizations nationally)

Directed and orchestrated the successful start-up of a niche-market law-enforcement-uniform company specializing in private-security and in-house-security organizations. Created a new market segment—wholesale—not previously available to this target audience. Divided time equally between sales and operations and built one of the most successful enterprises in the nation over a five-year period. Presently direct 11 employees, including warehouse manager, alterations manager, and office manager. Personally direct both sales and operations activities to ensure, "we deliver what we sell and sell only what we can deliver."

Specific Accomplishments

- Developed company in 1992 with $1,500 and $100 a week in sales to an industry leader with $1.6 million in sales by 1997
- Developed/managed company brand label (Great Scott!) to enhance market presence and maintain market dominance
- Private labeling efforts increased pant/shirt sales 47% and boosted gross profit margins 74%
- Spearheaded high-tech inventory JIT system—reduced inventory 18% while improving service
- Identified three solid acquisitions, performed due diligence, and negotiated successful purchase—adding $600,000 in sales
- Closed and managed four national accounts—IBM, Wackenhut Security, Pinkerton Security, and Raytheon Corp.
- Awarded "Distributor of the Year" by *Made to Measure* magazine (Industry Trade Publication)
- Awarded "Quality Dealer" award by *Made to Measure* magazine 7 consecutive years (Industry Trade Publication)
- Positioned company for successful sale—with one-year working contract

Allied International/Bromley's Security, Lynn, MA   1986 to 1992
(A security guard/alarm company serving accounts in Massachusetts)

Security Director
Recruited after graduating from UNH as a Management Trainee—working in a supervisory capacity to ensure security officers at client locations were performing as expected. Promoted, after three months, to Honeywell Manager—in charge of seven locations and 100 security offices throughout eastern Massachusetts for the lucrative Honeywell contract. Took over as Security Director in 1988 with full-charge responsibility for 13,400 weekly billable hours, or a $6.2 million operation, consisting of 350 security officers, servicing more than 60 accounts. Worked closely with VPs of sales and operations to ensure quality service and profitable performance. Purchased $85,000 a year in uniforms and equipment, oversaw alarm division personnel, and managed the operational integration of two major acquisitions.

Specific Accomplishments

- Managed unprecedented growth spurt from 6,000 weekly hours to more than 13,000 hours in 18-month period
- Increased profit margin from 3.9% net profit to 7.4%, or $242,000 to more than $458,000
- Negotiated significantly lower process and longer payment terms from vendors, saving more than $23,000/year
- Improved customer retention from 78% to 87.4% in highly volatile and competitive industry
- Reduced employee turnover from 357% to 89% in high-turnover industry
- Worked closely with management (Bromley's Security) to position company for sale to Allied International

EXERCISE 7: WRITE YOUR BILLBOARD

Create a four-line headline for your billboard. Your billboard should state clearly who you are, what you want to do, and the single most important benefit you can offer a prospective employer. Above all, it should answer the question, "Why should I hire you?"

Worksheet: Creating Your Own Billboard

Examples of Effective Billboards

Top-Producing Sales Professional/Account Representative
8 Consecutive Years Named to "President's Club" for High Achievement
National and International Experience
Fluent in English, Spanish, and French

Administrative Assistant/Executive Support
Project Management/Event Planning Expertise
Extensive Computer Skills
12 Years in High-Pressure Environments

Project Engineer
Expert in Nuclear Start-up Operations
12 Years Experience in Highly Responsible Positions
Project Engineer for Three-Mile Island Cleanup

Elementary School Teacher
17 Years of Outstanding Academic Training
Solid Classroom Management and Curriculum Development/Enhancement Skills
Selected as Delegate to National Teacher's Conference,
Washington D.C.—1995 through 2000

EXAMPLE: ERIC SCOTT'S BILLBOARD

TOP-PRODUCING SENIOR-LEVEL OPERATIONS MANAGER
Strategically Orchestrating Explosive Growth & Profits in
Highly Competitive, Global Markets
12 Years of Consistent, Verifiable, Uninterrupted Growth in Sales & Profits
Positioning Company as National and International Industry Leader

EXERCISE 8: WRITE YOUR RESUME!

You're ready to write your resume based on the information you've developed from the previous exercises you've completed in this Resume Workshop.

Your Contact Information and Showcase:

1. *Create your heading.* Include your name, address, and contact information listed in Exercise 1.

2. *Design your showcase.* Refer to your billboard in Exercise #7 and insert that under your heading.

3. *Insert your personal profile.* Under your billboard, insert your 2-3 line profile from your personal profile worksheet.

4. *Add your Keyword/Career Highlight section.* The final section of your showcase is the *Keyword* or *Highlights* section incorporating eight to ten vice presidential messages.

5. *Add your supporting-evidence section.* Now that you've completed your heading and showcase sections, the next step is to create your evidence section. Your evidence section substantiates your presidential message and provides supporting information for statements that describe your value to prospective employers. Determine what sections of your work history, education, and supporting activities best demonstrate proof of your value. Use the ranking system below.

Past employment	_____	Volunteer work	_____
Education	_____	Other	_____
Military	_____	Other	_____

Prioritize the sections in order of importance, depending on which section you want employers to read first. Add them to your resume in priority order.

Example: Eric Scott's Priority Ranking

Based on the sample resume below and the samples provided above, here's how Eric Scott prioritized his list:

Past employment	1	Volunteer work	4
Education	2	Other: Affiliations	3
Military	N/A	Other: Activities	5

THE FINISHED RESUME

At the end of this resume workshop, you should have a completed resume in hand—a resume that highlights your skills and accomplishments, sets you apart from other job candidates, and telegraphs your unique value to prospective employers. Best of all, your resume answers—right up front—that all-important question every hiring manager wants to know, "Why should I hire you?" Armed with this powerful selling tool, you can welcome interviews—and job offers—with confidence and satisfaction.

ERIC J. SCOTT
123 Diamond Street
Swampscott, Massachusetts 01970
Phone: (781) 555-1212/Cell: (781) 555-3232
Email: email@email.com

TOP-PRODUCING SENIOR-LEVEL OPERATIONS MANAGER
Strategically Orchestrating Explosive Growth & Profits in Highly Competitive, Global Markets
12 Years of Consistent, Uninterrupted Growth in Sales & Profits
Positioning Companies as National and International Industry Leaders

A team-spirited, growth-oriented, profit-centered operations professional with a proven, verifiable record for strategically orchestrating explosive growth and profits in highly competitive, global markets through creative, aggressive, and tactically designed marketing concepts—positioning company as industry leader. Strong conceptual, implementation, and organizational leadership skills.

CORE PROFESSIONAL STRENGTHS

Strategic Planning—Rapid Expansion Management

Corporate/Business Development

Building Strategic Alliances

Brand Development/Management

Customer-Service & Retention Management

Acquisitions Management

Product Development/Enhancement

Project Management/Leadership

New Technology Development/Transfer

Optimizing Personnel & Physical Resources

PROFESSIONAL EXPERIENCE

GREAT SCOTT ! Uniform Company, Boston, Massachusetts   1992 to Current
General Sales & Operations Manager

Directed and orchestrated the successful start-up of a niche-market law-enforcement-uniform company specializing in private-security and in-house-security organizations. Created a new market segment—wholesale—not previously available to this target audience. Divided time equally between sales and operations and built one of the most successful enterprises in the nation over a five-year period. Presently direct 11 employees, including warehouse manager, alterations manager, and office manager. Personally direct both sales and operations activities to ensure, "we deliver what we sell and sell what we can deliver."

Specific Accomplishments

- Developed company in 1992 with $1500 and $100 a week in sales to an industry leader with $1.6 million in sales by 1997
- Develop/manage company "brand label" (Great Scott !) to enhance market presence and maintain market dominance
- Private labeling efforts increased pant/shirt sales 47% and boosted gross profit margins 74%
- Spearheaded high-tech inventory JIT system—reduced inventory 18% while improving service
- Identified three solid acquisitions, performed due diligence, and negotiated successful purchase—adding $600,000 in sales
- Closed and managed four national accounts—IBM, Wackenhut Security, Pinkerton Security, and Raytheon Corp.
- Awarded "Distributor of the Year" by *Made to Measure* magazine (industry trade publication)
- Awarded "Quality Dealer" award by *Made to Measure* magazine 7 consecutive years
- Positioned company for successful sale—with one-year working contract

(Page one of two)

PROFESSIONAL EXPERIENCE (Continued)

Allied International/Bromley's Security, Lynn, Massachusetts   1986 to 1992
Security Director

Recruited after graduating from UNH as a Management Trainee—working in a supervisory capacity to ensure security officers at client locations are performing as expected. Promoted, after three months, to Honeywell Manager—in charge of seven locations and 100 security offices throughout eastern Massachusetts for the lucrative Honeywell contract. Took over as Security Director in 1988 with full charge responsibility for 13,400 weekly billable hours, or a $6.2 million operation, consisting of 350 security officers, servicing more than 60 accounts. Worked closely with VPs of sales and operations to ensure quality service and profitable performance. Purchased $85,000 a year in uniforms and equipment, oversaw alarm division personnel, and managed the operational integration of two major acquisitions.

Specific Accomplishments

- Managed unprecedented growth spurt from 6,000 weekly hours to more than 13,000 hours in 18-month period
- Increased profit margin from 3.9% net profit to 7.4%, or $242,000 to more than $458,000
- Negotiated significantly lower process and longer payment terms from vendors, saving more than $23,000/year
- Improved customer retention from 78% to 87.4% in highly volatile and competitive industry
- Reduced employee turnover from 357% to 89% in high-turnover industry
- Worked closely with management to position company for sale to Allied International

EDUCATION

University of New Hampshire, Durham, New Hampshire
Bachelor of Arts Degree: Business, 1986   (GPA: 3.1)

Relevant Continuing Education—Seminars/Workshops (1994–Current)

Dale Carnegie—Successful Selling
Tom Hopkins Sales Seminar
Anthony Robbins Sales Seminar
Lenore Johnston's "Customer Service Excellence," the Week-long Seminar
High-tech Inventory Management Systems, by Creative Software

PROFESSIONAL AFFILIATIONS

Co-founder: American Association of Uniform Retailers
Member: National Uniform Association of America (NUAA)
Member: American Society for Industrial Security (ASIS)
Member: Local Chambers of Commerce

VOLUNTEER/COMMUNITY SERVICE

Make-a-Wish Foundation
Special Olympics
Little League Coach
President/Member of the Board—POA

SELECTED ACTIVITIES

Collecting autograph books
Jet ski competitor
Downhill skier
Public speaking

References and Supporting Documentation Furnished upon Request

Turning a Two-Page Resume Into a One-Page Resume

If you are applying for a position in an industry that typically prefers one-page resumes, you may need to modify your resume format by eliminating your personal profile, keyword, or a highlights-of-experience sections. Here's an example showing how to condense your resume.

ERIC J. SCOTT
123 Diamond Street
Swampscott, Massachusetts 01970
Phone: (781) 555-1212/Cell: (781) 555-3232
Email: email@email.com

TOP-PRODUCING SENIOR-LEVEL OPERATIONS MANAGER
Strategically Orchestrating Explosive Growth & Profits in Highly Competitive, Global Markets
12 Years of Consistent, Uninterrupted Growth in Sales & Profits
Positioning Companies as National and International Industry Leaders

PROFESSIONAL EXPERIENCE

GREAT SCOTT ! Uniform Company, Boston, Massachusetts   1992 to Current
General Sales & Operations Manager

Directed and orchestrated the successful start-up of a niche-market law-enforcement uniform company specializing in private security and in-house security organizations. Created a new market segment—wholesale—not previously available to this target audience. Divided time equally between sales and operations and built one of the most successful enterprises in the nation over a five-year period. Presently direct 11 employees, including warehouse manager, alterations manager, and office manager.

- Developed company in 1992 with $1,500 and $100 a week in sales to an industry leader with $1.6 million in sales by 1997
- Developed/managed company brand label (Great Scott !) to enhance market presence and maintain market dominance
- Private labeling efforts increased pant/shirt sales 47% and boosted gross profit margins 74%
- Spearheaded high-tech inventory JIT system—reduced inventory 18% while improving service
- Identified three solid acquisitions, performed due diligence, and negotiated successful purchase—adding $600,000 in sales
- Closed and managed four national accounts—IBM, Wackenhut Security, Pinkerton Security, and Raytheon Corp.
- Awarded "Distributor of the Year" by *Made to Measure* magazine (industry trade publication)
- Awarded "Quality Dealer" award by *Made to Measure* magazine 7 consecutive years

Allied International/Bromley's Security, Lynn, Massachusetts   1986 to 1992
Security Director

Worked in a supervisory capacity to ensure security officers at client locations were performing as expected. Promoted, after three months, to Honeywell Manager—in charge of seven locations and 100 security offices throughout eastern Massachusetts for the lucrative Honeywell contract. Took over as Security Director in 1988 with full-charge responsibility for 13,400 weekly billable hours, or a $6.2 million operation, consisting of 350 security officers, servicing more than 60 accounts. Purchased $85,000 a year in uniforms and equipment, oversaw alarm division personnel, and managed the operational integration of two major acquisitions.

- Managed unprecedented growth spurt from 6,000 weekly hours to more than 13,000 hours
- Increased profit margin from 3.9% net profit to 7.4%, or $242,000 to more than $458,000
- Improved customer retention from 78% to 87.4% in highly volatile and competitive industry
- Reduced employee turnover from 357% to 89% in high-turnover industry

EDUCATION

University of New Hampshire, Durham, New Hampshire
Bachelor of Arts Degree: Business, 1986 (GPA: 3.1)

Relevant Continuing Education—Seminars/Workshops (1994–Current)

Dale Carnegie—Successful Selling; Tom Hopkins Sales Seminar; Anthony Robbins Sales Seminar; Lenore Johnston's "Customer Service Excellence," the Week-long Seminar; High-tech Inventory Management Systems, by Creative Software

PROFESSIONAL AFFILIATIONS

Co-founder: American Association of Uniform Retailers; Member: National Uniform Association of America (NUAA); Member: American Society for Industrial Security (ASIS)

6

Crafting Resumes to Use On-line

The Internet has had a dramatic impact on job-search campaigns. The Internet is used by thousands and thousands of employers worldwide, posting job openings on hundreds of job sites hoping job candidates will see them and send a resume. There are hundreds of thousands of job seekers posting their resumes to the Internet in hopes that companies seeking their skills and abilities will notice and and contact them for a follow-up interview. Job candidates are using the Internet to research companies they may want to work for; employers are using the Internet to gather corporate intelligence as well as labor statistics; and executive recruiters (headhunters) and employment agencies are using the Internet for all the same reasons. It has been estimated by the U.S. Department of Labor Statistics that currently, up to seven percent of all job positions filled are filled by using the Internet as a primary source. And it is estimated that by the year 2010, up to 20 percent or more of all job positions will be filled via the Internet. An on-line resume serves the same purpose as a regular resume in terms of its mission: promoting your value to prospective employers who need it. The major difference between on-line resumes and regular resumes is that regular resumes are created on paper and delivered by hand, mail, courier, or fax. On-line resumes are delivered electronically, by computers.

Regular resumes are created on paper and delivered by hand, mail, courier, or fax. On-line resumes are delivered by computer.

THREE TYPES OF HIGH-TECH RESUMES

There are three basic types of high-tech resumes:

1. Scannable
2. Electronic
3. Presentation

The Scannable Resume

The scannable resume is like a caterpillar that turns into a butterfly. It starts out as a regular resume on paper. When it reaches its destination, the resume is scanned into the employer's computer. The paper resume becomes trash (or it may be filed, though that is unlikely). The information on the resume, however, is stored away in the depths of a company's computer filing system. Inside the computer system, customized software seeks out information in the form of *keywords*. The software has yet to reach the level of sophistication where it can read a document as a human can, so it searches for predetermined, industry-specific, value-oriented words and phrases. Resumes with the "right" keywords are resumes that get read. Keywords are actually "code names" for value. Here are samples of keywords for five different positions.

- *Keywords for a salesman*: Business development, account management, retention management, new-product launch.
- *Keywords for an electrician*: Blueprint reading, commercial construction, troubleshooting, regulatory launch, high-impact presentation and closing skills, and revenue enhancement, compliance, estimating, and project management.
- *Keywords for an executive secretary/administrative assistant*: Client liaison, office management, staff development, meeting/event planning, records management, and sales support.
- *Keywords for a product marketer*: Product life-cycle management, project management, market-research and competitive analysis, authoring requirements/specifications, and sales support.
- *Keywords for a printing press operator*: Press configurations, setups, teardowns, project management, quality control, deadline oriented, matching, collating, fusing, trimming, and packaging functions.

The Electronic Resume

Electronic resumes fall into two separate and distinct categories: email attachments and ASCII Text Files.

Email Attachments: The beauty of an email attachment is that you can send your regular resume electronically, with all the **bolds**, *italics*, underlines, and shadows, as well as columns, shading, and any graphics or symbols ($, %, @, &, etc.) you have used on the resume, as long as the receiver of the resume has the same or compatible software to open the attached document when it arrives by email. This is the most popular method for sending and receiving on-line resumes.

ASCII Files: An ASCII File, in computer science, is also called a text file, a text-only file, or an ASCII text file. This is a document file in the universally recognized text format called ASCII (American Standard Code for Information Interchange). An ASCII file contains characters, spaces, punctuation, carriage returns, and sometimes tabs and an end-of-file marker, but it contains no formatting information. This generic format is sometimes referred to as "text" and is useful for transferring unadorned but readable files between programs that could not otherwise understand each other's documents. In some cases, an employer will ask you to send your resume electronically as an ASCII file. An ASCII file is a file made up of text—just plain words. The reason for using this format is that all computer systems and programs read ASCII files. Because the file only reads and acknowledges words, however, you cannot use **bolds**, *italics*, <u>underlines</u>, **shadows**, columns, shading, graphics or symbols ($, %, @, &, etc.). Unfortunately, the resulting document is dull and unexciting, and it looks like every other resume. When you send resumes in this format, selling and delivering the "right" value messages are paramount!

The Presentation Resume

The presentation resume is also known as the *Web* resume, the *multimedia* resume, or the *luxury* resume (because it can be very pricey to produce). The presentation resume is just that: a multimedia showcase presentation of your value, containing all supporting evidence. The presentation can be as simple as a one-page Web site containing your resume and some supporting information, or it can be as elaborate as a multimedia presentation with bells, whistles, music, video, and animation.

Most people don't need to use an elaborate presentation resume. If you work in media, the arts, design, and related professions, the presentation resume can be an exciting and powerful way to promote yourself.

ON-LINE HELP

This chapter is intended simply to introduce and review the subject of high-tech resumes. There are many comprehensive resources available that provide specific Web sites (thousands of them) and strategies on how to use the Internet effectively to post resumes and investigate posted job listings.

Resumes in Cyberspace, Pat Criscito, Barrons

Hook Up and Get Hired, Joyce Lain Kennedy, John Wiley & Sons

Using the Internet and the World Wide Web in Your Job Search, Fred Jandt and Mary Nemich, JIST

Job Hunting on the Internet, Richard Nelson Bolles, Ten Speed Press

REGULAR VERSUS ASCII: EXAMPLE

The following two resumes are in fact the same resume. One is a paper value-based resume, the other is the same document converted to ASCII text.

ANDREW J. KRAMER, C.C.C., C.E.C.
4823 Lake Shore Drive
Saukville, Wisconsin 53080
(262) 555-1212/email@email.com

CERTIFIED EXECUTIVE CHEF/CHEF INSTRUCTOR

Offering Solid Teaching, Motivation, & Leadership Skills

Contributing to the Growth & Advancement of Top-Ranked Culinary Organizations

---

Qualifications in 5-Star Dining as Executive Chef and Chef Instructor. Contribute to organizational growth/profits by enhancing individual/group productivity, expense management, and consistently delivering high-quality food products.

EDUCATION AND CREDENTIALS

THE CULINARY INSTITUTE OF AMERICA, Milwaukee, Wisconsin
- Associate of Science: Culinary Arts, 1987
- Externship, Ritz Carlton and Hyatt Regency, Waikoloa, HI

AMERICAN CULINARY FEDERATION, Milwaukee, Wisconsin
- Certified Executive Chef, Certified Chef de Cuisine, 1989

CULINARY AWARDS AND SELECTED RECOGNITIONS

Gold Medal, Awarded 1st Place, Hilton Head Island Seafood Cook-Off, 2001

Gold Medal, Awarded 1st Place, Atlanta Seafood Cook-Off, 1999

Silver Medal, Awarded Hot Food Competition, Orlando Food Expo, 1998

Silver Medal, Awarded S.E. Food Service Expo—Hot Food Mystery Box Competition, Atlanta, 1997

Silver Medal, Awarded S.E. Food Service Expo—Hot Food Mystery Box Competition, 1996

Bronze Medal, Awarded nationally to compete in NAFEM Culinary Competition, 1995

Featured in *Chef Magazine* (11/97, p.70): Article entitled "Char grilled Sea Bass," 2000

HIGHLIGHTS OF PROFESSIONAL EXPERIENCE

- As Chef Instructor, taught International Cuisine and coached student team to Gold Medal.
- Performed exclusive catering for U.S. Government Officials, Royalty, and International Guests.
- As Banquet Chef, planned and executed functions ranging in size from 20 to 15,000 people. Managed 62 chefs.
- As Garde Manager Chef, responsible for cold-food preparation, menu planning, and alterations.
- Coordinated costing & banquet planning, purchasing/inventory control, and projected/maintained food and labor costs.
- Current Advertising Chairman/Vice President: Atlanta Regional Chef's Association.

CHRONOLOGY OF PROFESSIONAL EXPERIENCE

Executive Chef	1992 to Current
The RCA Executive Club, Atlanta, Georgia	
Chef Instructor	1995 to Current
Atlanta Culinary Institute, Atlanta, Georgia	
Regional Executive Chef	1989 to 1992
Lockwood Food Service, Atlanta, Georgia	
Executive Chef/Banquet Sous Chef	1987 to 1989
Eastpointe Country Club, Atlanta, Georgia	

References Furnished Upon Request

Chapter 6: Crafting Resumes to Use On-line

ANDREW J. KRAMER, C.C.C., C.E.C.
4823 Lake Shore Drive
Saukville, Wisconsin 53080
(262) 555-1212/email@email.com

CERTIFIED EXECUTIVE CHEF/CHEF INSTRUCTOR

Offering Solid Teaching, Motivation, & Leadership Skills
Contributing to the Growth & Advancement of Top-Ranked Culinary Organizations

Qualifications in 5-Star Dining as Executive Chef and Chef Instructor. Contribute to organizational growth/profits by enhancing individual/group productivity, expense management, and consistently delivering high-quality food products.

EDUCATION AND CREDENTIALS

THE CULINARY INSTITUTE OF AMERICA, Milwaukee, Wisconsin
- Associate of Science: Culinary Arts, 1987
- Externship, Ritz Carlton, and Hyatt Regency, Waikoloa, HI

AMERICAN CULINARY FEDERATION, Milwaukee, Wisconsin
- Certified Executive Chef, Certified Chef de Cuisine, 1989

CULINARY AWARDS AND SELECTED RECOGNITIONS

Gold Medal, Awarded 1st Place, Hilton Head Island Seafood Cook-Off, 2001

Gold Medal, Awarded 1st Place, Atlanta Seafood Cook-Off, 1999

Silver Medal, Awarded Hot Food Competition, Orlando Food Expo, 1998

Silver Medal, Awarded S.E. Food Service Expo—Hot Food Mystery Box Competition, Atlanta, 1997

Silver Medal, Awarded S.E. Food Service Expo—Hot Food Mystery Box Competition, 1996

Bronze Medal, Awarded nationally to compete in NAFEM Culinary Competition, 1995

Featured in *Chef Magazine* (11/97, p.70): Article entitled "Char grilled Sea Bass," 2000

HIGHLIGHTS OF PROFESSIONAL EXPERIENCE

- As Chef Instructor, taught International Cuisine and coached student team to Gold Medal.
- Performed exclusive catering for U.S. Government Officials, Royalty, and International Guests.
- As Banquet Chef, planned and executed functions ranging in size from 20 to 15,000 people. Managed 62 chefs.
- As Garde Manger Chef, responsible for cold-food preparation, menu planning, and alterations.
- Coordinated costing & banquet planning, purchasing/inventory control, and maintained food and labor costs.
- Current Advertising Chairman/Vice President: Atlanta Regional Chef's Association.

CHRONOLOGY OF PROFESSIONAL EXPERIENCE

Executive Chef The RCA Executive Club, Atlanta, Georgia	1992 to Current
Chef Instructor Atlanta Culinary Institute, Atlanta, Georgia	1995 to Current
Regional Executive Chef Lockwood Food Service, Atlanta, Georgia	1989 to 1992
Executive Chef/Banquet Sous Chef Eastpointe Country Club, Atlanta, Georgia	1987 to 1989

References furnished upon request

7

How to Write Winning Cover Letters

Unless you plan to present your resume in person, you will need to construct a well-written, visually pleasing, and rapport-building cover letter to accompany your resume. Most employers, hiring professionals, recruiters, personnel professionals, and human-resource managers agree that cover letters are critical. Another point they agree on is that the cover should *not* simply rehash the resume. Otherwise, why not just send two resumes and forget the cover letter? Instead, the cover letter should introduce the resume, capture an employer's attention, and build immediate rapport. Simply put, a good cover letter entices an employer to read the accompanying resume with interest and enthusiasm.

WHAT IT TAKES TO WRITE A COMPELLING COVER LETTER

Cover letters must complement resumes, not emulate them. First and foremost, a good cover letter builds rapport and establishes a "relationship" with a prospective employer.

Contrary to popular belief, opposites do *not* attract, at least not in the world of work, and not for the long term. Commonality attracts. Your cover letter builds rapport by identifying and addressing points you have in common with the hiring manager. You can accomplish this in several ways: by including information about what you know about the company or organization and how you believe you "fit." You can accomplish this by doing some research and intelligence gathering about the company culture or the person to whom you are sending the cover letter, and by flattering the reader in a professional way. Your ultimate goal is to *build a bridge of commonality* between yourself and a prospective employer.

Building Rapport = Building Bridges of Commonality

Most career coaches advise job candidates to be observant and look around for *subject clues* just before the start of an interview. Subject clues identify ice breakers that establish immediate rapport with a hiring manager. They identify interests that you and the hiring manager have in common, and they help to create a bond between you. Look around the office and lobby. You might see a bookcase filled with soccer trophies because the company sponsors soccer teams in town. You might notice military plaques, impressionist paintings, tropical gardens, or sales awards. By taking notice of these subject clues, you can pick a few out that you can talk about to warm up the interview at the start and make both you and the interview more comfortable. One case in point, "I see you have a beautiful garden off the entranceway. I just want to compliment you on it. I love gardening—I've been doing it for over 10 years." Another, "I noticed that your company sponsors youth soccer teams. Judging from the number of plaques on your lobby wall, it looks like your teams have done very well. They've sure won a lot of championships. I am a big soccer fan myself. Do you coach, or are you personally involved with the sport?"

At this stage, you probably won't have had the advantage of visiting an employer's office and making a personal observation. Even so, you must strive to build the same kind of bridge of commonality in your cover letter. To do it, you'll need to be creative. Your approach will depend on your individual circumstances. If, for example, you are responding to a blind newspaper ad and have no idea who the company is, default to your *value*—but introduce it in an exciting way, emphasizing your character traits. Normally, it is best to leave character traits off your resume, as employers tend to perceive them as wordy. Character traits can strengthen a cover letter, however. Here is an example, "While I cannot determine the identity of your company from your advertisement in the newspaper, I assure you that as a seasoned office manager, I can improve office efficiency and productivity in an energetic, creative, and professional manner. I am a team leader able to carry out and enforce your company's policies and procedures and exceed your most stringent expectations."

If, on the other hand, you have a contact in the company who knows the hiring manager, you have an advantage. Find out what's most important to him or her and incorporate it into your cover letter. Let's say, for example, that you want to send your resume to the Controller of ABC Company. A friend who works for ABC has told you that the Controller has three important priorities: reducing outstanding monies owed, willingness to work as long as it takes to do it, and getting the job done in a professional manner that reflects favorably upon ABC Company.

With this information, you can write an effective, rapport-building cover letter, "I am a hard-working accounts-receivable professional with a verifiable track record of success that includes dramatically reducing outstanding accounts receivable in a highly ethical and professional manner. I am recognized, in all past positions, as one who is willing and determined to work as hard and as long as it takes, to make a significant contribution to the goals and objectives of my department. In this light, I would like the opportunity to be able to contribute to your department's goals and objectives, and I believe I can accomplish them in a way that reflects the integrity and reputation of ABC Company."

Deliver Your Presidential Message in Your Cover Letter

One of the best ways to build rapport and establish commonalities between yourself and a prospective employer is to deliver the power of your *presidential message* (see Chapter 2) strategically within your cover letter. Of course, your presidential message will be the main theme and key message of your resume as well. Remember, however, that your presidential message answers this single all-important question, "Why should I hire you?" If you answer this question immediately and effectively in your cover letter, the hiring manager will be enticed into reading your resume with great interest. For example, "I have the expertise to manage your warehouse using proven, verifiable systems of control that will contribute to your bottom line."

Make a Strong First Impression

Your cover letter delivers that all-important *first impression* to a prospective employer. A hiring manager will read your cover letter first, before he reads your resume, and before he invites you in for an interview. Presentation and professionalism are critical. Along with building rapport, your cover letter should be well organized, well written, and *absolutely free of spelling or grammatical errors*. Spell check and proofread your cover letter carefully before you send it. Double-check the spelling and job title of the recipient, along with the spelling of the company name.

TEN GUIDELINES FOR WRITING EFFECTIVE COVER LETTERS

Following are ten guidelines for writing effective cover letters—letters that build rapport and interest in hiring managers.

1. Develop a master team of advisors to help you write and edit your cover letters. You can't do it alone! Team up with family, friends, hired employment professionals—anyone who would inspire and help achieve career goals and objectives.
2. Personalize and customize your cover letter for each prospective employer. At the very least, include the name of the recipient, his title, and company name.

3. Keep the letter short. Two to three paragraphs is generally sufficient. Your goal is to get the hiring manager to read your resume—quickly and with interest!

4. Don't rehash what is already in the resume. Instead, focus on your pertinent character traits and the hiring manager's specific interests. Write with the reader in mind. Build rapport by building bridges of commonality.

5. Entice your prospective employer. Give him or her a compelling reason to read your resume and invite you in for an interview.

6. Include your presidential message. Answer the question, "Why should I hire you?"

7. Differentiate your cover letter from your competitors' by using distinctive formats, type fonts, and stationery. Don't overdo it, however. Your cover letter should appear professional, not tacky.

8. Do not mention money or compensation unless requested.

9. Initiate action. End your cover letter by asking for an interview, a phone conversation, or other appropriate action that will take you closer to landing the job.

10. Thank the reader for his or her attention and sign off.

Sample #1: Responding to a Classified Advertisement

David H. Grant
9 Star Bright Avenue
Peoria, Arizona 85371
(602) 555-5555/email@email.com

April 18, 2002

Mr. Maxwell Justin, Vice President of Human Resources
The Donovan Corporation
147 Windy Breeze Road
Phoenix, Arizona 85440

Dear Mr. Justin:

This is not just another cover letter and resume team responding to your advertisement in the *Phoenix Chronicle* for Accounts Receivable Manager. You will see from my resume that I have over seven years of verifiable success as a contributing member of aggressive, state-of-the-art accounting departments. I am a hard-working accounts-receivable professional recognized for dramatically reducing outstanding accounts receivable in a highly ethical and professional manner to reflect the integrity and reputation of my employer. I would like the opportunity to be able to contribute to The Donovan Corporation's goals and objectives.

Your Criteria for Employment	My Credentials
Minimum 3 years experience in A/R	7 years experience in A/R
Strong communications skills	Strong verbal and written communication skills
Excellent telephone skills	7 years of A/R using the phone as primary tool
A team player	A team player with outstanding interpersonal skills
Strong analytical skills	Analytical and problem-solving proficiency

I am very much aware that The Donovan Corporation is an industry leader and recruits individuals who are team players in pursuit of greater growth, expansion, and profits. I am confident that I can be a contributing member in pursuit of your goals and objectives by controlling outstanding receivables and enhancing the company's cash position.

After reviewing the enclosed resume, if you believe, as I do, that my qualifications, experience, and supporting references would be valuable to The Donovan Corporation, I would welcome the opportunity of meeting you in person. I will call you next week to discuss this further. Thank you for your time and consideration.

Sincerely,

David H. Grant
Encl: resume

Harold C. Cooper
18 Forest Street
Loretto, Pennsylvania 15941
(814) 555-5555/email@email.com

> "Harold Cooper is one of the finest finishing carpenters I have had the pleasure of working for me in more than 30 years of being in business."
>
> —Chester Williams, former employer

July 22, 2002

Mr. Michael Gordon, Owner/President
Gordon Contracting, Inc.
2300 Park Lane
Pittsburgh, Pennsylvania

Dear Mr. Gordon:

I am exploring employment opportunities as Lead Finishing Carpenter with your company. I have enclosed my resume for your review and consideration.

I am very proud of the testimonial above, as Mr. Williams has employed thousands of carpenters over his long and successful career as owner and President of Cabinets International. There is no doubt that I can be of value to you and your company as well.

I am a young, energetic, quality-oriented professional who takes great pride in his work. I strive to be the very best I can be, go the extra mile, and I know that by providing an exceptional quality of work—on time and within budget—I can add to the growth and reputation of your company.

I would like to meet with you personally to introduce myself and my portfolio of work that I have done over the past five years. If you have an employment opportunity and feel I would be a "fit" with your company, I would enjoy getting together. I will take the liberty of calling you next week to discuss this matter.

Respectfully,

Harold C. Cooper

Sample #3: Executive Recruiter—Unsolicited

Susan P. Brandt
171 Smith Avenue
Denver, Colorado 30003
(303) 555-5555/email@email.com

October 7, 2002

Mr. Winston Betts, Executive Vice President
International Marketing Consortium, Ltd.
195 Wellington Place
Los Angeles, California 98649

Dear Mr. Betts:

Jerry Billings referred me to you and mentioned I might be a person you might like to meet.

I am currently the General Sales and Business Development Director for Walker Enterprises based in Denver, Colorado. In less than three years in this position, I have built an international team of sales professionals that have dramatically improved sales in global arenas by over 600 percent—from $8.2 million in 1998 to more than $51 million in 2000. Furthermore, I have helped my company strengthen the market position of our key clients, including Pepsi, New Balance Shoe, General Electric, and The Body Shop. These efforts alone have led to significant additional sales from our existing customer base.

Your recruiting firm is considered one of the top firms in serving the types of clients that would be a perfect fit for me. My goal is to attain an executive-level position where I can direct international sales, marketing, and business-development efforts in high-tech, solution-focused environments.

I am pursuing new opportunities at this time as I am seeking new challenges with corporations offering opportunities for professional growth, management, and leadership. Presently, I am earning $180,000 as a base salary with incentive bonuses based on exceeding production standards.

Please note that I am fluent in three languages (English, Spanish, and German) and am conversant in French and Italian, offering extraordinary cross-cultural business and sales/marketing experience.

I will call you at the end of next week to explore employment opportunities that will surely benefit you, your client companies, and myself.

Sincerely,

Susan P. Brandt

Encl: Resume

Sample #4: Responding to an Internet Job Posting—ASCII Text File

Ellen Richmond
89 Grant Boulevard
Nashville, Tennessee 38456
(615) 555-5555/email@email.com

To: Matt Henderson, HR Director: The Whealen Companies
RE: Director of IS—Posted 10/20/02

November 2, 2002

Technological excellence lies in one's ability to integrate strategy with tactics, to assess and meet the needs of each department, and to deliver and support the technologies and applications appropriate to each functional department.

I am presently the Manager of IS and Technology Development for Kingston International, and have spent the past 10 years providing technology solutions and leadership for a $280 million, top-rated health-care organization. Under my direction I have reorganized the IS department to reflect the evolving health care industry and positioned the new technology to:

- speed up reporting
- track key data and information
- support sales, marketing, operations, finance, and customer service efforts
- spearhead the development of a $1.9 million Web site
- enhance the financial position—bottom line and cash management

My resume, enclosed in an ASCII Text File, reflects my core responsibilities and key achievements and contributions. At this point in my career, I am seeking new challenges and opportunities to again lead a technology department in a high-growth market. The Whealen Companies would certainly fit that profile.

I would welcome an in-person or telephone interview at your earliest convenience and will furnish any additional and supporting documentation that you might need to make the right decision for this important position.

Sincerely,

Ellen Richmond

Sample #5: Responding to Inquiry from Executive Recruiter (Asking for Salary History)

Daniel Wallace Charles
1225 W. 32ND Avenue
Reno, Nevada 80001
(709) 555-5555/email@email.com

September 20, 2002

Ms. Janette Hastings, Senior Recruiter
Executive Gaming Recruiters, Inc.
1200 Main Street
Las Vegas, Nevada 89022

Dear Janette:

It was a pleasure speaking with you on the telephone today and am very pleased that, based on our brief conversation, I might be a leading candidate for the position of Gaming Manager for the Silver Slot Corp. You asked me to send you a resume, and that is enclosed for your review. You also requested that I send a salary history, which I provided for you below—along with production/bottom-line results.

To briefly reiterate what we covered in our conversation today, you noted you were seeking a gaming manager with start-up management experience, strong organizational and leadership skills to lead an organization with more than 1,500 employees, and the ability to deliver consistently above-industry-standard profit results. You will note from both my resume and salary history, I have succeeded in all these areas.

Company	Year	Title	Salary	Sales	Profits
The Reno Corp	1995 current	Gaming Manager	$111,000	$101 million	$16.2 million
HRT, Ltd.	1989–1995	Gaming Manager	$84,000	$71 million	$11.4 million
Dock St. Corp.	1984–1989	Asst. Gaming Mgr.	$76,000	$89 million	$13.1 million

In closing, I hope this information is what you are looking for. I will call at the end of the week to follow up with you.

Again, thank you for your efforts on my behalf. Have a good week.

Sincerely,

Daniel Wallace Charles

Encl: resume

Sample #6: Responding to Blind Classified Advertisement (Company not known)

Vicky Garcia
87523 Edward Boulevard, Apt. #505
Edwards, Wisconsin 53927
(908) 555-5555/email@email.com

June 29, 2002

Human Resource Manager
JP # 405B—*Wisconsin Tribune*
RE: Executive Assistant to the President
PO Box 89000
Madison, Wisconsin 52454-9000

Dear Hiring Manager:

Based on your advertisement in the *Wisconsin Tribune*, I am unable to determine the identity of your company, but I assure you that as a seasoned office manager and executive assistant, I can improve office efficiency and productivity in an energetic, creative, and professional manner. I am a team leader able to carry out and enforce your company's policies and procedures and to exceed your most stringent expectations.

There are five areas I feel I can excel in, based on the criteria you noted in your advertisement which includes:

- Meeting and event planning and coordination
- Executive-level customer-service and client-relations management
- Strong writing skills (former English teacher) and computer experience
- Excellent interpersonal skills—a team player
- A highly professional demeanor

My objective is to help you and your company achieve yours! I would welcome the opportunity to explore this in more depth—possibly via telephone or an in-person interview.

I thank you for reviewing my experience and qualifications, and I hope to hear back from you at your earliest convenience.

Sincerely,

Vicky Garcia

Sample #7: Referral

Jennifer Wong
508 University Club Drive
Dallas, Texas 75203
(210) 555-5555/email@email.com

December 3, 2002

Mr. Graham Todd, President
Dallas Interior Design Corp.
3124 Westin Blvd., Suite 305
Dallas, Texas 75111

Dear Mr. Todd:

Melanie Rogers suggested that I contact you regarding a position as Interior Designer for your business-to-business and commercial division. Melanie is well aware that I have been in the commercial/business-to-business arena for the past 12 years throughout Texas, and I offer your company a number of valuable areas where I believe I can significantly contribute to your future growth and profits.

1. I have key contacts throughout Texas (and beyond) to assist in future business-development efforts.
2. I have worked (start-to-finish) on major interior design projects from $250,000–$4.7 million.
3. I am recognized for exceeding customer expectations while meeting ALL deadlines and budgets.
4. I am strong in turning around underperforming or "troubled" projects—quickly and effectively.
5. I am experienced in successfully opening new offices and territories in highly competitive markets.

I have enclosed my resume for your review. Melanie mentioned that you might be out of town for the next two weeks, so I will plan on contacting you upon your return.

Thank you for your time in reviewing my resume. I look forward to getting together in the near future.

Respectfully,

Jennifer Wong

Encl: resume

Bailey C. Hughes
111 College Drive
Arlington, Massachusetts 01933
(617) 555-5555/email@email.com

May 15, 2002

Mr. Howard Enterman, President
Enterman Construction, Inc.
720 Commonwealth Avenue
Boston, Massachusetts 01926

Dear Mr. Enterman:

I will be graduating from Boston University in less than three weeks and hope to utilize my academic and work experience as an architect to contribute to a well-respected architectural firm. I have enclosed my resume for your consideration. Thank you in advance for reviewing it.

Anyone who has lived or worked in the Boston area surely has heard of Enterman Construction, Inc. Your company is recognized as the premiere commercial construction firm in the Boston area—and based on my research, I understand you have an in-house architectural division. I am very interested in working for this division. I can offer you the following:

- A graduate who finished in the top 15 percent of his class and completed an Internship with Maslow, Inc.
- A person with seven years of architectural experience—full/part time while attending school.
- A creative, highly disciplined worker able to meet all job functions, including CAD.

I have a strong portfolio of references including college professors (architectural department), former employers, and clients, who would support my resume. I would like to share them with you in an interview setting where I can introduce myself and my qualifications. Please expect my telephone call in the coming week to see if such a meeting can be arranged.

Again, I thank you for your time and look forward to speaking with you next week.

Sincerely,

Bailey C. Hughes

Encl: resume

Part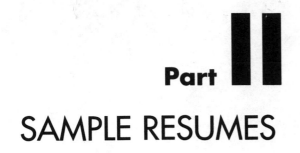

SAMPLE RESUMES

Business

RETAIL COORDINATOR

JENNIFER du PONT

1209 The Pointe Drive • Cincinnati, Ohio 45373
(413) 555-1212 • email@email.com

RETAIL COORDINATOR
Exclusive Designer, Apparel-Related Environments

Sales, New-Business Development, and Special-Event Coordination
Product-Assortment Management, Merchandising Specialist

Four years' high-visibility positions in conjunction with major high-end retailers and specialty stores.

Recognized for enhancing sales 56% each season for past four years.

CORE STRENGTHS

Market research and analysis of buying trends	Advertisement selection; strategic marketing
Selective buying and procurement	Relationship building; developing strategic partnerships
Trend forecasting	Recruiting, training, and managing of sales specialists
Identifying new and current market trends	New-account acquisition
Turning around underperforming operations	Research and analytical aptitude

PROFESSIONAL EXPERIENCE

MICHAEL KORS, Cincinnati, Ohio   1995 to Current
(Michael Kors is an American design company consisting of three divisions—Michael Kors, a designer collection line; KORS Michael Kors, a diffusion line; and KORS Michael Kors Petites.)

Regional Retail Coordinator
Develop/grow existing accounts through detailed selling strategies on an individualized basis (31 current accounts). Introduce and orient retail management/staff on products via facilitation of monthly seminars. Develop/implement regional buying strategies at seasonal markets, coordinate special events, and recruit/manage selling specialists.

- Fall, 1999–Spring, 2000—increased volume by 58% for total region
- Develop and manage 38% of the company's total U.S. business
- Spring, 2001—two accounts to be increased from $175,000 to $250,000/season

SAKS FIFTH AVENUE, Cincinnati, Ohio   1987 to 1995
(Worked with four departments—Woman's Footwear, Handbags, Accessories, and Hosiery—in two positions over two year period.)

Assistant Department Manager
Achieved and exceeded planned sales increases through varied sales and clientele strategies. Compiled EOM reports and reviewed them with the general manager. Constructively coached/evaluated associates relative to sales-performance and customer-service levels, conducted weekly staff meetings, identified key trends, and communicated specific assortment needs to vendors/buying office.

- Elected to serve on the Service and Selling Committee
- Awarded "Best Support Team"
- Recipient of "Spirit Award"

EDUCATION

ROLLINS COLLEGE, Winter Park, Florida
English Major; Communications Minor, 1995–1997

Sales Seminars: Dale Carnegie Selling for Profit, 2001; Sanders Sales Training, 1997–2001
Computer Literate: Windows, Excel, Word, PowerPoint, Access, Act, and the Internet

References Furnished upon Request

BUSINESS DEVELOPMENT/RELATIONSHIP MANAGEMENT

COURTNEY KRISTINE FROST

312 Belleview • Palm Beach Gardens, Florida 33410
Day: (561) 555-1212 • Evening: (561) 555-5454
email@email.com

BUSINESS DEVELOPMENT/RELATIONSHIP MANAGEMENT
Seven Years' Experience in Diversified Environments—Pharmaceuticals/Automotive
"Top producer in all positions held"

- **Senior-level presentation and closing skills**
- **Start-up and turnaround management experience**
- **New-product rollout-management expertise**
- **Team/organizational leadership**

A highly competitive, tenacious, and results-oriented professional combining polished interpersonal and rapport-building skills to significantly enhance growth, profits, and return on investment.

Core Strengths

Total account-relationship management (long-term)	Strategic market domination and leadership
Tactical alliance/partnership development	Negotiating complex contracts/special terms
Product, service, and sales training—all levels	Brand development and management
Customer-service and retention management	Time management

Professional Experience

PharmCo, Inc., Central/South Florida   2000 to Current
Institutional Account Specialist
Full accountability in developing mutually productive business relationships with key influencers and decision-makers to gain formulary access for new products. Responsible for maintaining stringent sales quotas for designated priority accounts. Work with sales management in investing resources with priority customers to optimize sales and return-on-investment.

"100% of accounts added new product on formulary"

- Promoted to highest performance category—only 19 professionals out of 298 in the United States.
- Achieved 105% of quota with successful launch of Zyvox.
- Attained 110% increase in sales of Fragmin over 1999 sales in the Miami market.
- Promoted after four months—as a result of top performance.

Pfizer Pharmaceuticals, Miami, Florida   1995 to 2000
Institutional Healthcare Representative (1999–2000)
Directed sales and account-management activities targeting institutional accounts. Mentored and trained institutional healthcare representatives, initiated and led institutional sales projects, and demonstrated and provided key information to increase sales.

"Ignited Sales from $556,000 to $2.1 million"

- Trained and mentored 25+ new pharmaceutical representatives—elevating district to #1 ranking status.
- Consistently ranked in top 5% of institutional representatives—exceeding quotas in all product areas.
- Achieved formulary acceptance (all products) at Jackson Memorial, Miami VA, and Mt. Sinai Medical Center.
- Created sales rep. resource book that was adopted by Pfizer USP Training and Curriculum Department.
- Contributing team member in developing a cost-analysis program for specialized treatment program.

BUSINESS DEVELOPMENT/RELATIONSHIP MANAGEMENT (CONT.)

Courtney Kristine Frost
Page 2

Professional Experience

Pfizer Pharmaceuticals
(Continued)

Professional Healthcare Representative (1995–1999)
Managed physician and hospital accounts in the private sector. Developed efficient call cycle, managed district projects, implemented and assessed sales-action plans, and managed formulary approvals.

> *"Increased sales from $600,000 to $3.1 million"*

- Initiated new sales tactics to achieve maximum productivity and profit.
- Achieved 222% of quota—for all products sold.
- Successfully and professionally exceeded all established sales objectives.
    - Awarded: Circle of Excellence
    - Awarded: Topper Club
    - Named: Rookie of the Year

Ford Motor Company, Dallas, Texas   1/94 to 4/96
Market Area Manager
Sales and marketing liaison between Ford Motor Company and 17 Ford/Mercury dealerships—wholesaling 16 vehicle lines. Traveled among the 17 locations providing consultative advice and support on key areas, including inventory management, advertising and marketing, pricing, and profit building.

> *"Ranked #1 in sales for both car and truck offerings"*

- Ranked #1 in sales—managed $250 million in annual sales (17 dealerships)—wholesale sales.
- Earned *#1 Select Manager Award* honors for achieving highest percentage of quota.
- Coordinated and facilitated high-energy motivational programs to achieve top levels of individual/team performance.
- Promoted four times in recognition of sales and marketing achievements.

Education/Professional Development

Florida State University, Tallahassee, Florida
Bachelor of Science: Marketing Major; Management Minor, 1993
GPA: 3.75/Summa Cum Laude

Selected Professional Development
Target Account Selling, Targeted Selection, Conflict Resolution, Speed Reading, Public Speaking

License
220 Insurance License (General Lines)

Computer Skills
Windows, Word, WordPerfect, Excel, PowerPoint, and Internet Applications

Activities

Running, Physical Fitness, Skiing, Interior Decorating, Reading/Personal Development, and Community Service

References and Professional Portfolio Furnished upon Request

COMMUNICATIONS EXECUTIVE

JANET CHASE

1610 Donovan Hill Road
Upperville, Virginia 20184
Phone/Fax: (540) 555-1212
email@email.com

SENIOR-LEVEL COMMUNICATIONS EXECUTIVE
20 Years' High Visibility in Washington, D.C.
Best-selling Author/Crisis Management Expert

Government, Media, Communications, and Public-Relations Specialist
Top-level Speech Writer/Resource and Economic-Development Management

---

A **well-connected, achievement-driven Public Relations/Communications Executive** with outstanding qualifications in all phases of corporate/governmental communications, with particular emphasis on strategic crisis management. Spearheaded the public-relations efforts for national and international crises, including:

- Tylenol Crisis
- Three-Mile Island Crisis
- Teamsters/Government Takeover

HIGHLIGHTS OF EXPERIENCE

- Association-management executive for trade associations
- Spokesperson for International Union representing more than two million members and affiliate members
- Director of Public Relations and Congressional Liaison for the American Revolution Bicentennial Administration
- Presidential Appointment, Vice Chairman, National Parks Advisory Board, 1991 to 1995
- Appointed Vice Chairman, Presidential Inaugural Committees, 1969, 1981, and 1989
- Nominee, National Mediation Board, 1995
- Featured guest on *Nightline*, *The Today Show*, *Dateline*, and all network news, including CNN
- Speechwriter (White House and three U.S. Senators); best-selling author of *Devil's Pact: Inside the Teamsters*

PROFESSIONAL EXPERIENCE

SOUTHEAST THOROUGHBRED ASSOCIATION, Warrenton, Virginia   1992 to Current
Executive Director

Developed programs to enhance breeding of native thoroughbred industry while promoting racing in Virginia. Created and implemented high-impact programs and interfaced closely with industry leaders, breeders, government officials, and the legislature to meet association goals and mandates. Oversaw budget processes, administered state breeders' fund, directed educational seminars, spearheaded fundraising activities, and serviced association members.

- Increased membership 12% a year, adding $124,000 a year to new business efforts
- Reduced attrition rate by 8%—from 12% down to 4%, through improved member-service management
- Increased profit center revenue by 32% between 1999 and 2001 by successful target-marketing efforts
- Significantly improved bottom-line results by an average of 11% per year

INTERNATIONAL BROTHERHOOD OF TEAMSTERS, Washington, D.C.   1978 to 1992
Director of Communications/Executive Assistant to the President

Served as international spokesperson, fully responsible for all communications and media-relations efforts for the two million-member union and its affiliates. Managed a staff of 20 in producing all publications, educational and policy material, and other pertinent collateral information for the membership.

- Served as Executive Assistant to the President, and Director of Government Relations
- Served as Senior Assistant and White House Liaison for international union activities

(Page one of two)

COMMUNICATIONS EXECUTIVE (CONT.)

Janet Chase
Page two

PROFESSIONAL EXPERIENCE (Continued)

NATIONAL CAUSE, Washington, D.C.   1976 to 1978
Assistant Director/Vice President

Established efforts to promote U.S. international policies, commerce, and trade, to enhance targeted causes with government, industry, and business leaders. Wrote speeches and directed press/communications efforts.

- Directed policy development and communications on domestic and international policy for national think-tank organization founded by Senators George Murphy, John Stennis, and others, including the late John Wayne

AMERICAN BICENTENNIAL ADMINISTRATION, Washington, D.C.   1971 to 1976
Director of Public Relations/Congressional Liaison

Contributing leadership role in developing and implementing all aspects of communications and public relations, including promotional planning, for the National Bicentennial Celebration. Liaison with Congressional members relative to administration and federal development and planning for national observance.

- Chief of the News Bureau, responsible for all press relations, publications and media development, marketing, and high-level speech writing

HILL AND HILL PUBLIC RELATIONS, INC., Washington, D.C.   1967 to 1971
Vice President/Account Executive

Directed government-liaison activities and public-relations campaigns for several major accounts, including Ernest & Ernest, American Airlines, The Wine Institute, Gillette, Owens Illinois, Miles Laboratories, Procter and Gamble, Continental Can, Zenith Radio Corp., and the *New York Times*.

- Developed crisis-management strategies for the Tylenol Crisis and the Three-Mile Island Crisis

EDUCATION

Bachelor of Arts: Communications, Journalism	George Washington University	1966
Associate's Degree: Political Science	Dartmouth College	1962
International Law and Foreign-Relations Studies	Georgetown/Catholic University	1966–67

AFFILIATIONS

Virginia Society of Association Executives   Public Relations Society of America
National Press Club   Who's Who in American Politics

REFERENCES

Senator John W. Warner (603) 555-1212   Congressman Tom Davis (603) 555-1213
Lawrence J. Brady (603) 555-1212   Richard Quinn (603) 555-1232

MEDIA AND PUBLIC RELATIONS PROFESSIONAL

DEBORAH ALLISON

12 Birch Street
Tequesta, Florida 33469
(561) 555-1212/email@email.com

MEDIA & PUBLIC RELATIONS
Successfully Combining Academic Training with Experience in Professional Sports
Proven Track Record for Enhancing Attendance and On-Site Sales

---

A self-motivated, high-energy, and results-oriented individual with a solid record of success in communications/ public relations within diversified environments--including **professional sports, recreation, fashion, and media**. Recognized for outstanding verbal/written communications skills to enhance organizational growth and profitability.

CORE STRENGTHS

Strategic planning and implementation	Public, community and media relations
Key project/event management	Presentation/public speaking skills
Negotiation and proactive persuasion skills	Advertising, marketing, sales, and promotion
Research and "intelligence" gathering	Lead generation and referral management
Project/event budgeting and expense control	Team leadership and staff development

PROFESSIONAL EXPERIENCE

ROGER DEAN STADIUM, Palm Beach Gardens, Florida   1998 to Present
Communications Coordinator / Public Relations / Special Events

- Immediately revamped Communications department and established/reestablished strategic contacts with all local and regional media. Developed programs and special events to captivate the community's attention.

- Direct the "Shark Patrol Kids Club," consisting of 3,200 children ages 3–13. Answer questions from parents concerning all program issues. Deal with problems during kids club baseball games that involve members and family. Handle all questions and concerns from recreation centers/summer camps. Work closely with the ticket office personnel and sales people as well as local Little League Baseball organizations in securing sponsors. Respond promptly to all phone calls concerning members. Manage event budgets and expenses.

- Spearhead Youth Day at the Ballpark attracting 3,000+ people. Contact summer program members and follow up with phone calls. Perform public/community/media relations work (Write press releases and media kits), building key partnerships to enhance exposure and program attendance. Establish strong relationships with local media and business community. Secure major sponsors (and advertising dollars) for the stadium including the Discovery Channel Store and Don Olson Tire Company. Sell ads for program and inserts and PA announcements to local businesses and individuals. Train and Develop staff and interns for on field promotions during games.

PROFESSIONAL EXPERIENCE (While Attending School)

Sales Associate	Bloomingdale's	1999 to 2000
Sports Anchor, Sports Producer & Editor	Virginia Tech News	1997 to 1999
Public Relations Committee Coordinator	New River Valley Fashion Show	1998 to 1999
Production Assistant	ESPN	1997
Volunteer	Ronald McDonald Children's Charities	1993 to 1997

EDUCATION

VIRGINIA POLYTECHNIC INSTITUTE AND STATE UNIVERSITY, Blacksburg, Virginia
Bachelor of Arts: Communications (Concentration in Mass Communication), 1999

- Computer Skills: Word, Excel, PowerPoint, and Internet Applications

References Furnished upon Request

PHARMACEUTICAL SALES/ACCOUNT MANAGER

JESSICA MARIE KAPLAN

45 Yacht Club Drive, #202
Chicago, Illinois 60662
(312) 555-1212/email@email.com

Seeking Position as...

PHARMACEUTICAL SALES/ACCOUNT MANAGER

"Six Consecutive Years of Enhancing Growth and Profits"

**Lead Generation/Customer Service & Referral Management
Start-up & Turnaround Management/New Product Launch**

CORE STRENGTHS

Strategic marketing and goal setting
Communication skills (verbal/written/listening)
Presentation/public-speaking skills
Relationship/consultative sales techniques

Building/maintaining key strategic alliances
Direct mail/marketing expertise
Research and intelligence gathering
Negotiation, persuasion, and closing skills

HIGHLIGHTS OF PROFESSIONAL EXPERIENCE

PITNEY BOWES, INC.
Chicago, Illinois/1995 to Current

Major-Account Representative (1999 to Current)
Senior Sales Associate (1995 to 1999)

Develop and maintain large/corporate accounts through strategic/targeted marketing efforts and high-impact relationship-building skills. Enhance revenue stream by increasing customer base, improving average transaction value, and increasing customers' frequency of purchase.

Accomplishments/Contributions

- ❑ Leadership role in pioneering virtual office concept—utilizing expertise to help grow clients' businesses
- ❑ Closed and managed 600+ accounts contributing $3.94 million in sales over past six years
- ❑ Averaged $970,000 in annual revenues over past two years with a stunning 81% closing ratio
- ❑ Recognized for strong mentoring abilities—assisted six new representatives, achieving $900,000 in production
- ❑ Pacemakers Club; Member: President's Roundtable; First Honors Club

DELMAR TITLE COMPANY
Chicago, Illinois/1990 to 1995

Real-Estate Title/Transaction Closer
Responsibilities included closing real-estate transactions on a daily basis utilizing research and customer-service skills and abilities. Evaluated projects, prepared written reports, addressed customer inquiries, and trained new employees.

Accomplishments/Contributions

- ❑ Recognized as the center's primary training facilitator—able to inspire top levels of production
- ❑ Average 39 closings per month—14 closings above industry average
- ❑ Elevated to Senior Closer—coordinating activities of four Junior Closers

EDUCATION/TRAINING/CERTIFICATIONS

B.A. Degree: Sociology, 1989, State University of Illinois, Chicago, Illinois
<u>Computer Skills</u>**:** Microsoft certified, Windows, Word, Excel, and Pathfinder, Internet applications and research

References and Supporting Documentation Furnished upon Request

OFFICE MANAGER/EXECUTIVE SUPPORT

MARY JO REDDING

3205 Brook Street • Charleston, West Virginia 34552 • (304) 555-1212 • email@email.com

OFFICE MANAGEMENT/EXECUTIVE SUPPORT
15 Years' Successful Experience in Responsible, High-visibility, and Multitask Environments

"Solving Problems and Taking the Initiative"

Organizational & Personnel Leadership/Sales Support/Event-Planning Expertise
Excellent Computer Skills/Assignment & Project Management

A positive-thinking, results-oriented, and team-spirited Administrative/Executive Support Professional recognized for proactively exceeding organizational mandates over past 15 years in diverse work environments.

CORE STRENGTHS

Communications skills (verbal & written)	Project and assignment management
Sales and marketing support	Interpersonal and relationship-building skills
Staff training, development, and empowerment	Time management—deadline sensitive
Document control—information processing	Customer service and client retention

Computer Skills: Windows, MS Office 2000 (Word, Excel, PowerPoint, Outlook), Publisher, and Internet research

PROFESSIONAL EXPERIENCE

GE Medical Systems Clinical Services, Charleston, West Virginia   1996 to Current
Human Resources Assistant
Provide support to the Human Resources Department with various duties, including preparing benefits binders. Update spreadsheets, prepare offer letters, follow up on necessary paperwork and procedures. Update policy and procedure manuals, screen prospective new-hires and follow up on employment interviews, set and coordinate training schedules, and assist in all areas of EEO and regulatory reporting.

- Assisted with special programs—Diversity Training, EHS Quality Training, and Employee Recognition Awards.
- Designed flyers and invitations for the Young Executives Division and assisted with the implementation of their community programs, including *"Teens Speak Out," "Aspiring Youth,"* and *"Minority Outreach."*
- Member of the computer help group, "WIZARDS"—designed to assist coworkers with software questions/problems.
- Promoted to Document Control Administrator after one year as document specialist.
- Participated in the formation of policies in the area of traditional engineering documentation and compliance.

STATE BAR OF WEST VIRGINIA, Charleston, West Virginia   1989 to 1996
Executive Secretary to the Director of West Virginia Center for Law-Related Education
Assisted the Director in preparing and monitoring annual reports, fiscal budgets, departmental budget packets, grant applications, and other reports and surveys. Handled renewals for dues, subscriptions, and memberships. Processed management requests for conference and educational seminars. Assisted with assignments and special projects for the Bar Foundation Board of Directors and other bar associations, organizations, and attorney and nonattorney groups.

- Coordinated with Director on *Project Citizen* and *We the People*—statewide civic education programs. Designed program booklet, handled registrations, reserved rooms at the state capitol, and recruited volunteers.
- Helped plan the *Civitas Bosnia Teachers' Delegation* visit to West Virginia, including hotel and meal arrangements. Designed itinerary booklet and welcome packets. Accompanied the delegation on visits.

EDUCATION & TRAINING

Courses in Liberal Arts and Computer Networking, Broward Community College, Charleston, West Virginia, 1985–89

Continuing Education—Seminars—Workshops
Seminar—"Management Skills for Administrative Assistants and Support Staff"   Fred Pryor Seminars, 2001
Seminar—"Meeting Planning and Contract Negotiation"   WVSA Executives, 2000

References upon Request

DIRECTOR OF ARTS IN MEDICINE

RENEE JEAN ALLEN

1081 Siena Oaks Circle East
Philadelphia, Pennsylvania 19108
Phone: (215) 555-1212/Cell: (215) 555-1234
Fax: (215) 555-4321/email@email.com

Seeking Position as...

Director of Arts in Medicine
At St. Ann's Hospital and the Richard & Judy Jones Children's Hospital

Recipient: "Non Profit Professional of the Year"

- 14 Years' Experience as Professional Artist
- 16 Years' Experience Working with Seriously Ill Patients
- 16 Years' Successful Fundraising and Volunteer-Coordination Experience
- 16 Years' Management and Organizational Leadership Skills
- 16 Years' Successful Event and Program Development/Management Experience

CORE STRENGTHS

Oil painting and Impressionism style
Project and program development and coordination
Senior-level presentation and public-speaking skills
Ability to integrate the arts as a healing process

Free sculpture—modern style
Using art as a fundraising tool
High-impact marketing and public relations
Strong affiliation with art world—internationally

EXPERIENCE

ALLIE CHRISTOPHER CHILDREN'S FUND, Middleton, Pennsylvania   1984 to Current
Founder/Director of Volunteers/Case Manager/Fundraising Manager

- Established a nonprofit 501 organization to help needy children throughout Pennsylvania
- Developed community-partnership efforts for fundraising events using the arts as the pull
- Made public appearances/speaking engagements for up to 800 people
- Recognized by the state of Pennsylvania as the "Nonprofit Organization of the Year"
- Recognized by the Student Council of Philadelphia and awarded grant money for 1995 and 1998
- Established and directed a full-time volunteer staff

WORLD CLASS FINE ARTS, Philadelphia, Pennsylvania   1990 to Current
Founder—Sales/Promotion/Public Relations

- Directed start-up operations for contemporary art works by major artists
- Created strategic alliances with dealers and national buyers
- Bought and sold art—inventory exceeded $1 million, including Picasso, Caulder, and Miro

EDUCATION/PROFESSIONAL TRAINING

BA: Arts—Syracuse University, Art Studies, 1980
-    Art Studies: UCLA, 1981–82; San Francisco Fiber Arts Institute, 1983; Philadelphia Art Center, Current
-    PC Professor, Computer Training, 1998 and 1999

COMMUNITY AFFILIATIONS

Board Member, Stop Children's Cancer
Board Member, Children's Miracle Network
Member, Shumei Arts Council of America

References Furnished upon Request

MANUFACTURING OPERATIONS EXECUTIVE

ROLAND DeMAZIO
11601 Fir Street • Columbus, Ohio 43211
(614) 555-1212/email@email.com

MANUFACTURING OPERATIONS EXECUTIVE
Driving Growth & Profits in Industrial/Manufacturing Environments
**Product Development & Enhancement/Start-up & Turnaround Leadership
Market & New-Business Development/P&L Responsibility**

Dynamic operating/management professional offering extensive and successful leadership positions in industrial and manufacturing arenas. Successfully integrate solid management, business development, personnel leadership, and technical expertise in pursuit of bottom-line goals and objectives. Additional areas of expertise include:

Strategic planning and logistics management	**Regulatory compliance oversight**
Budget/expense control—financial reporting	**Efficiency/productivity enhancement**
Customer-service and quality-control management	**Sales, marketing, and business expansion**

PROFESSIONAL EXPERIENCE

Walters Coatings, Inc., Columbus, Ohio   1996 to Current
Director of Operations
Direct all aspects of the Columbus facility ($3.2 million operation) for a recognized leader in the application of industrial coatings—serving a diverse clientele as a Dupont-licensed applicator of Teflon® finishes. Company also applies specialized coatings from other manufacturers of liquid and powder coatings. Oversee daily production by coordinating activities with plant manager to assure production meets deadlines, quality standards, and customer/sales requirements. Spearhead sales and new-business activities—identifying and capitalizing on new and emerging market opportunities. Full charge P&L responsibility—ensuring proper pricing, expense control, and systems/technology integration.

- Built up and service more than 300 accounts, exceeding $3 million in sales.
- Turned around an unprofitable operation ($100,000/yr. loss) to a profitable operation ($336,000) in 23 months.
- Maintain an average net operating profit of 13%—some 5% above industry standards.
- Closed and manage key accounts, including Motorola, Ford, Heinz Food, and Panasonic.
- Developed and introduced new coating technologies resulting in $450,000 in added revenue per year.

Coat-Up, Inc., Chester, Pennsylvania   1983 to 1996
General Operations & Sales Manager
Company specialized in custom industrial finishing and coating (liquid and powder fluorocarbon coatings—Teflon, Kynar, Halar, PFA, etc.) serving diversified industries, including equipment manufacturers, electronics, chemical, petrochemical manufacturers, plastic molders, and aero space. Directed day-to-day operations and sales/marketing activities, hired, trained, and supervised employees, oversaw production efforts, and ensured regulatory compliance. Full P&L responsibility.

- Orchestrated all sales and marketing efforts for start-up company, resulting in $750,000 in new business.
- Closed and managed key accounts, including Polaroid, IBM, Litton, and Boeing Corp.
- Oversaw production activities—optimized both labor and physical resources to achieve projected profits.
- Developed new and highly unique coatings/processes to maintain competitive edge and meet customer needs.

EDUCATION & LICENSES

Penn State University, Springfield, Pennsylvania
Bachelor of Science: Business Administration, 1982

References and Supporting Documentation Furnished upon Request

OPERATIONS/MANAGEMENT EXECUTIVE

HAROLD R. CONNORS

17177 Northway Circle
Boston, Massachusetts 01977
Phone: (617) 555-1212/Cell: (617) 555-3232
email@email.com

SENIOR-LEVEL OPERATIONS/MANAGEMENT EXECUTIVE
Increasing Shareholder Value in Both Publicly Traded and Private Companies

SEC Reporting & Compliance/Start-up & Turnaround Management
Technology Integration/Business Development & Expansion
P&L Responsibility/Cash-Flow Management

A market-driven Senior Executive with outstanding qualifications in directing multimillion-dollar operations in global theaters. Recognized for capitalizing on existing product potential and identifying new growth opportunities.

CORE STRENGTHS

Visionary leadership/innovation management
Production and efficiency optimization
Customer service and retention management
Business development and expansion

Strategic-alliance/partnership development
Multiple-project/location management
Multichannel product distribution
Organizational/team leadership

PROFESSIONAL EXPERIENCE

HEALTH CARE INTERNATIONAL, INC., Boston, Massachusetts   2000 to Current
Senior Executive

- Business advisor to the President of a NASD Company in the health-care industry with annualized run-rate revenue of $220 million. Wrote comprehensive business plan to acquire new company and merge into existing division.
- Directly responsible for filings of past-due Form 10 K (fiscal year 1999) and subsequent Form 10 K for the four ensuing periods (through 6/2000). Prepared initial drafts of these filings and coordinated between SEC counsel, CFO, and Board of Directors. Settled more than $250,000 of payables for $45,000 in cash payments. Successfully reorganized an unprofitable division—turning around an operation draining more than $80,000/month in cash.
- The Company was in default on a note of $200,000 that was previously renegotiated. The lender, as part of the note, had obtained a Confession of Judgment, precluding the Company from entering any defenses to the note. Successfully negotiated payment of note with Company stock, not only saving the Company $200,000 in cash, but transformed a debt into an equity on the Company's balance sheet.
- Spearheaded all litigation with outside counsel and negotiated a fee reduction from $10,000 to $2000/month. Re-assigned workload of HR department, saving $50,000/year while improving output. Coordinated all insurance matters, prepared leases and physician contracts and developed comprehensive analysis for in-house billing/collection efforts.
- Successfully renegotiated a $1.2 million billing contract (far in excess of normal costs) and arranged a contract buyout for $350,000 in stock—and obtained a new contract on more favorable terms.

MACKENZIE CONSULTANTS, Boston/New York   1990 to 2000
Full-time Consultant for Multioffice OB/GYN Practice

- Recruited to restructure and turn around an underperforming, unprofitable high-volume medical practice (six physicians) with operations throughout five South Florida counties—with revenues exceeding $3.5 million.
- Restructured $750,000 fully recourse loan with Merrill-Lynch to a nonrecourse loan with more-favorable interest and advance rates. Initiated and installed new accounting systems of control to evaluate each office's productivity and profitability. Developed new accounting-control systems for in-house certified clinical laboratory.
- Analyzed cost benefits of closing targeted offices without compromising patient revenue or quality patient care. Improved cash flow by reorganizing billings and claims department with a $300,000 reduction in A/R.
- Acquired new medical-practice congruent with strategic goals and objectives for seeking marketshare dominance.
- Successfully negotiated contract with state agencies to provide additional sources for new business.

(Page one of two)

Harold R. Connors
Page two

PROFESSIONAL EXPERIENCE

KFC—KENTUCKY FRIED CHICKEN—INTERNATIONAL OPERATIONS, Curacao/Aruba   1979 to 1990
Franchise Owner

- Purchased two international franchise businesses in Curacao and Aruba—both of which were losing propositions. Developed strategic business plans (operations/marketing) and initiated core organizational changes and began to consistently turn a profit in less than 10 months.
- Opened three additional stores in Curacao—total combined revenues exceeded $4 million with net earnings between 8% and 18%. These stores were among the highest-volume franchised units in the world.
- Recruited, trained, and developed strong management team to contribute to corporate success—with an overall workforce consisting of 120 people. Implemented ironclad financial systems of control—accounting for over 240,000 pieces of chicken per month with less than a 1.4% loss factor.
- Implemented incentive program for employees to enhance sales and operating profit margins. Negotiated long-term supplier contracts at fixed and favorable prices with U.S. companies to provide consistent source of supply and to ensure measurable gross profit margins.
- Returned investor's initial capital investments within 24 months and continued to pay dividends thereafter.

EDUCATION/TRAINING

HOFSTRA UNIVERSITY, Hempstead, New York
Bachelor of Arts: Accounting, 1978

Additional/On-going Training

- Master's Degree Coursework in Taxation, St. John's University
- Real Estate License, Poes Institute
- Computer Courses in IBM RPG Programming and Cobol
- Coursework in Windows, Excel, Lotus, Solomon Accounting Software, Timberline, Word, T-Value
- Sales, Customer Service, and Quality-Management Training

BOARD POSITIONS

Board of Governors, St. Andrews Country Club (Three Years)
Board of Directors, NASD Listed Company (Four Years)

References and Supporting Documentation Furnished upon Request

MARKETING EXECUTIVE

MICHAEL GORDON

606 Alexander Drive West
Albany, Ohio 45023
Tel: 740–555-1234 Fax: 740–555-4321
Email: email@email.com

INTERNATIONAL MARKETING, SALES & BUSINESS-DEVELOPMENT EXECUTIVE
Expert in U.S. and Latin American Business/Commerce

A Verifiable Record of Building Growth & Profits in Competitive Markets

Key Top-level Contacts/Cultural Savvy/Regional Reputation/Organizational Leadership
Fluent: English, Spanish, & French

Professional qualifications include 13+ years of International sales/marketing experience with senior-level P&L accountability. Develop profitable distribution networks, initiate successful sales operations, and manage key accounts in existing/emerging Latin American markets.

CORE SKILLS

Latin American import/export & business protocol
Developing key strategic partnerships/alliances
Turning around underperforming sales efforts
New-product/service launch

Strategic market-analysis/business-plan development
Building active dealer/distributor networks
Start-up and new-business-development management
High-level presentation, public speaking & training

PROFESSIONAL EMPLOYMENT

CONCO MEDICAL COMPANY, Rock Hill, Ohio   1993 to Current
Export Sales Manager

- Full charge sales/marketing responsibility for Latin America, with concentration on locating, engaging, developing, and consulting with "dealerships" in marketing high-quality medical products.
- Successfully opened new markets throughout Latin America—an instrumental contributor to the company's successful sales/profit growth that generated $2.7 million (annualized) in first nine months of operation.
- Created export-marketing plans customized for individual markets in South and Central America and the Caribbean, and developed complete pricing policies for each area.

B.E.I. International, Bloomfield, Ohio   2/87 to 1993
General Manager

- Complete P&L responsibility in managing all operations for company selling diversified medical supplies and equipment, including H.P. Imaging Systems, Amsco Auto Claves, Surgical Hardware and Cardiac specialty lines of related hospital equipment. A $5.6 million operation.
- Devised highly effective export-marketing strategies that incorporated logistical contingencies and government policies for numerous enterprises interested in start-up operations in Argentina, Bolivia, Brazil, Chile, Colombia, Ecuador, Paraguay, Peru, and all Central American markets.

EDUCATION/TRAINING

OHIO WESTERN UNIVERSITY, Belmont, Ohio
Bachelor of Arts Degree, 1984, Major: International Business/Global Marketing

Languages: Fluent English, Spanish, and French; solid working knowledge of Portuguese and Italian.

References Furnished upon Request

HUMAN-RESOURCE MANAGEMENT

MICHAEL P. DYER
27 Hanover Street
South Portland, Maine 04106
(207) 555-1212/email@email.com

HUMAN-RESOURCE MANAGEMENT
Recruitment Specialist—Recruiting Productive and Contributing Team Members

Strategic Planning/Policy & Procedure Development/New-Program Conceptualization & Implementation
Personnel Training/Benefits Management/Regulatory Compliance

Solid experience in human resource management, encompassing personnel recruiting, training, and supervision, benefits coordination, policy development/enforcement, office administration, training-curriculum development/facilitation, and financial management/budgeting. Contributing to bottom-line objectives through enhanced efficiency and labor resources.

CORE STRENGTHS

Program development; enhancing existing programs
Working with governmental agencies/policies
Turning around underperforming operations/departments
Career management and design (internal and outplacement)

Organization and administration—time management
Building key local/national alliances and partnerships
Reengineering and functional-change management
Personnel recruiting and job placement

PROFESSIONAL EXPERIENCE

UNITED STATES NAVY
San Diego, California—1989 to 1998

Administrator/HR Specialist
Responsible for the training and performance reporting of individuals in administrative ratings. Provided administrative services to more than 1800 enlisted and retired personnel. Coordinated shipboard activities with auxiliary service and non-service agencies, including the American Red Cross, Navy Relief Society, Navy Drug and Alcohol Rehabilitation Centers, and local community resource centers.

Trained and experienced in such contemporary issues as sexual harassment, personnel administration, wage and salary administration, administrative discharge, as well as solid knowledge of EEO regulations and guidelines. Experienced in policy and procedure development/enhancement.

- Developed training-resource materials and presented seminars in Human-Resource Management.
- Recipient: Navy Achievement Medal for "Excellence in Administration."
- Played significant role in Naval Reserve Centers Portland SELRES retention figures while conducting RESFIRST system.
- Recipient of SOQ/SOY Award for building/maintaining "vibrant morale" and maximizing command productivity.
- Saved more than $1.7 million in training costs over five-year period by developing in-house training programs.

EDUCATION

Bachelor of Science: Public Administration, 2002
(High Honors)

University of Maine at Augusta, Augusta, Maine

Workshops and Seminars
Management by Objectives
Work-Flow Management
Time Management
Cultural Expression

Human-Resource Management
Equal Opportunity
Supervisory and Leadership Training
Evaluation/Performance Systems

- Computer Skills: Word, Excel, Access, PowerPoint, and the Internet

References and Verifying Documentation Furnished upon Request

HOSPITALITY MANAGEMENT PROFESSIONAL

CHRISTOPHER D. DUNCAN

701 SE Oak Street
Detroit, Michigan 72530
Phone: (912) 555-1212/email@email.com

FOOD & BEVERAGE/HOSPITALITY MANAGEMENT PROFESSIONAL
Food-Distribution Management/P&L Management

"Enhancing Growth and Profits in Hospitality Environments"

Offering more than 15 years of successful, recognized achievement in F&B/Hospitality/Food Distribution

AREAS OF STRENGTH

Employee recruiting, training, and empowerment
Regulatory compliance, health & safety management
Front and back-of-the-house management
Customer-service and quality-control management

Strategic planning and implementation
Communication skills (verbal/written)
Productivity and efficiency enhancement
Sales, marketing, and business development

PROFESSIONAL EMPLOYMENT

MARRIOTT INTERNATIONAL, Detroit, Michigan   1989 to Current
Senior Account Manager/Customer Service (1997–Current)

- Act as liaison between MDS and the customer, responsible for strategic partnerships. Provide training for new account managers, support national account activities, ensure quality customer service, resolve disputes, and take strategic action to ignite sales and territorial growth.

- Develop high-impact marketing and sales strategies, perform ongoing market/competitive analysis, and survey existing customers to maintain and improve quality standards. Revenue increases averaged 13% above projections.

- Oversee and supervise customer service—maintaining open communications with customers. Coordinate orders, handle credit requests, and respond to customer inquiries. Retention rates increased from 91% to 97%.

Unit Manager/Host, Marriott (1989–97)

- Managed and handled all day-to-day operations of a travel plaza generating $6.6 million in annual food sales. Interacted with a 15-member management team and a staff of more than 100, ensuring high-quality service and customer satisfaction. Specific duties and responsibilities included weekly employee scheduling, ordering food products and supplies, equipment and facilities management, and overall profit-and-loss accountability.

MR. LAFF'S RIVERFRONT RESTAURANT & MARINA, Detroit, Michigan   1987 to 1989
Restaurant Manager

- Directed a 260-seat, high-volume facility with annual sales of more than $3.5 million. Supervised a staff of 110, including a four-man management team and a head chef. Responsible for hiring, training, and supervision.

- Budget and shared-P&L responsibility; also in charge of advertising and promotion; oversaw menu planning, food and liquor inventory control, live entertainment, and special events.

EDUCATION

Associate of Arts Degree, Liberal Arts, 1974, EL CAMINO COLLEGE, Torrence, California

Certifications:
- Management Certification: Burger King Corp., Marriott International., Sbarro Italian Eatery.
- Health Department Certifications: Dade, Broward, Martin, and St. Lucie Counties; National Assessment Institute

References Furnished upon Request

CUSTOMER-SERVICE REPRESENTATIVE—BANKING

BETTY CARSTACK

2370 Waterside Drive
Natick, Massachusetts 01760
Phone: (508) 555-1212 * Cell: (508) 555-6262
email@email.com

Seeking Position as...

CUSTOMER-SERVICE REPRESENTATIVE —BANKING
Promoting Goodwill and Customer Retention

**Customer-Service Expert/Sales & Business-Development Support
Organizational Leadership/Relationship Building
Bilingual—English & Spanish**

A highly energetic, personable, and results-oriented professional with outstanding customer-service skills. Offering more than 10 years' successful experience in fast-track customer-service-oriented environments.

CORE STRENGTHS

Opening new accounts (all types—including IRAs)	Wire-transfer/stop-payment coordination
Account transfers	Employee training and mentoring
ATM coordination and supervision	Bookkeeping and accounting
Communication skills—written and verbal	Time management—deadline sensitive

▪ Computer Skills: Windows, Word, Proprietary Banking programs, and Internet applications

HIGHLIGHTS OF PROFESSIONAL EXPERIENCE

REPUBLIC NATIONAL BANK, Natick, Massachusetts   1998 to Current
Customer Service

- Work with up to 200 customers a day—resolving simple to complex issues.
- Improved customer-service branch rating from 92.4% to 98.1% in first year.
- Train new tellers and assist/mentor existing personnel.

FIRST UNION BANK, Wesley, Massachusetts   1993 to 1998
Customer-Service Leader

- Led four-person customer-service team, with emphasis on commercial clients—(approximately 350 accounts).
- Resolved all problems/conflicts and developed successful programs for proactive problem avoidance.
- Assisted bank manager in a variety of areas, including sales, training, and operations improvement.

WINN HARBOR YACHTS, Boston, Massachusetts   1990 to 1993
Customer-Service Coordinator

- Followed up with clients purchasing yachts—averaging $1.5 million.
- Liaison between sales, financing, service/prep, and operations, to ensure total customer satisfaction.
- Developed high-impact follow-up customer survey, resulting in constant and never-ending service improvements.

EDUCATION

Roland Junior College, Brookline, Massachusetts
Associate's Degree: Communications, 1989

Seminars/Training: Customer Service (Dale Carnegie); The Power of "WOW" (Tom Peters); The Winner's Circle (The Hanegan Group); Computer Classes: Windows, Word, Excel, Act, PhotoShop, and the Internet

References Furnished upon Request

NEW-BUSINESS DEVELOPMENT

CHARLET S. SONY

1257 Southwest 52st Street
Davie, Florida 33331
Cell: (954) 555-4343/Home: (954) 555-0066
email@email.com

Seeking a Position in...

NEW-BUSINESS DEVELOPMENT/SALES & MARKETING
Four Years of Successful Experience in Building Construction & Development Environments
Utilizing Solid Civil/Architectural-Engineering & Project-Management Experience
"Solid Construction Background to Drive Sales and Growth"

A dynamic, highly motivated, and results-driven professional with qualifications in all phases of residential and commercial building construction/project management.

Seeking to combine outstanding practical/educational experience in civil and architectural engineering with desire to sell and promote industry products/services to enhance organizational growth and profitability.

AREAS OF STRENGTH

- Sales, marketing, and lead generation
- Advertising, marketing, and promotions
- Organizational skills, deadline management
- Interior design
- Customer-service and retention management

- Networking and strategic-contact development
- Project/event coordination and supervision
- Regulatory and code compliance
- Training and customer/client education
- HVAC and illumination design

Computer Skills:
Lotus 1-2-3, Excel, WordPerfect, Word, PowerPoint, Access; Windows and DOS Environments; PCs and Macintosh Systems; FORTRAN Language; Lode Application; AutoCAD

PROFESSIONAL EXPERIENCE

AT&T, Miramar, Florida   1995 to Current
Project/Construction Coordinator
   * Managed and directed construction of telecommunications building—a 32,000 sq. ft. project.
   * Utilized Lode Applications technology to control and reduce project costs on all 12 projects.
   * To date, completed 12 building construction projects—260,000 total sq. ft. ($75 million in construction).
   * Worked effectively in team environment to meet project goals, budgets, and deadlines.

NATIONAL PARTITIONS, Hialeah, Florida   1993 to 1995
Structural Engineer/Sales & Marketing Support
   * Worked with sales and marketing team to assess and meet customer needs. Exceeded projections by 23%.
   * Member of the Brand Sales Team to insure design goals are consistent with project vision and budget.
   * Designed steel structures for nonprogressive wall systems and modular buildings, including structural-member details, floor plans, and electrical and HVAC layouts. Used AutoCAD for drafting assignments.
   * Utilized Microsoft Access database to generate itemized invoices for materials required for each project.

(Page 1 of 2)

117

NEW-BUSINESS DEVELOPMENT (CONT.)

PROFESSIONAL EXPERIENCE (Continued)

R.C.T. ENGINEERING, INC., West Palm Beach, Florida   1990 to 1993
Civil Engineer/Administrative Accountant

* Recipient: 1998 Third Quarter Recognition Award for high achievement.
* Made high-impact marketing presentations—and budget proposals for upcoming projects.
* Developed and implemented aggressive public relations and marketing efforts.
* Performed on-site analysis and project review—made appropriate recommendations as needed.
* Prepared contract documents and project specifications.

CHARLES W. LYNCH BUILDING, INC., Hackensack, New Jersey   1987 to 1990
Operations Manager

* Formulated marketing-program elements for commercial properties; prepared employee construction schedules.
* Managed residential properties; responsible for designing floor plans of residential properties.
* Checked drawings for code compliance; implemented standards for traffic control and pedestrian safety.
* Supervised up to 40 employees; coordinated payroll.
* Assisted with interior decorating.

EDUCATION/SEMINARS & WORKSHOPS

UNIVERSITY OF MIAMI, Coral Gables, Florida
Bachelor of Science, Dual Major: Civil & Architectural Engineering, 1990

Internships

AGENCY FOR HEALTH-CARE ADMINISTRATION, Miami, Florida
University of Miami Master Program/Plans and Construction Internship, 1990
* Selected by the Head of the Department of Plans and Construction to participate in this program.
* Reviewed building plans for the construction and remodeling of hospitals, nursing homes, and surgical centers, for code compliance.
* Inspected health-care facilities for quality and safety during all phases of construction; tested the performance of equipment and systems for HVAC and fire protection.

PASSAIC VALLEY SEWERAGE AND COMMISSIONERS, Newark, New Jersey
Chief Engineering Assistant Internship, 1989
* Arranged, analyzed, and presented annual budget of the entire wastewater treatment plant.
* Assisted in obtaining the Oxygen Uptake Rates (OUR) on the site.
* Developed spreadsheets for collected data.
* Attended Technical Review Committee meetings.

- References and Supporting Documentation Furnished upon Request -

INTERNATIONAL-RELATIONS PROFESSIONAL

LAURA MARIE CARROLL
22 Jones Union
Brunswick, Maine 04011

Email: email@email.com
Home Phone: (207) 555-1212

Graduate Student Seeking Position In International Relations
Intellectual/Analytical/Solution-Focused

PERSONAL STATEMENT

My recent internships required that I put my analytical skills to practical use in organizing and synthesizing data into meaningful conclusions and practical solutions. I have been trained to think logically, respond quickly and creatively, and communicate effectively; I am highly adaptable to change, work well with culturally diverse people, and thrive in fast-track, high-pressure environments. I have excellent language ability in Chinese and Spanish and am computer proficient in MACS/PCs; Windows/DOS; Word, Excel, Lotus, PageMaker, PowerPoint, and Internet applications.

EDUCATION

Bowdoin College, Brunswick, Maine: Summa cum laude with departmental honors expected 5/2000
Bachelor of Arts: 1) Asian Studies with focus on China and 2) History with focus on Latin America
- GPA 3.8 Overall (3.9 in Asian Studies and 3.8 in History).
- Capital University of Economics, Beijing, China, Fall,1998 (Studies Abroad).
- Harbin Institute of Technology, Harbin, China, Spring, 1999 (Studies Abroad).

HONORARIES:
- Received full scholarship to attend The Fund for American Studies Program at Georgetown University.
- Received American Financial Systems Scholarship for Academic Excellence.
- Received Freeman Fellowship to pursue Chinese language study at the Stanford Center at National Taiwan University.
- Recognized as *Sarah and James Bowdoin Scholar for Outstanding Academic Achievement* every semester at Bowdoin.
- Co-editor of *The Bowdoin Forum, Journal of International Affairs*.
- Bowdoin Crew Treasurer.
- Received *Peace Action Grant* to participate in a Washington, D.C. workshop on "Proliferation of Chemical Weapons."

HIGHLIGHTS OF WORK EXPERIENCE

THE UNITED STATES EXPORT IMPORT BANK, Washington, D.C.   6/99 to 9/99
David Carter, Vice President of Communications: Project Assistant
- Researched and prepared speeches/press briefs for Chairman James A. Harmon.
- Assisted upper management personnel with key projects.
- Researched and published "The Export Import Bank in China: a Marketing Analysis."

FHI INTERNATIONAL, Beijing, China   9/98 to 12/98
Gary Kong, Beijing Office Chief: Academic Consultant
- Assisted Chinese students with their MBA and graduate school applications.

KOREA ECONOMIC INSTITUTE OF AMERICA, Washington, D.C.   6/98 to 9/98
Melanie Miller, Director of Congressional Affairs: Research Assistant
- Worked with the Congressional Affairs Director and attended hearings on Capitol Hill and related programs that addressed Korean/Asian issues. Summarized these events into a consolidated document, which was distributed to Korean Embassies and Economic Consulates worldwide.
- Summarized economic news pertinent to Asia, from all major newspapers, periodicals, and research documents, daily.
- Helped organize and facilitate conferences hosted by Korean Economic Institute.

BOWDOIN COLLEGE DEAN OF ACADEMIC AFFAIRS, Brunswick, Maine   1/98 to 6/98
Office of Dean Wells: Research Assistant
- Organized process of faculty committee's appointment into database that could be easily modified each year.

References and Supporting Documentation Furnished upon Request

9
Construction and Engineering

ESTIMATOR

MICHAEL BOBROWS

3111 Crows Nest Circle
Ashville, NC 87163
(912) 555-1212

ESTIMATOR—for General Contractor
17 Years' Successful Experience—Field, Office, Project-Management Estimating
Hard-Bid & Negotiated Work

"A Competitive Estimator Who Knows How to Make You Money"
- J. Kline, Former Employer

SUPPORTING STRENGTHS

- ❑ Estimating costs in relation to manpower, equipment, and materials; preparing bid packages/proposals.
- ❑ Clarifying and interpreting bids; writing/developing scope of work and construction-related specifications.
- ❑ Supervising commercial, municipal, and residential construction projects—estimating/project management through completion.
- ❑ Assessing needs, and hiring, training, and scheduling men, contractors, and equipment, to ensure maximum efficiency.
- ❑ Monitoring work progress to ensure quality work.
- ❑ Ensuring compliance with blueprints, and specifications; change order management.
- ❑ Developing and maintaining good customer relations.

PROFESSIONAL EXPERIENCE

CLARK CONSTRUCTION SERVICE, INC., Ashville, North Carolina   1992 to Current
Lead Estimator
- ❑ Responsible for estimating total job costs on commercial projects ranging in price from $400,000 to $4 million.
- ❑ Prepared project estimates through contract negotiation, and supervised construction operations and personnel—start-up through completion/acceptance. Worked on government/municipal bids/projects.
- ❑ Initiated key contact, drew up bid specifications for $3.2 million school-renovation project, and was awarded the contract.
- ❑ Successfully estimated and awarded contract to refurbish Ashville City Hall—a $2.6 million project.
- ❑ Turned around a troubled project—six weeks behind and over budget. Came in on time and met all financial/quality goals.

INTERNATIONAL HOSPITALITY SERVICES, Greenville, North Carolina   1988 to 1992
Purchasing Agent, Estimator & Superintendent
- ❑ Initially employed as superintendent, responsible for providing on-site supervision in all phases of construction. Subsequently promoted to estimator—preparing estimates for hotel construction projects. Elevated to purchasing agent, responsible for negotiating contracts with subcontractors and purchasing materials for commercial projects.

MULCATHY, INC., Ashville, North Carolina   1986 to 1988
Carpenter
- ❑ Employed by company providing carpentry-subcontractor services on various government and institutional projects, such as schools, museums, and government-works buildings.
- ❑ Performed carpentry duties for the installation of acoustical tile ceilings, freezer panels, and freezers, on various commercial construction projects.

Prior employment included eight years in various positions in the Construction Industry.

TRAINING/AFFILIATIONS

Harding Vocational and Technical School—Successfully Completed Two-Year Program   1975–77
Carpentry Apprenticeship, Ashville, North Carolina   1978
Member, American Society of Architects & Estimators
Computer Skills:
     - Timberline Estimating/Business software
     - Word, Excel, and Internet applications

Letters of References Furnished upon Request

ELECTRICAL ENGINEERING INTERN

SHANNON YATES

15857 60th Street North
Austin, Texas 78620
(512) 555-1212
email@email.com

ENTRY-LEVEL/INTERNSHIP
Electrical Engineering

Utilizing Outstanding Technical & Problem-Solving Skills
Currently Enrolled in Electrical Engineering Curriculum

A highly dynamic, team-spirited, and results-oriented individual seeking *entry-level or intern position in the area of power sources and systems as an electrical engineer trainee* while attending Austin Community College. Highly dependable, with a strong desire to learn, contribute, and make a difference.

AREAS OF STRENGTH

Technical problem-solving and troubleshooting
Maintenance and repair (grounds and equipment)
Statistical analysis; factual recall and evaluation
Communication and rapport-building skills
Project planning and coordination

Logical reasoning and deduction
Purchasing and inventory control
Staff training and development
Organization and time management
Customer service and quality control

■ Computer Skills: Microsoft Office 2000 (Word, Excel, Access) and Internet research & applications

EDUCATION

PALM BEACH COMMUNITY COLLEGE, Lake Worth, Florida
Bachelor of Science: Electrical Engineering, In Progress (EGD: Winter, 2002)

Selected Coursework:

Calculus
Trigonometry

Chemistry I and II
Biology

Environmental Conservation
Microcomputer Applications

HIGHLIGHTS OF PROFESSIONAL EXPERIENCE

* More than six years of working in electrical engineering (helping father in his engineering business)
* Utilizing technical and maintenance skills, ensuring proper maintenance and care related to equipment
* Assisted in the automation of Stellar Equine Center—installed retail and inventory software
* Selected as lead project engineer for college project—junior year

CHRONOLOGY OF PROFESSIONAL EXPERIENCE (While Attending School)

Southgate Electrical Engineering Group, Austin, Texas
Electrical Engineering Apprentice (part-time and summers)

1996 to Current

Stellar Equine Center, Austin, Texas
Sales Representative—Horse Trainer (Summers)

1990 to Current

References and Supporting Documentation Furnished upon Request

ELECTRONICS ENGINEER

LORNE D. GINSBURG

335 Waterside Drive
Evansville, Indiana 47734
(812) 555-1212/email@email.com

ELECTRONIC ENGINEERING/TECHNICAL PROFESSIONAL
Contributing to Growth & Profitability via Technical Project/Product Leadership

Product Delivery/Customer Relations/Quality Assurance
Complex Problem Solving/Organizational Leadership

A dynamic, team-spirited, and bottom-line-oriented Electronic Engineer/Technician offering outstanding qualifications in equipment/product development to include **prototyping, testing and debugging, layout and documentation, production coordination, final testing/documentation, and delivery to end-user (installation, training, and follow-up).**

CORE STRENGTHS

Analytical and technical aptitude	Team leadership and staff development
Assimilating and communicating complex information	Computer skills, including programming
Presentation and public-speaking skills	Cooperative interdepartmental interface
Total quality management and customer service	Automated testing experience

PROFESSIONAL EXPERIENCE

TECH SERVICES, Indianapolis, Indiana
Electronic Engineering Technology Services
1994 to Current

Consistent and ongoing technical work assignments for three key client companies

MOTORLA, Indianapolis, Indiana
(1999 to Current)
Testing Engineer/Technician
Constructed automated test stations, including robotics, for the development of personal communication devices. Utilize Hewlett Packard Test and Measuring equipment as well as Rhodes and Swartz and proprietary interfaces. Construct prototypes and design simple circuits and mechanical subassemblies to ensure proper interface with personal communication devices.

- Significantly reduced mechanical construction time by introducing templates and predrilled and tapped rails and plates.
- Decreased wiring time by using harness technicians.
- Successfully performed much of the work without formal documentation.

GEO FOCUS, Springfield, Indiana
(1995 to 1999)
Electronic Engineer/Technical Consultant
Responsible for building prototypes, testing, and coordinating with manufacturing for development of prototypes, ordering parts, field installation, testing, and service/repair to component level. Developed documentation, and built drawings and bills of materials. Designed simple mechanical and electronic subassemblies.

- Involved in the installation of Train Tracking System (GPS) on tri rail trains and platforms.
- Installed computer network at the Tri Rail Customer Relations Center, including wireless radio.
- Reduced downtime by reprogramming boards in the field.
- Dramatically reduced service calls by redesigning computer-networking connections.

(Page 1 of 2)

ELECTRONICS ENGINEER (CONT.)

PROFESSIONAL EXPERIENCE

IMAGE GRAPHICS, INC., Holden, Indiana
(1994 to 1995)
Customer-Service Technician
Responsible for troubleshooting and maintenance of EBR (Electronic Beam Recorder) micrographics, and image setter used in micropublishing. Worked with Unix system—both hardware and software. Coordinated customer-service efforts at customer site—troubleshooting both digital and analog systems.

- Successfully troubleshot equipment and systems, causing no downtime to the client.
- Effectively trained customer personnel in EBR operations.

PROFESSIONAL EXPERIENCE (Other)

QUANTA CHROME CORP., Westin, Indiana   1992 to 1994
Electronics Technician
- Built and calibrated scientific equipment—repair to component level (digital and analog).

ENGINEERED COMPUTER SYSTEMS, Torrance, California   1991 to 1992
Systems Consultant
- Designed, installed, and trained on electronic publishing systems (including software applications).

AMP BUSINESS SYSTEMS, LTD., Dartmouth, Nova Scotia   1987 to 1991
Systems Consultant
- Designed, installed, and trained on 3M Optical Disk and Micrographic Systems.

BELL & HOWELL, Toronto, Canada   1985 to 1987
Assistant Regional Manager
- Hired, trained, and directed staff for presentations made in academic environments throughout eastern Canada to recruit students for Bell & Howell's DeVry Institute of Technology.

ACADEMIC/TRAINING HIGHLIGHTS

DeVRY INSTITUTE OF TECHNOLOGY, Toronto, Canada
Bachelor of Science: Electronics Technology, 1984

ROYAL CANADIAN NAVY, Halifax, Canada
Radar and Electronics Technician, 1980–84

References and Supporting Documentation Furnished upon Request

ENVIRONMENTAL ENGINEER/CONSULTANT

DUMMA KROSTAC

3121 Village Crossing • West Palm Beach, Florida 33409 • (561) 555-9638 • email@email.com

---

ENVIRONMENTAL ENGINEER/CONSULTANT
3 Years' National and International Experience Working with Fortune 500 Companies/Clientele
Master's Degree in Environmental Engineering

A dynamic, team-spirited, and bottom-line-oriented Project/Environmental Engineer offering outstanding qualifications in all areas of Environmental Engineering—with emphasis on working on multimillion-dollar projects for key international clientele, as well as smaller national projects.

Environmental Management System/Water & Air Management/Waste Management
Environmental Impact Assessment/Environmental Annual Report/Cleanup and Remediation
Environmental Audit/Project Management/Power-Plant Water & Sewer Management

CORE STRENGTHS

Regulatory compliance
Contract negotiation/administration
Budget and expense management
Complex problem solving/troubleshooting

Project cost analysis
Field-performance supervision
Multiple-project management
Policy/procedure development

Computer Skills: Windows, MS Office (Word, Excel, PowerPoint, Outlook), Visio, and Internet applications

PROFESSIONAL EXPERIENCE

DELOITTE & TOUCHE LTD, Budapest/Miami   1992 to Current
Environmental Engineer/Consultant
Project Manager/Team Member in directing environmental engineering projects. Work in a team environment on diversified projects, interfacing closely with clients to ensure quality work and that all project/budgetary objectives are met.

- Prepared environmental report for multibillion-dollar, international corporation for the purchase of a $50+ million-dollar power plant. Provided comprehensive evaluation, including environmental-risk analysis and cost analysis.
- Managed the improvement of one of the largest Hungarian wine company's water and sewage system, and worked with environmental authority to accomplish stringent goals.
- Worked for local government—assessed the cleanup of polluted property (oil and gas), and analyzed cleanup strategy. Determined cost to complete work, and oversaw the completion of the project.
- Project leader for Phase 1 Environmental Audit for Macedonian Government—a large-scale lead battery firm.
- Successfully directed a Phase 1 Environmental Audit for Punch Hungary LTD—a plastics-materials manufacturer serving the computer industry.
- Performed environmental risk analyses for European Union PHARE Programs for financing viable investment projects, with specific concentration on determining "environmental benefits" of the projects.

BUDAPEST POWER PLANT LTD, Budapest   1989 to 1992
Environmental Engineer
Prepared company's first annual environmental report, contributed to remediation procedures and the improvement of the water-management system.

- Set up company's comprehensive environmental procedures program and improved company's image.
- Managed remediation project and helped complete project to come in under budget.
- Improved the safety and quality of the water system—addressing/resolving acid and oil contaminates.

ACADEMIC HIGHLIGHTS

Master's of Science in Environmental Engineering, 1989   University of Veszprem, Hungary
Course Certification (Environmental Industry and Ecology), Summer, 1996   University of Stockholm, Sweden

- Fluent in English, German, and Hungarian

OCCUPATIONAL SAFETY ENGINEER

ROLANDO P. QUINNEY

230 Pennsylvania Avenue
Liberty, Iowa 45372
(333) 555-1212/email@email.com

OCCUPATIONAL-SAFETY ENGINEER/LOSS-CONTROL MANAGER
Contributing to Organizational Growth/Profits via Safety & Loss-Control Management
16 Years' Experience in Diversified Environments

Construction & Facilities Safety Management/Regulatory Compliance Expertise
Program Development/Organizational Leadership & Training/Claims Management

---

A dynamic, team-spirited, and bottom-line-oriented Safety Engineer/Loss-Control Specialist offering outstanding qualifications in, and a verifiable record of, reducing work-related injuries and the severity of work-related accidents. Contribute to growth and profitability by significantly reducing liability exposure and claims.

A solid track record for successful leadership in staff/personnel training, development, and empowerment. Recognized for strong Worker's Compensation claims management, investigative/inspection aptitude, and meeting and exceeding regulatory compliance mandates.

CORE STRENGTHS

Reducing work-related injuries (severity of injuries)
Claims management and control
Staff training, development, and empowerment
Efficiency and production-improvement management

Program development and enhancement
Presentation and public-speaking skills
Complex problem solving/troubleshooting
Quality-control assurance/management

ACADEMIC HIGHLIGHTS

EMBRY RIDDLE AERONAUTICAL UNIVERSITY, Daytona Beach, Florida
Master's in Aeronautical Science, 1991

SOUTHERN ILLINOIS UNIVERSITY, Carbondale, Illinois
Bachelor of Science: Industrial Technology, 1988

COMMUNITY COLLEGE OF THE UNITED STATES AIR FORCE, Maxwell AFB, Alabama
Associate in Applied Science: Safety Technology, 1986

Certified Environment Compliance Manager
United States Air Force Safety Specialist Course
Triple A Driver-Improvement Instructor

OSHA 500 Basic Instructor's Course
United States Air Force Supervisor's Safety Course
CPR Instructor—National Safety Council

PROFESSIONAL EXPERIENCE

THERMA SEAL ROOFING, INC., Liberty, Iowa   2000 to Current
Safety Manager
Direct Occupational Safety Program for high-volume roofing contractor with more than 200 employees throughout the state of Iowa. In high-risk work environment, proactively develop/implement policies, procedures, programs, and systems, to reduce work-related injuries and the severity of such mishaps. Establish strategies to limit Worker's Compensation claims, develop one-on-one/group training to reinforce safety issues, and take aggressive action to ensure a drug-free work environment. Coordinate accident investigations, conduct thorough site/workforce inspections, and spearhead all regulatory compliance matters.

- Significantly reduced numbers of and severity of injuries.
- Wrote company's comprehensive Safety Manual and a Subcontractors Training Manual.
- Developed a highly effective disaster/hurricane preparedness action plan.

(Page one of two)

128

PROFESSIONAL EXPERIENCE (Continued)

NU-TEC ROOFING CONTRACTORS, INC., Johnson, Iowa   1997 to 1999
Safety Administrator
Directed the Occupational Safety and Worker's Compensation programs for the seventh-largest roofing contractor in the United States—program encompassed more than 200 employees in Florida. Performed accident investigations and daily job-site inspections to ensure program/regulatory compliance. Conducted pre-inspections of all new projects and submitted pragmatic recommendations to project managers. Created and employed Employee-Safety-Training program, spearheaded the Return-to-Work program, and developed modified work responsibilities for injured employees. Maintained all safety records.

- Identified the requirements for, approved, and procured personal protective equipment for employees exposed to safety and occupational health hazards—significantly reducing liability and injury probability.
- Developed and managed Drug-free Workplace program and associated training curriculum.
- Authored and initiated company's Safety Manual and established a new Bilingual Employee Manual.
- Reduced Worker's Compensation costs by $500,000-plus, via aggressive claims management and in-house training.

FRSA/SIF, Winter Park, Iowa   1990 to 1997
Loss Control Consultant/Manager
Provided professional, high-tech risk-management services to more than 500 policyholders throughout the state of Iowa. Assisted policyholders in the prevention and reduction of risk and losses—with emphasis on safety, health, and Worker's Compensation-related issues. Hired and trained loss-control consultants and safety engineers. Responsible for budget management and contributing to the bottom-line via safety/loss-control management.

- Dramatically reduced the number of injuries and severity of majority of policyholders.
- Reduced loss ratio by 30%—and improved account retention considerably.
- Author of monthly safety column for the *Iowa Forum Trade Association Magazine*, 1990–1997.

MILITARY SERVICE

UNITED STATES AIR FORCE   1981 to 1990
Ground Safety Technician
Contributing team leader in planning, development, and execution of the Occupational Safety Program for the 56th Tactical Training Division (F-16 Fighter Pilot Training Unit). Program encompassed more than 8,000 personnel, including on and off-duty mishap-prevention programs. Prepared annual operating budget for the Occupational Safety Program. Maintained liaison with federal, state, and local safety organizations and officials. Conducted comprehensive investigations entailing all classes and categories of mishaps/accidents, including fraud and workplace safety risks.

- Selected as *Tactical Air Command's Exceptional Performer in Ground Safety*, 1988.
- Awarded *Air Force Commendation Medal*, 1986 and 1990.
- Author of monthly safety column for the *Mac Dill Air Force Base Newspaper*, 1985–1990.

COMPUTER SKILLS

MS Windows, Word, Publisher, Excel, PowerPoint, Access
Internet applications

AFFILIATIONS

Member: American Society of Safety Engineers
Volunteer/Participant: Youth Soccer

References and Supporting Documentation Furnished upon Request

REAL-ESTATE SALES PROFESSIONAL

ANITA JOHNSON
3426 Island Drive • Billings, Washington 55234 • (888) 555-1212

REAL-ESTATE SALES PROFESSIONAL
Residential / On-Site Developer Sales
Outstanding Presentation and Closing Skills

A dynamic, enthusiastic, and highly motivated individual with six+ years' professional sales experience in landscape/real-estate-related environments. A resourceful, solution-focused individual combining solid sales and management skills with landscape background—pursuing a career in real-estate sales.

AREAS OF STRENGTH

Prospect development; lead generation
Financing skills—contract administration
Communications skills—verbal/written
Knowledge of Washington laws/regulations

Networking; building strategic alliances
Creative problem solving
Organization and time management
Landlord experience—asset management

PROFESSIONAL EXPERIENCE

ADMIRALS COVE, Jupiter, Washington   1997–Present
Real-Estate Sales
Generate leads and develop book of clients. Assist customers buy/sell homes/property. Market and sell homes in the $125,000–$600,000 range—concentrating on Martin, Granger, and Madison Counties.

- Average a closing every two weeks—with the average home selling for $189,000, or $4.9 million in property/year.
- Member of Million-Dollar Club, President's Club, and Silver Achiever's Club.

GAZEBO LANDSCAPE, INC., Holden, Washington   1992–1997
Sales
Sold landscape design and materials to existing client base. Managed six commercial sites in addition to individual home accounts, supervising two crews consisting of eight people.

- Average commercial contract represents $80,000 in annual revenues. Managed key developments, including Broken Sound and the Office Depot Headquarters in Delray Beach.

RUPPERT LANDSCAPE, INC., Ashton, Washington   1987–1992
Sales
Sold landscape design, materials, and maintenance to commercial and residential clients. Heavy prospecting and cold canvassing—qualifying and closing new prospects.

- Promoted to Manager in 1993 for $50 million commercial landscaper with more than 600 employees. Managed two crews consisting of ten people. Responsible for 13 properties, including Westinghouse and the University of Maryland (Baltimore). Managed annual contracts in the $80,000–$150,000 range.

EDUCATION/LICENSES/CERTIFICATIONS

Bachelor of Arts: Real Estate, 1986
Associate of Science: Turf Management, 1990
Real Estate—Sales Course I

Gordon College
State University of Washington
Gold Coast Real Estate School

- Washington Real Estate License
- Certified Horticulturist
- Computer Literate

References Furnished upon Request

PROPERTY MANAGEMENT PROFESSIONAL

ANDREW S. BOWDEN

4655 Rocky Road West, #123 • Blue Skies, Montana 99877
Phone: (987) 555-1212 • Cell: (987) 555-3232
email@email.com

CONSTRUCTION MANAGEMENT/PROJECT SUPERINTENDENT
PROPERTY MANAGEMENT PROFESSIONAL
"On-Time/On-Budget Management History"

**30+ Years' Successful Residential and Commercial Experience
Contributing Team Member for Growth and New-Business Development**

STRENGTHS

Full charge construction and development management	Project troubleshooting and problem solving
Multiple-project management and coordination	Project scheduling and deadline management
Project budgeting and expense management	Quality control and customer/client relations
Contract negotiation and administration	Residential and commercial property management

PROFESSIONAL WORK EXPERIENCE

MERIDIAN MANAGEMENT CORP., Hopeville, Montana   1998 to Current
Project Manager
Direct day-to-day operation and maintenance of physical plant and mechanical aspects of college campus (FAU, John D. MacArthur Campus, High Fall, Montana). Full-charge responsibility for all human resources vis-à-vis custodial and maintenance staff. A liaison between university officials and corporate offices in Los Angeles. Responsible for all preventative maintenance and computer operations of HVAC system. Gather bids and spearhead appropriate maintenance and repair contracts with vendors.

- o   Recognized by university officials for unprecedented project performance.
- o   Raised systems and operations to peak performance levels through creative, hands-on leadership.

THE GOODMAN COMPANY, Blue Skies, Montana   1990 to 1997
Commercial Property Operations Manager
Liaison between the tenants and owners for several properties, including prime locations—The Esplanade on Royal Avenue and Okee Square Shopping Center in Blue Skies. Provided appropriate staffing and services to ensure smooth facilities operations as it related to mechanical, structural, and landscaping needs.

- o   Assisted in arranging special events, including the gallery opening for Tico Tores (Drummer for Bon Jovi).
- o   Implemented cost-saving, energy-efficient cuts, resulting in cost savings of $47,000.

CUSTOM COMMERCIAL CONSTRUCTION, Hanover, Maryland   1986 to 1990
Construction Supervisor
Coordinated construction projects throughout MO, AR, WA, SN, and ND—from prebid through final inspection and opening. Gathered bids and negotiated and administered contracts for all aspects of the projects. Projects included office buildings, shopping centers, restaurants, and supermarkets.

- o   Successfully managed large-scale multiple projects concurrently.
- o   Projects completed on time and on schedule—exceeded expectations.

TRAINING / CERTIFICATIONS

Associate's Degree: Business, Monroe Community College, Rochester, New York, 1985
- o   Licensed Community Association Manager (CAM), Montana
- o   EPA Certification
- o   Certified Pool/Spa Operator, National Swimming Pool Foundation

10
High Tech

ELECTRONICS ENGINEER

ENRICO HERNANDEZ

710 Winter Park Drive, Apt. #7 • Miami, Florida 33459 • (305) 555-6341/email@email.com

Position in the design management, implementation, and operation of high-speed data and video networks using associated optical and electronic equipment

Enhancing the Speed of Information for Corporate Planning and Decision Making

PROFESSIONAL EXPERIENCE

SENIOR TELECOMMUNICATIONS SERVICE SPECIALIST
ASSISTANT TO DIRECTOR/PROJECT MANAGER
• Telecommunications Department... Florida Atlantic University, Boca Raton, Florida
February 1997 to Present

Main duties as Project Manager include: Planning and overseeing major building rewiring projects for enhanced CAT-5 standards and fiber optics. Interface with outside networking/technical vendors for timely completion of all projects. Responsible for the configuration of all FAU's PBX systems. Manage a staff of network technicians, direct all field installations, and troubleshoot for the Telecommunications Department. Selected as a member of the Internet II Engineering Committee.

NETWORK FIELD ENGINEER
• Mindspring Enterprises, Atlanta, Georgia
October 1996 to January 1997

Main responsibilities included the activation and conversion of T1s and PRI Telco lines into modem banks for connecting to an Enterprise Internet Service-providing network. Planning and interfacing with telecommunication providers and network engineers for the timely activation of these circuits. Duties also included the logistical planning of all hardware in circuit upgrades and installations.

SENIOR TELECOMMUNICATION SERVICE SPECIALIST
• Network Management for UFNet... University of Florida, Gainesville, Florida
January 1992 to October 1996

UFNet is the University of Florida's data and video network provider. Duties in this position involved performing highly skilled technical duties associated with the development of the campus-wide network. Configurations, planning, and design and installation of UFNet data and video network; also designing plans for installation of specific telecommunications equipment and their implementation. Supervised and carried out installation work with support from OPS employees. Performed analysis of current network configurations involving preventative maintenance and repair of existing network. Data collection for analysis regarding network traffic. Presented proposals for network configurations and provided technical data along with cost estimates for implementation.

NETWORK TECHNICIAN
• Digital Design Facilities... University of Florida, Gainesville, Florida
August 1988 to December 1991

Duties included design and implementation of Local Area Networks in campus environment. Using Ethernet and Broadband technologies with emphasis on fiber-optic media. Installation and configuration of such devices as bridges, hubs, repeaters, etc. Supervised installation crew, performed preventative maintenance, repair and inventory of equipment, and maintained documentation of network topology.

Duties included installation of campuswide fiber-optic and broadband network, including termination, testing, and activation of all networking devices. Implementing and operating multi-channel video distribution C and KU band satellite dish downlink station. Trained other personnel on fiber-optic termination and testing as well as several network-implementation procedures for analysis and purchase.

(Page 1 of 2)

ELECTRONICS ENGINEER (CONT.)

ENRICO HERNANDEZ

Page two

EXPERIENCE (OTHER)   Additional employers during college: HBO Sports, ESPN Sports Network, and J&E Service.

<u>Hardware</u>: I have experience in the following hardware: Bay Systems (Wellfleet), CN, LN, BN, Cisco, and Alantec 7000 switch/routers. Bridges, Hubs, Repeaters, and transceivers. Network General Sniffer. RMON test devices, Cabletron Systems, 3-COM Equipment, US Robotics, and terminal servers. Fiber-optic and LAN test equipment, and fiber-optic video and audio network devices. Also experienced with FDDI, Ethernet, Tokenring, and SONET network topologies.

<u>Telecommunications Equipment</u>: TBERD, Seimens/RDM; 9751, 8000, and 9000 Series PBX; CSU/DSU, and various test equipment.

<u>Software</u>: I have experience with the following software: UNIX, DOS, Windows 98, NT, IP, IPX, and Appletalk Protocols. Plus software packages, such as MacDraw, WordPerfect, AutoCAD, ProComm Plus, EMML 9006.3, and various spreadsheet programs.

EDUCATION   University of Florida, Gainesville, Florida
Bachelor of Science, 1987

Miami-Dade Community College, Miami, Florida
Associate of Arts Degree, August 1985

PERSONAL BACKGROUND   Foreign language proficiency: Fluent in English and Spanish
Recreational Interests: Water sports, music, and the outdoors

- References Furnished upon Request -

TECHNOLOGY EXECUTIVE/CONSULTANT

RICHARD D. LLOYD
1168 Jason Way
Los Angeles, California 90223
Home: (213) 555-2121/Cell: (213) 555-6565
Email: email@email.com

**INDUSTRY LEADER—TECHNOLOGY EXECUTIVE/CONSULTANT
CIO/CTO/INFORMATION TECHNOLOGIST**

Orchestrating Explosive Growth in Volatile and Down DOT COM Markets

**Expanding & Re-engineering Organizations/Start-up Management Expert
Organizational/IS Leadership of Public and Private Enterprises**

High-profile career spanning 25 years, spearheading the development, commercialization, and implementation of emerging technologies across key industry sectors, including Internet, healthcare, and high-tech environments.

CORE PROFESSIONAL STRENGTHS

Strategic Visioning/Planning	Management/IT Team Development
Corporate/Business Development	Product Development/Enhancement
System Integration/IT Infrastructure	Project Management/Leadership
Building Strategic Alliances and Partnerships	New-Technology Development/Transfer

PROFESSIONAL EXPERIENCE

COURT-LAND, INC., Boca Raton, Florida   1998 to Current
Chief Technology Officer
- Spearheaded team to develop an Internet Healthcare plan that became the basis for Cybear's vision.
- Core-management-team member that took this developmental-stage Internet company public.
- Designed and implemented Court-Land's HIPAA-ready National ISP network and Network Operations Center (NOC).
- Drafted initial specifications and developed "Dr. Cybear Internet Portal."
- Integrated strategic business partner's applications into the product.

CYBERMATRIX CORP., West Palm Beach, Florida   1995 to 1998
Chief Information Officer
- Directed IT strategic planning and implementations in preparing PhyMatrix for its IP.
- Built a national network to support corporate Medical-Practice Management, Managed Care, and Data Warehousing systems.
- Worked with the top management to identify, evaluate, and integrate organizations into PhyMatrix's core business systems.

PALM BEACH COUNTY HEALTHCARE DISTRICT, West Palm Beach, Florida   1991 to 1995
Chief Technology Officer
- Re-engineered the internal infrastructure and implemented a new managed-care system.
- Developed team to plan countywide managed-healthcare network.
- Managed internal and consulting resources during this effort; project was on time and under budget.

DIGITAL OFFICE SYSTEMS INTERNATIONAL, West Palm Beach, Florida   1986 to 1990
Chief Technology Officer
- Developed the first Cable TV (CATV) Facilities Resource Management System for integration into the advance Geographic Information System (GIS) and Cable TV Engineering software.
- Headed the development team responsible for the D-tain House Arrest System. Developed all facets of the system: Hardware, systems software, imbedded microprocessor software, unit fabrication, and manufacturing. Product deployed nationally in 1987.
- Founded and managed DOSI operations and development teams.

EDUCATION & TRAINING

Bachelor of Science: Analytical Chemistry	University of Florida	1985
Associate Faculty Member	College of Engineering	1990–Current

Comprehensive Resume, Specific Achievements, & References Furnished upon Request

SYSTEMS ENGINEER

ANTHONY TRAINER

1985 Devron Avenue, South, # 244
Boca Raton, Florida 33445
Phone: (561) 555-1212/Cell: (561) 555-1212
email@email.com

MICROSOFT-CERTIFIED SYSTEMS ENGINEER

Accomplished in Maintaining Enterprise Local Area Network
Four-plus Years' Manufacturing and Database Experience
ERP Systems Experience/Financial-Data Reporting
Network Architecture/Citrix-Metaframe Experience

A highly creative, technically skilled, and results-focused professional recognized for providing technical solutions to maintain business infrastructure in a timely and cost-effective manner.

Professional Experience

DiMARZZIO MANUFACTURING SERVICES, INC., Boca Raton, Florida   1998 to Current
Network Administrator/DBA

- Set up/maintain all user accounts, access rights, and permissions; support of desktop computers and Thin clients.
- Maintain SQL and Exchange 5.5 servers, and maintain connectors with NY, SC, TX, and Netherlands facilities.
- Configure and maintain Citrix Metaframe servers.
- Administer Fourth Shift ERP system. Support nine servers, including the WINS and DNS servers.
- A team member for completing an IT Roadmap project—that was adopted as the company's five-year plan to further integrate the facilities and provide better services through sharing information with customers and vendors. Emphasis was on sharing the needs of the organizational database infrastructure to accomplish this task.
- Transferred reporting system from an old FoxPro for DOS system to a newer, Web-enabled Brio Enterprise environment, resulting in…
  - The management team being able to acquire accurate, up-to-date information more easily and rapidly, therefore enhancing the critical decision-making process.
  - The setting up and maintenance of an MS SQL server acting as a data warehouse of the information included in Fourth Shift.
  - The process of transforming the data being automated and updated on a regularly scheduled basis.
  - The Brio Enterprise receiving the data through a connection to the SQL server rather than affecting the performance of Fourth Shift.
- Set up and maintain a corporate intranet server using Internet Information server 4.0.
- Monitor Cisco Switches and Routers to ensure network connectivity within the facility and to remote locations.

KRASHAW MARKETING GROUP, INC., Boca Raton, Florida   1993 to 1998
Systems Integrator—Microsoft Technician

- Implemented, designed, and supported LAN for small-to-medium-size businesses, using Windows NT/95/98 Operating Systems and 10/100baseT topologies.
- Set up and implemented Microsoft Exchange 5.5, Microsoft SQL server 7.0, and various configurations, using BackOffice 4.0 and 4.5.
- Provided NT-server administration on a contract basis—maintaining and supporting all clients.
- Custom configured hardware to specifications required for client systems. Provided Help Desk support.
- Setup various configurations of IIS 4.0.

(Page one of two)

138

Professional Experience

MOTOROLA, Plantation, Florida   1988 to 1993
Robotic Automation Trainer

- Specifically dealt with the development and implementation of operator-training systems for high-end robotic equipment. Position included technical writing for operator-training manuals based on ISO standards.
- Training of machine operators according to ISO-approved documentation to better enhance the productivity of the department, and therefore increasing revenue due to higher-quality products and increased production.
- Certification of operators to ensure production was utilizing qualified individuals to increase performance.
- Continuing documentation of qualified individuals to ensure production was consistently utilizing and updating the skills of their employees.
- Participated in the development of virtual-reality training systems.

Education/Training

UNIVERSITY OF PHOENIX, Phoenix, Arizona
B.S.I.T., 1987

Microsoft Certification Track/Training
- Windows 2000 Training for Accelerated Exam (70-240), 2001
- MSCE—Microsoft Certification Systems Engineer, 1998–99
    - Network Essentials
    - Windows NT Workstation
    - Windows NT Server
    - NT Server in the Enterprise
    - TCP/IP
    - Internet Information Server 4.0
- MCDBA—Microsoft Database Administrator, 2000
    - Administering SQL Server 7.0
    - Implementing and Designing an SQL 7.0 Database

Microsoft TechNet—Implementing a Windows 2000 Network, 2000
Self-study: Introduction to Visual Basic 6.0, 2001–Current
Fourth Shift ERP Administration Training, 2000

Certifications

Microsoft-Certified Systems Engineer
Microsoft-Certified Database Administrator

References and Supporting Documentation Furnished upon Request

INFORMATION TECHNOLOGY ACCOUNTING PROFESSIONAL

WENDY CONNERS

8339 Old Forest Road
Harbor View, Georgia 87644
(545) 555-1212/email@email.com

INFORMATION TECHNOLOGY
ACCOUNTING PROFESSIONAL
Enhancing Corporate Financial Position & Shareholder Value

Outstanding Computer Application, Configuration, & Troubleshooting Skills
Leadership Skills in Financial (P&L) & Cash-Flow Management
Strong Organizational-Leadership & Customer-Service Skills

A dynamic, team-spirited individual recognized for successfully integrating advanced technology and accounting to improve organizational growth and profitability. Experience includes Director of Information Systems, Manager of Data Processing, Systems Engineer, Controller, and Accounting Professional.

CORE STRENGTHS

Technical Experience
Mssql 6.5, Mssql 7, Btrieve, Visual Foxpro, Visual Basic, RPG, Cobol, NT Server, Novell Server, AS/400, IBM-5340-5360, Website-Design Management, E-commerce Integration

Technical/Financial Applications
Solomon IV, Platinum, Abra Suite, Microsoft Office Suite (Word, Excel, and Access), Lotus, WordPerfect, Crystal Reports, R&R Report Writer, FRx

Organizational Leadership
Productivity & Efficiency Enhancement, Long and Short-Term Strategic Planning/Forecasting, Accounts Receivable & Cash-Flow Management, Personnel Training & Development, Regulatory Compliance & Reporting Management

PROFESSIONAL EXPERIENCE

TECHNOLOGY CONSULTANTS, Atlanta, Georgia   1994–Current
Consulting Assignments—IT Accounting, System Engineer, IT Integration

Assignments:

BLYDER INDUSTRIES, Atlanta, Georgia (1999 to Current)

- Established/managed the IS department, consisting of IBM midrange and Novell Servers for a holding company with a labor force of 3,000 employees (revenues exceeding $375 million). Directed database-support activities, project planning, and software development for commercial and in-house-designed applications. Implemented a corporate widely centralized payroll system to replace individual subsidiary systems. Supported an office staff of twenty-eight employees. Oversaw all accounting systems.

- Made modifications to the 401 K data files based on the new requirements of the plan administrator.

ROBERT HALF INTERNATIONAL, Atlanta, Georgia (1997 to 1999)

- Reconditioned desktop/laptop computers, installed Windows operating systems, Microsoft office products, Internet access, and e-mail software. Setup odbc data sources for access to the Solomon IV Mssql server.

- Documented all installation procedures and created handout documents covering each area of the financial applications for training purposes. Provided customer training to client employees for G/L, A/P, A/R, inventory, purchasing, and order management.

(Page 1 of 2)

Wendy Conners
(Page two)

PROFESSIONAL EXPERIENCE (Continued)

CLIENT SERVER TECHNOLOGIES, INC., Jacksonville, Florida (1995 to 1997)

- Installation of Mssql7 and Solomon IV ver 4.21 software for a company specializing in the installation of accounting, human-resource, and payroll applications. Implemented data conversions to extract, modify, and import financial history from existing client databases to the Solomon IV application databases.

- Reconciled all financial modules by accounting period, and audited all financial information and reports for accuracy. Planned the company Web page, page layouts, pull-down tabs, and page links with a Web site developer, which included a mission statement, software-solution applications, and e-mail contacts.

INTERNATIONAL SERVICE CORPORATION, Atlanta, Georgia   1986 to 1994
Director Information Systems (1988–94)

Supervised a data-processing manager, 25 computer operators, and support for an office staff of 50 employees, for a broker servicing military installations worldwide. The client base exceeded 100 manufacturers and provided revenues in excess of $200 million. Financial Applications: General ledger, payroll, A/R, A/P, sales, budgeting, contractor billings, independent-labor distribution, 1099 and W2 electronic filings with the IRS, sales support, merchandising and expenses, sales invoices and commissions, customer service, purchase-order processing, and distributor-item pricing.

Designed an EDI (UCS and ANSI xX12) bridge application to interface with the Sterling software interpreter and generator to pass information to/from the client or purchasing agency based on their unique EDI requirements. Processed 2,000+ transaction sets daily, including credit/debit adjustments for distributors/clients, purchase orders from military installations, price changes, and invoices, to the internal accounting system. Significantly decreased the cost of using a third-party network (Sterling software), 80%, by enhancing software applications.

Controller/Financial Officer (1986–88)

Managed all corporate accounting and computer operations for the parent and subsidiary corporations comprised of 80 cost centers. Supervised twenty-five employees in general accounting, accounts payable, accounts receivable, and payroll. Reconciled cash receipts, prepared monthly accruals, asset depreciation schedules, federal and state tax liabilities, closing entries, and P&L statements. Monitored cash management, investments, forecasting, employee health, 401K, disability insurance, budgeting, and the personal financial portfolio of the owner of the corporation.

EDUCATION/TRAINING

UNIVERSITY OF RHODE ISLAND, Providence, Rhode Island
Bachelor of Science: Business Administration, 1985

Selected On-going Training

NCR programming and operations, 1975   RPG programming and operations, 1978
AS/400 operations and utilities, 1994   FoxPro 2.6, 1996
Visual FoxPro 5 and 6.0, 1997, 1999   Sql database architecture, 1998
Solomon IV implementation and system administration, 2000   Solomon IV distribution series, 2000

MILITARY SERVICE

UNITED STATES AIR FORCE
Inventory Management Specialist, 1978–81

References and Supporting Documentation Furnished upon Request

ONLINE CONTENT PRODUCER

Confidential Resume

MICHAEL L. LOCKE

234 Winston Trail ▪ Concord, New Hampshire 12243
Phone: (603) 555-1212/Cell: (603) 555-2121 ▪ email@email.com

WEBSITE & GRAPHIC DESIGN/ONLINE CONTENT PRODUCER
Award-Winning Design Skills/Outstanding Visual Marketing & Concept Development
12 Years' Successful Experience in National & International Environments

Solid Computer Graphics Experience
Extraordinary Writing and Strategic-Marketing Expertise
Excellent Interpersonal & "People" Skills

A highly creative, energetic, and growth-oriented Website/Content Professional dedicated to taking a leadership role in helping to expand organizational growth and profits through expert Website/content-development management.

CORE STRENGTHS

Internet Website design, layout, and development/enhancement
Production scheduling and project management
CAD details and shop drawings development and review
Teaching, leading, and empowering team members
Relationship development skills; building strategic alliances

Graphic design/authoring—concept marketing
Engineering (windload) analysis and review
Professional technical/communications skills
Technical problem solving/troubleshooting
Customer-service/quality-control management

COMPUTER/TECHNICAL STRENGTHS

Photoshop, GoLive, ImageReady, QuarkXPress, Illustrator, Word, Excel, Painter, Acrobat/Reader/Distiller, Netscape Communicator, Explorer, Mac OS, and Windows

PROFESSIONAL EXPERIENCE

DOWNTOWN DESIGNWORKS, Concord, New Hampshire/Boston, Massachusetts   1993 to Current
Web/Graphic Designer
Recruited by established graphics business in the area of Web/graphic design. Responsible for concept development, design, artwork, and printing services. Provide services incorporating design, layout, and presentation materials for print, as well as Website design & site development. Assess needs, develop cost-effective solutions, and prepare proposals/presentations to secure new business. Prep file formats, optimize image files, and prep HTML for new and existing Websites. Consult in key areas of Website management.

- Successfully captured the vision of new business owners and designed effective collateral and promotional materials.
- Designed and created high-impact logos for profit and nonprofit clientele.
- Created initial Websites for organizations/private enterprise—conceptual design through launch and debugging.

BOLLA DOOR CO., INC., Manchester, New Hampshire   1988 to 1993
Senior Sales Engineer
Direct responsibility for processing factory orders in preparation for fabrication documents and order acknowledgments for custom manufacturer of high-quality architectural sliding glass door systems for national and international export markets. Additional responsibilities included supervision of estimates, personnel training and efficiency management, and technical support to domestic and foreign-industry clients (including architects, contractors, and glazing companies). Provided CAD and technical details. Scheduled orders for factory production. Oversaw purchasing and inventory-control processes. Authorized financial signatory. Analyzed and assessed product-performance criteria with design specifications.

- Drafted proposal for company Internet business strategy and online resources.
- Composed logic and assisted implementation of customized PC-based computer program to automate estimates and orders—resulting in significant improvement in efficiency and reduction of paperwork.

(Page 1 of 2)

142

MICHAEL L. LOCKE
234 Winston Trail ▪ Concord, New Hampshire 12243
Phone: (603) 555-1212/Cell: (603) 555-2121 ▪ email@email.com

PROFESSIONAL EXPERIENCE

BOLLA DOOR CO., INC.,
(Continued):

- Designed automated (spreadsheet) interface and system to facilitate and simplify shipping-department packaging methods and enhance professional corporate image; designed and updated company instructional literature.
- Recognized as the company's first CAD operator—developed system of providing computer-generated detail drawings for project specifications and architectural support.

JELLER TROTTA ARCHITECTS, Concord, New Hampshire   1985 to 1988
Draftsman
Primary responsibilities included CAD drawings under architects' supervision. Additional duties included blueprinting and project presentation for clients.

- Prepared detailed CAD drawings for key architectural projects.

EDUCATION/TRAINING/CERTIFICATIONS

Bachelor of Science: Graphic Design Technology, New Hampshire College	1985
Associate in Science: Drafting and Design Technology, New Hampshire College	1983
Certified Internet Web Designer, (Novell CIP), New Hampshire College	1988
Certified Internet Business Strategist, (Novell CIP), UNH	1990
CEU Certificates/Credits—"PC Graphic Tools" and "Desktop Publishing," UNH	1993

Awards & Recognitions
First Place (Graphic Design), New Hampshire College Student Show
Winner (Advertising Design), Palm Beach Community College Student Show
President's Honor List, Palm Beach Community College

References, Studio Portfolio, and Supporting Documentations Furnished upon Request

EXECUTIVE-LEVEL HIGH-TECH SALES

JOSEPH A. MURRAY

5767 Newton Circle • Melbourne, Florida 32940
Phone: (321) 555-2233 • Cell: (321) 555-5353
email@email.com

EXECUTIVE-LEVEL HIGH-TECH SALES
KEY-ACCOUNT/RELATIONSHIP MANAGEMENT

Eight Years' Top Producing Sales Experience in High-tech/Dot Com Environments
Closed/Contributed to $87.4 Million in New Business Over Past Eight Years

- Expert start-up management and sales strategist
- High-impact presentation and closing techniques (Fortune 1000/key accounts)
- Strategic and global account development
- Rapid, " immediate-to-market" deployment sales/management strategies

---

Areas of Strengths

Total account relationship management (long-term)	Strategic market domination and leadership
Tactical alliance/partnership development	Executive-contract negotiations expert
Product, service, and sales training—all levels	Highly diverse, industry-technical knowledge
Cross-functioning team building and leadership	Customer-service and retention management

Professional Experience

> *Exceed quota—performing at 121%*

PULLO.COM, Melbourne, Florida   1998 to 2001
Strategic Account Manager
(The largest privately held data colocation provider in the United States. A start-up company with 28 facilities expanding rapidly.)
Managed strategic and global accounts for Florida region. Heavy focus on retention control as well as high-impact presentations for executive-level meetings. Focused primarily on Fortune 1000 flagship accounts. Helped launch and market new collocation data center in Orlando, Florida with heavy emphasis on product ubiquity and flexibility. Turned start-up sales into millions by implementing strategic selling versus typical tactical sales.

- Directly responsible for over $70 million in total gross revenue.
- Expert in negotiating strategic and global accounts at the executive level with Fortune 1000 corporations.
- Consistent top performer in southeast region beating quota by 121%.
- Designed high-impact proposals for executive-level management.
- Solely responsible for sales for $12 million collocation data center in Orlando, Florida.

> *Turned around underperforming sales division in 90 days*

BTAL TELECOM, Orlando, Florida   1996 to 1998
Regional Data Specialist/Data Sales Manager
(A rapidly expanding company with annual sales of $300 million—providing broadband access to customers worldwide)
Directed daily operation of all data sales in Central Florida. Used effective strategies to implement new training techniques for all data sales that were later incorporated into different regions. Managed a team of 32 people, trained regional directors (35+ people) on the latest development in the data industry, and strategized how to increase bottom line and time-to-market with new products. Product expert on ATM, ISDN, Frame Relay, SONET, and *(x)*DSL.

- Exceeded quota objective for 12 months straight.
- Turned around data-sales division from deep losses to black ink in less than 12 months.
- Serviced key accounts with extraordinarily high industry-retention rate.
- Contributing team member to *(x)*DSL releases in Florida territory.

Joseph A. Murray
Page 2.

Professional Experience

> **Ignited start-up sales from $0 to more than $900,000 in 16 months**

DDR-WEB, Melbourne, Florida   1993 to 1996
Vice President of Sales and Marketing
(A start-up Web-hosting, broadband-access, and Internet-business-consultation firm)
Directed firm with no sales and exploded into the Florida market with $900,000 the first year—$1.2 million second year—and $1.9 million the third. Business consulting and broadband services grew from one small company to over 100 companies in a single year, including *FOX Sports* and *MTV*. Managed a sales team, selling broadband services to the rapidly expanding corporate market. Helped launch two new key critical products that "turned the red ink black." Assisted with the design and launch of industry advertisements in national publications including *Internet World* and *Internet Week*.

- Directly responsible for $2.1million gross sales from new start-up company.
- Ignited "Data Sales Team" performance 104%.
- Successfully launched new products and achieved rapid market deployment.
- Managed sales team of six people, responsible for over 80% of gross revenue.
- Developed and maintained strategic, multimillion-dollar accounts.

> **Top Sales Producer—1995**

METROLINK INTERNET SERVICES, Melbourne, Florida   1991 to 1993
Corporate Data Sales/Sr. Technical Advisor
(A start-up Internet firm with gross revenues of $1 million+ in first year. ML provided direct Internet access to 10,000+ customers as well as over 800 Web-based accounts. ML grew over 250% per year until it was bought out at the end of 1998.)

Directed all sales and marketing efforts in the Florida territory. Solely responsible for managing all key accounts and consummating any deal worth over $5,000 MRR for the company. Served as a technical advisor to president. Helped launch key products to the market such as ISDN, Clear Channel T-1, and Frame Relay services.

- Contributed to total revenue of $1 million from zero; named "top sales producer" 1995.
- Managed Florida territory, contributing to new development of key accounts.

Military Service

UNITED STATES ARMY—82nd Airborne Division   1987 to 1991
Airborne Combat Infantry Brigade
Staff Judge Advocates Intelligence Division—System Network Coordinator (LAN-based networks)
- Member: US Army Parachute Team; Honorable Discharge, 1994

Education/Professional Development

UNIVERSITY OF CENTRAL FLORIDA, Orlando, Florida.
Bachelor of Arts: Philsophy—Expected Date Graduation—2001
- GPA: 3.85/Summa Cum Laude

Selected Professional Development

Highly specialized in ATM/SONET/*(x)*DSL/ISDN/Frame Relay/Corporate Broadband Services

Activities

Costa Rica—built homes for indigent families; Assistant to *Guardian Ad-Litem* program for abused children
Pilot—VFR certified

References and Professional Portfolio Furnished upon Request

IT CONSULTANT

STEPHEN N. HOLLAND

120 Cambridge * Berkley, Michigan 48072 * (248) 555-1212 * email@email.com

---

IT Consultant

Manager in Big5 Consulting Firm
Successful Manager of People, Process, & Technology
eCommerce Expertise in Growth & Profit Generation

A motivated, innovative, growth-oriented IT Consultant with positive, contagious energy who builds teams, creates relationships, and earns trust. Strategically and tactfully resolves and troubleshoots problems. A high-impact, multidimensional IT professional respected by his peers/superiors with a verifiable record of achievement of exceeding expectations.

CORE STRENGTHS

Information systems issues, risks, development, implementation	Business process analysis and improvement
Vision, strategy, and assessing market opportunities	Product development and enhancement
Teaching, leading, and empowering team members	Business and technical acumen
Relationship development skills; building strategic alliances	Web design and E-commerce technology

PROFESSIONAL EXPERIENCE

ERNST & YOUNG, LLP, Detroit, Michigan   1997 to Current
Manager
Professional Services Manager in the Information Systems Assurance & Advisory Services (ISAAS) practice. Has a history of success delivering measurable value to a myriad of clients in multiple industries, from Fortune 1000 to small, high-growth companies. Extensive experience managing risk as organizations apply technology to complex internal and external business processes. Strategically focused in eProcurement, Internet security, venture acceleration, business process analysis/design, and IT strategy. Helped Ernst & Young develop eProcurement and eCommerce methodologies and build market share. Creates teams, empowers people, and delivers results. Innovative thinker. Pursuit leader on sales efforts. Delivers measurable value on every project.

- Lake Erie region ISAAS eProcurement and eCommerce leader
- Selected to deliver eCommerce presentation at the annual National Ernst & Young Accounting update meeting
- Selected as ISAAS leader on Ann Arbor territory expansion and pursuit team
- Increased revenue streams through demonstrating value to client's IT organization and business processes
- Successfully managed client expectations on all projects, resulting in additional work/favorable client referrals
- Instrumental in building the ISAAS practice, trained staff/senior consultants in successful client service delivery
- Industry expertise includes health care, insurance, manufacturing, banking

Listing of Ernst & Young Major Projects:

Project Name	Description
Venture Acceleration	Accelerated venture business plans to first round of funding. Activities include business modeling, revenue modeling, content sourcing, value-chain analysis, competitive analysis, and product definition and design.
Business Plan Assessment	Assessed start-up business plans.
eProcurement	Managed and led strategic eProcurement ROI and diagnostic assessments.
Internet Security	Implemented Axent's Technologies NetProwler and Intruder Alert host and network-based intrusion-detection software.
Internet Security	Assessed online systems security of B2B transportation provider.
Business Process Analysis	Defined business-process improvement opportunities for a myriad of clients in multiple industries.
IT Strategy	Conducted an IT departmental budget assessment.
Due Diligence	Assessed ASP internet start-up as due diligence for potential Venture Capitalist.
Systems Consulting	Defined and assessed technical and functional requirements.

IT CONSULTANT (CONT.)

PROFESSIONAL EXPERIENCE

BLUE CROSS & BLUE SHIELD OF MICHIGAN, Southfield, Michigan   1994 to 1997
Work flow & Imaging Consultant, Contract through Computer Methods Corporation
Assisted Blue Cross Blue Shield in the design of the dental claims imaging system. Was the only consultant on the business side of the imaging project. Led client teams in defining business process and system requirements for various automated work-flow queues. Defined detail-process flows for work-flow and imaging-system design. Codeveloped system-reporting requirements with client-management team.

- Selected by users/management to facilitate business process improvement initiatives with Orthodontic work team
- Defined and established benchmark criteria for the Dental Imaging System to measure overall project success
- Designed, developed, and implemented dental-claim-appeals-tracking database that is still in use today

COMPUTER METHODS CORPORATION (CMC), Livonia, Michigan   1987 to 1994
Project Manager (1992–94)
Employed with CMC for over 5 years as a Project Manager, Account Executive, and Business Analyst for this $30 Million software consulting firm. Reported directly to the President and CEO for 3 years. Selected in 1997 to lead the Imaging Technologies business unit after much employee turnover, customer dissatisfaction, and lack of organizational structure. Instrumental in achieving stability, increasing revenues, cutting costs, consolidating resources, and ultimately, improving customer confidence.

- Directed Imaging Technologies business-unit operations, responsible for $1.2 million in annual revenues
- Successfully negotiated new-business and renewal contracts with small and Fortune 1000 clients
- Consistently increased group profitability on a quarterly basis
- Comanaged implementation of OCR technology integrated with custom-developed claims-adjudication software
- Successfully managed department's staff of 30+ people (programmers, network admin., and administrative staff)
- Responsible for business unit financial planning and budgeting

Account Executive (1990–92)

- Responsible for high growth, middle-market-clientele sector, successfully increased annual sector revenue
- Sold client/server solutions, wrote and presented comprehensive proposals for custom application development, established new revenue streams
- Main liaison between customer and development team, managed customer expectations
- Selected as Sales and Marketing contact for Microsoft's Solution Provider program

Business Analyst (1987–90)

- Defined user, business, and system requirements for scope and design documents
- Identified & tracked corporate quality measurables, lead contributor to Ford's on-site Q1 quality audit

EDUCATION/TRAINING

Bachelor of Arts Degree, 1993   **ALBION COLLEGE, Albion, Michigan**

Dual Majors: **Mathematics**, GPA: 3.8/4.0; **Economics** GPA: 3.8/4.0
Concentration: Carl A. Gerstacker Professional Management Program; Business Study Exchange, Germany, Summer, 1993

Training: Certified Document Imaging Architect (expected 2/2001); Commerce One eProcurement Technical Training; PeopleSoft Application Controls Training

ACTIVITIES

Junior Achievement High School Economics Teacher and Consultant
Troy High School, Volunteer Football Coach
Albion College Class Agent, Class of '93; Albion College Leadership Campaign Committee Member

References Furnished upon Request

TECHNICAL-SUPPORT PROFESSIONAL

WILLIAM C. HANLEY

7725 Mountain Lane
Colorado Springs, Colorado 80909
Phone: (719) 555-1212/Cell: (719) 555-1234
email@email.com

TECHNICAL-SUPPORT PROFESSIONAL
Hardware/Software Installation, Application, Troubleshooting, & Configuration

"Gets it Right the First Time"

**Help Desk Technician/Tech Support Engineer/Product Specialist/Systems Analyst
Network Specialist or Engineer/PC-Support Specialist/Computer Operations**

More than twenty years of responsible experience with the United States Navy (and Secret Service) highlighted by high achievement and increasingly responsible decision making in the areas of management/administration, and the development, installation, and support of information systems.

CORE STRENGTHS

Strategic development of hardware/software-technology solutions
Organizational leadership—personnel training and development
Customer-service management—quality control

Project management and budget control
Problem-solving and conflict resolution
Technical writing

▣ Computer Skills

Hardware/Systems:	PCs—installation, application, configuration, and troubleshoot; DOS, Windows, NT, HTML
Software:	Word, Excel, PowerPoint, Access, Outlook, Express, Visio, Project, WordPerfect, Corel Draw Internet Explorer, Netscape, and Internet applications

HIGHLIGHTS OF EXPERIENCE

Awarded two Navy Commendation Medals for successful implementation of technology solutions.

Managed over $4,000,000 in operations and claims budgets throughout career. Reduced operating costs 22% annually on average while boosting acquired services from providers through negotiation.

Authored 125-page shipboard legal manual and numerous other legal documents that provided guidance for the administration of command-discipline programs and other administrative procedures.

PROFESSIONAL EXPERIENCE

THE BOWDEN GROUP, Denver, Colorado   1999 to Current
Help Desk Support Technician / IBM Customer Support Specialist
- ❑ Provide expert technical support to end-users for all IBM ThinkPad, Aptiva, and Work Pad computers. Perform problem determination/resolution on all installed hardware and user-added IBM hardware. Provide additional support on operating systems (W95/98/NT/2000) assisting customers with software adjustments and system recovery.
- ❑ Awarded "President's Commendation" Award for outstanding performance and leadership.

U.S. SECRET SERVICE, Washington, D.C.   1992 to 1999
Special Officer
- ❑ Performed a wide range of security/protective-support functions at Headquarters and associated areas. Monitored/operated U.S. Secret Service computerized security system.

UNITED STATES NAVY   1979 to 1999
Discipline Officer—Naval Air Technical Training Center, Pensacola, Florida (1995–99)
- ❑ Developed/administered an MS Access database for training command of 5,000+ students and 600 staff. Dramatically improved accountability and simplified data analysis. Awarded a Navy Commendation Medal as a result.
- ❑ Provided desktop and hardware support for MS Office 97, Windows 95 in an NT environment, and Internet Explorer and Lotus cc:Mail, to Legal Office personnel.

(Page 1 of 2)

PROFESSIONAL EXPERIENCE (Continued)

U.S. Navy (Continued)

Administrative Officer—U.S. Sending State Office for Italy, U.S. Embassy, Rome, Italy (1990–95)
- ❏ Initiated the conversion of office computers from Windows 3.1 to Windows95, installed and configured all network hardware/software on systems establishing an additional domain on the U.S. State Department's worldwide telecommunications system. Developed the project plan, prepared a detailed written justification for expenditures, and provided technical assistance/support to U.S. State Department Information Systems personnel.

- ❏ Served as Budget Officer, Customs Officer, Law Librarian, Assistant Passport Reviewing Officer, and International Transportation Office Supervisor. Awarded a Navy Commendation Medal for outstanding performance.

Discipline Officer, USS CANOPUS (1988–90)
- ❏ Developed a detailed report-tracking system using Borland dBase for this shipboard command of 1,400 crewmembers. Established a peer-to-peer network in Windows for Workgroups environment to establish file and resource sharing.

Student, University of North Florida (1987)
- ❏ 1 of 100 sailors selected Navy-wide to participate in the U.S. Navy's enlisted degree completion program.

Legalman (Paralegal), Naval Legal Service Office, Mayport, Florida (1982–87)
- ❏ Technical Support Representative for a legal staff of 30 personnel. Implemented/supported all headquarter IT initiatives, including hardware/software upgrades and establishing/maintaining remote-access service to headquarters.

- ❏ Budget Officer, Claims Office Supervisor. Managed a $300,000 annual operating budget and $300,000 annual claims budget. Adjudicated over 2,000 claims against the U.S. government. Increased collections by 200%.

- ❏ Leading Petty Officer of the Legal Department. Prepared courts-martial and administrative-procedures documents. Operated and maintained office automated data-processing equipment.

Medical Laboratory Technician, U.S. Naval Hospital, Bremerton, Washington (1979–82)
- ❏ Operated and maintained computerized laboratory equipment.

EDUCATION AND CERTIFICATIONS

B.A. (Summa Cum Laude), Criminal Justice/Minor, Business   UNIVERSITY OF NORTH FLORIDA

Graduate Studies: Business Administration (18 Semester hours)   UNIVERSITY OF WEST FLORIDA

CERTIFICATIONS: A+, Network+, Microsoft-Certified Professional (MCP—Networking Essentials, NT Workstation)

CONTINUING EDUCATION: Completed training in Technical Support, Total-Quality Management, and Equal Opportunity

References and Supporting Documentation Furnished upon Request

PRODUCT MARKETING/BUSINESS-DEVELOPMENT EXECUTIVE

STEVEN D. GILLMAN
30667 Willow Road
Decatur, Georgia 30335
Phone: (404) 555-5511/Cell: (561) 555-1155/email@email.com

PRODUCT MARKETING/BUSINESS-DEVELOPMENT EXECUTIVE

20 Consecutive Years of Successful Product Life-Cycle Management and New-Product Introduction ...

*Electronic Publishing/Software and Internet Products for the
Automotive/Aerospace/Petro-Chemical/Pharmaceutical/Construction industries.*

Product Life-Cycle Management	Project Management
Strategic & Business Planning	Market Research & Competitive Analysis
Authoring Requirements and Specifications	Marketing & Sales Support
Corporate Acquisitions	Business Development

Well versed in JAVA, HTML, XML, Relational Database, and other technologies.

Professional Experience

e-AUTOALLIANCE, Atlanta, Georgia   1996 to Current
Vice President of Product Development
(Provider of customer-relationship management, e-Commerce, and software tools to the automotive aftermarket)
Strategic planning, product management, and business development for automotive aftermarket start-up.

- Worked with the CEO and closed $6.7 million initial round of funding.

- Worked with CEO on the acquisition of three leading automotive-business-management-system providers, increasing the company's customer base by 8000.

- Established national-distribution agreement with a major manufacturer's 200-person sales force.

- Created product specifications for customer-relationship management and B2B e-Commerce systems.

- Managed an eight-person software-development organization.

- Consistent record of consecutive on-time product releases.

DATAPROTECH, Decatur, Georgia   1990 to 1996
Product Marketing Director
(The leading provider of electronic automotive-diagnostic information to the automotive aftermarket—a $75 million company)
Established a product-marketing department with eight direct reports.

- Responsible for the identification, creation, and rollout of company's next generation product resulting in...
  - A 250% ($14 million) growth in sales.
  - Customer-retention growth from 85% to 93%.
  - Pretax-profit performance 33% over plan.

- Managed $3 million *Popular Mechanics* consumer product, marketed through retail channels, including Kmart and Autozone.

- Launched Internet consumer product, currently accounting for over 25,000 new customers and $500,000 contribution margin (Conducted all phases of market research, field testing, planning, project management and rollout).

- Worked with the database-development organization on outsourced projects in India and Romania.

- Phased out DataProTech's mature product line, saving in excess of $500,000.

- Involved in the creation of a B2B e-Commerce company funded by Internet Capital Group.
  - Conducted market research, cowrote business plan, authored product specifications, designed prototypes, and established partnerships.

- Conducted business and technical evaluations and recommendations for the acquisition of third-party e-Commerce software (Commerce One, Ariba, Interworld, Broadvision, etc).

Confidential

(Page 1 of 2)

150

STEVEN D. GILLMAN
Page Two

Professional Experience (Continued)

INFORMATION HANDLING SERVICES, Englewood, Colorado   1982 to 1990
Senior Business-Development Manager
(A $400 million electronic publisher of technical, regulatory, and product information)

- Conducted extensive market research and executive management interviews (engineering, purchasing, and finance) with market leaders (Boeing, Caterpillar, General Motors, Lockheed, Arco Petroleum, General Electric) to identify new business and product opportunities.
- Led a cross-functional team, developing partnerships with automated CAD suppliers (Mentor Graphics, Cadence Design, CATIA).
- Authored requirements and specifications for a multimillion-dollar software-development project as part of a $15 million product line.
- Conducted a six-month business development project (market research, business planning, and product definition) covering the automotive aftermarket.
- Participated in sales training and customer visits, giving executive-level presentations in support of the company's new business strategies.
- Team member involved in developing the strategy to move the company's product lines to the Internet.
- Participated in evaluating various acquisition candidates for the company.
- Worked closely with CEO and management to implement company strategies.

Education/Personal Development

Bachelor of Science: Life Cycle and Product Development	University of Florida	1979
Post Graduate Studies toward Master of Environmental Engineering	University of Florida	1980–81
Associate Faculty Member	College Engineering	1974 to 1976

- Microsoft Certification—Intermediate Visual Basic
- Advanced Project Management
- Finance & Accounting for the Nonfinancial Manager (Droms)

References on Request

Confidential

11
Education

HIGHER-EDUCATION ADMINISTRATOR

SHIRLEY F. GRAHAM

3820 Victoria Drive • Minneapolis, Minnesota 55443 •((612) 555-1212/email@email.com

---

ADMINISTRATIVE POSITION IN HIGHER EDUCATION
Student Affairs/Public Affairs/Governmental Affairs
Certified Educational Planner

"Helping Students Build an Inspiring Life"

A highly dynamic, team-spirited, and results-oriented individual seeking to combine academic training with excellent work experience to make a solid contribution to organizational goals in higher education.

AREAS OF EXPERTISE

College admission and financial-aid counseling
Personnel recruitment, training, and development
Marketing, promotions, and public/community relations
Counseling and guiding students to resolve key challenges

Program development and implementation
Curriculum development and enhancement
Policy/procedure development/enforcement
Public-speaking and presentation skills

☑ <u>Systems</u>: Mac, PC, IBM AS400; <u>Software</u>: Office 2000, WordPerfect, Lotus, ACT 2000, and Internet Applications

EDUCATION

BALDWIN SOUTHEASTERN UNIVERSITY, Minneapolis, Minnesota
Doctorate of Higher Education (Higher Education Administration), 2001

DEPAUL UNIVERSITY, Chicago, Illinois
Master of Science in Education, 1996
Bachelor of Arts in Communications/Sociology, 1990

PROFESSIONAL EXPERIENCE

INDEPENDENT EDUCATIONAL CONSULTING SERVICES, Minneapolis, Minnesota   1995 to Current

GSW EDUCATIONAL CONSULTANTS
Educational Consultant
- Work closely with students and parents with career assessment/development, college selection/placement, and financial-aid processes/procedures.
- Conduct extensive research and compose comprehensive newsletters and other materials related to the admissions process for institutions of higher education.
- Consistently invited by colleges and universities throughout the nation to visit their campuses to see, first-hand, their variety of resources and curricula, to ensure highly effective counseling/coaching to clients.
- Conduct college-planning workshops at high schools and private institutions.

HAYWARD COLLEGE, Minneapolis, Minnesota   1990 to 1995
Senior Admissions Counselor/Articulation Officer
- Worked closely with account representatives from various educational publications to coordinate advertising program for Enrollment Services Office.
- Developed and coordinated recruitment activities for transfer-student population. Prepared transfer-student informational brochures and correspondence.
- Planned and facilitated Independent Colleges and Universities of Minnesota Articulation Workshops for community and private college personnel on campus.
- Interviewed, counseled, and advised prospective students on academics, financial aid, and career services.

(Page 1 of 2)

Shirley F. Graham
Page Two

PROFESSIONAL EXPERIENCE (Continued)

CONTINUUM INC./STEELCASE INC., High Point, Minnesota · · · · · 1988 to 1990
Sales & Marketing Assistant
- Coordinated and managed company trade shows, events, and expos (high-volume furniture manufacturer).
- Assisted the VP of Sales and Marketing in devising creative and high-impact marketing material.
- Developed first company employee manual; handled company vendor-certification process.

GREENSBORO COLLEGE, Greensboro, North Carolina · · · · · 1986 to 1988
Admissions Counselor
- Managed all recruitment activities for large territory—Southeastern United States.
- Served as Chairperson of the campuswide Human Relations Committee for Student Affairs Department.
- Coordinated multicultural and college visitation programs for the college.

THOMASVILLE HOUSING AUTHORITY, Thomasville, North Carolina · · · · · 1983 to 1986
Office Assistant/Management Intern
- Researched and assisted with writing grants and proposals.
- Assisted with the coordination of agency programs, including Crime Prevention and Drug Awareness.
- Interviewed tenants and maintained tenant records database.

CERTIFICATIONS

Certified by and Member of: Independent Educational Consultants Association (IECA)
Certified by and Member of: American Association of Independent Educational Consultants

PROFESSIONAL AFFILIATIONS

Minneapolis Teacher Advisory Board
Minneapolis County Journalist Association
Toastmasters
Women in Leadership

References and Supporting Documentation Furnished upon Request

ART TEACHER

DENISE ACKINSON

1883 Bridgeport Boulevard
Old Bridge, New Jersey 53427
(908) 555-1234/email@email.com

ART TEACHER
College/High School

A creative, motivating, and highly qualified art teacher seeking position to enhance art program and to provide extraordinary environment for students to recognize their full creative potential.

EDUCATION

UNIVERSITY OF VERMONT, Burlington, Vermont
Bachelor of Arts in Animation Science (3.77 GPA), 1994

Internships:

UNIVERSITY OF VERMONT, Burlington, Vermont
Art Internship Department of Creative Arts, 1993—94

Museum of Fine Art, Burlington Museum
Intern Special Projects

EMPLOYMENT

Janet Dempsy High School, Old Bridge High, New Jersey	**Art Teacher**	1998—Present
Henderson Copley School of the Arts, Old Bridge, New Jersey	**Art Teacher**	1995—1998
New Jersey Animation Society, Newark, New Jersey	**Cartoonist**	1994—1995

AWARDS

ACA National Honorarium Award, 2001	NACA International Recognition, 2001
IACA International Recognition, 2000	ISUL Top Achievement in Creative Art, 1999

CHRISTIAN EDUCATOR/COUNSELOR

TAI EDWARD LAO

1345 Stoneway Lane
Wilmington, Delaware 19866
(302) 555-1212/email@email.com

CHRISTIAN EDUCATOR/COUNSELOR
Three Years' Experience in Student Service/Higher-Education Administration
Master of Divinity—Boston University
"Enhancing the Quality of Life for Clients in a Cost-Effective & Expeditious Manner"

Intellectually grounded and results-oriented educator/counselor with a proven record of success in working with diverse populations, including students and college graduates of color and GLBT. Guide GLBT communities towards healing and wholeness in a Christian-based environment—assisting them to navigate their way through the maze of complex issues of faith, relationships, commitments, empowerment, and identity.

Core Strengths

Individual and group counseling/case management
Client assessment and intervention coordination
Bridging cultural diversities and conflicts

Christian-based curriculum development
Public-speaking and high-impact presentation skills
Motivating/empowering clients of color and GLBT

Education/Continuing Education

Master of Divinity, 2000
Bachelor of Arts In American History, 1997

Boston University, School of Theology
Boston University, College of Arts and Science

Highlights of Experience

- Recipient: Boston University School of Theology Fellowship Award
- Five years as Facilitator—Harlem Renaissance African American History Lecture
- Four years' experience designing Christian-based curricula
- Developed three family plans that served as the benchmark for counseling training

Professional Experience

DEPARTMENT OF CHILDREN & FAMILIES, Wilmington, Delaware   1991 to Current
Family Service Counselor
Conduct investigations concerning allegations of child abuse, neglect, and threatened harm. Provide crisis counseling for families in which children are in imminent danger. Assess families' strengths and weaknesses relative to child care and develop family-treatment plans for high-risk families. On-Call for 40 families, and serve three monthly 24-hour On-Calls for Northern Palm Beach County. Attend court advocacy for clients vis-à-vis custody cases and juvenile adjudication.

- Reunited several families from which children had previously been removed as a result of abuse and neglect.
- Developed three family plans that served as model for future training.
- Prevented the disruption of a number of families through intensive counseling and community intervention.

BOSTON UNIVERSITY OFFICE OF RESIDENCE LIFE, Boston, Massachusetts   1986 to 1991
Senior Resident Assistant for Training and Development (1998–2000)
Directed the supervision of a staff of 45, administered job-performance evaluations, planned and chaired biweekly staff meetings, and designed, developed, and organized mandatory staff-training sessions. Designed programs to enhance the quality of staff relations.

- Created Recognition Program for Outstanding Resident Assistants.
- Delivered African American History Lecture series during African American History Month (Invited back three years).
- Facilitated a Conflict-Resolution Workshop given twice during Resident Assistant Training.
- Created program to troubleshoot and resolve staff-relations issues.

References and Supporting Documentation Furnished upon Request

ATHLETIC COACH

ROBERTA LYNDA GREENBERG

320 Brandies Street • Springfield, Illinois, 62232 • (618) 555-1212 • email@email.com

ATHLETIC COACH
Basketball

9 Years' Successful Experience in High-visibility Athletic Programs

"Improving Skills—Improving Character—Improving Basketball Programs"

Discipline/Reward/Growth

A positive-thinking, results-oriented, and team-spirited athletic coach with a sound, verifiable record of success in building winning programs and developing values-based students into contributing citizens in their communities.

CORE STRENGTHS

Athletic conditioning and fitness expert
Strategic planning—sound basketball fundamentals
Program marketing and promotions—on/off campus

Nutritional certification
Staff development
Concentration on grades and sport

EMPLOYMENT

Springfield County School System, Springfield, Illinois   1992 to Current
Girls Head Basketball Coach/Math Teacher—McKenner High School

Coaching Highlights:

2001	American Midwest Regional Finals—Top 12 in State
2000	American Midwest Regional Finals—Top 10 in State
1999	NCCA—Runner-up
1998	Northwest Conference Champions
1997	Northwest Conference Champions
1996	Runner–up Northwest Conference Champions

Coaching Record:

	WINS	LOSSES	PERCENTAGE	COMMENT
2001	15	3	83%	First in conference
2000	14	4	77%	Second in conference
1999	16	2	88%	First in conference
1998	12	6	66%	Third in conference
1997	13	5	72%	Third in conference
1996	13	5	72%	Third in conference
1995	9	9	50%	Sixth in conference
1994	10	8	55%	Fifth in conference
1993	9	9	50%	Sixth in conference
1992	6	12	33%	Last in conference

EDUCATION & TRAINING

Providence College
Rhode Island

Master in Athletic Coaching	1991
Bachelor of Science: Sports Science: Providence College	1988 (Dual)
Bachelor of Arts: Education: Mathematics and Statistics	1988 (Dual)

AFFILIATIONS

National Coaches Federation—Member/Former Board Member, Springfield County Chapter
American Heart Association—Board Member—Springfield County Chapter

References upon Request

ELEMENTARY SCHOOL TEACHER

VIVIAN WALKER

50 Ferne Lane
Seattle, Washington 98366
(941) 555-1212/email@email.com

ELEMENTARY SCHOOL TEACHER
Enhancing Academic Experience for All Children

A highly motivated, intuitive, and results-focused individual with 18+ years of successful experience in diversified environments—the past eight years as an educator

A team player with solid leadership skills able to generate new ideas, analyze and resolve challenges, and advance organizational goals and objectives

Creative, detail-oriented, and highly dependable; work effectively in stress/high pressure situations; flexible and adaptable to ever-changing environments

Fluent in English and Spanish

Strengths

Communication skills (presentation/writing skills)   Coaching, teaching, and training
Interpersonal and "people" skills   Multiple/complex project management
Organization, administration, and time management   Problem solving and conflict resolution
Start-up operations supervision and coordination   Curriculum development/enhancement

Education

UNIVERSITY OF ILLINOIS, Urbana-Champaign, Illinois
Bachelor of Science: Psychology, 1983
- Specialization: Developmental Child Care Program
- CDA Equivalency through Seattle Community College, Early Childhood Educators Network

Professional Experience

BEGINNINGS PRESCHOOL, Seattle, Washington   1993 to Current
Teacher

- Plan and implement daily classroom activities for preschool education program. Assist children in academic and personal/social growth development—to include interpersonal, organizational, and conflict-resolution skills. Organize and prepare materials for daily activities; maintain clean, well-organized learning environment; and direct the children to appropriate activities throughout the day.

- Perform written evaluations three times a year and work as a team member in developing/enhancing academic curriculum. Create weekly lesson plans, train new teachers/staff in classroom procedures and curriculum development, and provide quality support to both the children and their parents/families.

- Played a team leadership role in the creation of a new library, including classification of books and category determination. Ensured all logistical efforts were in place for meeting Grand Opening deadline.

- Member—Teacher Parent Advisory Council, 1995 to Current

Professional Experience, Other (1983 to 1993)

Retail Experience/Customer Service   Byrons/Toys-R-Us, Seattle, Washington
Teaching—Pre School and Public School   Seattle School System, Seattle, Washington

References and Supporting Documentation Furnished upon Request

LIBRARY POSITION

BETTY C. BROWN

810 Clear Water Avenue
Palm Beach, Florida 33401
(561) 555-1234/email@mail.com

LIBRARY POSITION

"A retired elementary school principal seeking to conclude her educational career contributing to the growth and organizational enhancement of a state-of-the-art library."

Qualifications

Chairperson:	West Palm Beach Library Board, 1995–1997; Active Member, 1983 to current
Active Member:	West Palm Beach Library Long-Range Planning Ad Hoc Committee, 1994–current
Delegate:	To the Florida Governor's Conference on Library Information Services, 1995, 1997, 2000
Delegate:	To the White House Conference on Library Information Services, 2000
Librarian:	Five years as Pharmacy Librarian, Florida A&M University, School of Pharmacy, 1977–82
Change Agent:	Change leader for Palm Beach County School

Professional Experience

PALM BEACH COUNTY SCHOOL SYSTEM
Palm Beach County, Florida
1970–Current

Principal	**1991 to Current**
Assistant Principal	**1983 to 1991**
Reading Consultant/English Teacher	**1976 to 1983**
Reading/English Teacher	**1970 to 1976**

- One of 55 educators selected from DE US to participate in U.S.A. Reading Revival Program
- One of 35 educators selected to participate in State of Florida's Summer Read for Fun Program
- Selected to analyze, evaluate, and redesign reading and studying environment for Florida's libraries
- Principal of one of Palm Beach County's largest elementary schools—The JB Darren Elementary School—720 students and a faculty exceeding 19 professionals.

Education

M.A. in Education:	University of South Florida, Tampa, Florida, 1969
B.A. in Education and Library Science:	University of South Florida, Tampa, Florida, 1968

Certified:	State of Florida
CRI:	Certified Reading Instructor
CSET:	Certified: Special Education

Computer Skills:
PC/Mac; Windows, Office, Internet applications, and a host of Teacher/Student Proprietary Software

Portfolio of References Furnished on Request

ACADEMIC ADMINISTRATOR

JODY LEAH ALWERT

63 Penn Street
Little Rock, Arkansas 72239
(501) 555-1212/email@email.com

ACADEMIC ADMINISTRATION
PROJECT MANAGEMENT/PROGRAM DEVELOPMENT

Utilizing Solid Network of Contacts in Washington, D.C.

Marketing/New-Business Development
Community & Public Relations/Special-Events Management

A successful and diversified work history to include seven years of high-visibility positions in Washington, D.C. in project management for numerous agencies, including the Resolution Trust Corporation, Office of Thrift Supervision, Office of Personnel Management, and General Services Administration.

"Enhancing Community Awareness"

More than four years' experience as Owner/Manager of Norrell Services in Little Rock, AK, directing a high-volume temporary-employee operation serving 300+ clients. The past two years have been spent at Northwood University as Director of Corporate liaison, incorporating outstanding interpersonal, team-building, and resource-utilizing skills.

AREAS OF STRENGTH

Project management and execution	Strategic planning (creative short/long term planning)
Budget management and expense control	Building key alliances and partnerships
Personnel training and development	Presentation and closing/persuasion skills
Consensus building—team leadership	Sales, marketing, and promotion

PROFESSIONAL EMPLOYMENT

NORTHWOOD UNIVERSITY, Little Rock, Arkansas   1996 to Current
Director, Corporate Liaison

- Promote and market the University College Management Programs at Northwood University—a unique accelerated A.A. and B.B.A. program for adults. Responsible for promoting the program to corporations and community organizations, recruiting individual students, and creating special events to best enhance exposure and enrollment.
- Network with 14 key organizations to increase program exposure. Selected for Leadership Northeast, Class of 2000 that will further build bridges between the university and the private/community sectors.
- Created, funded, and managed the Northwood University Working Women Management Scholarship, a first-of-its-kind scholarship in honor of The Executive Women of Little Rock County, The Women's Chamber of Commerce, National Association of Women Business Owners, and The Association of Women in Communication.
- Developed and sustain close alliances as an active contributor with all above associations. Sit on various boards and committees to maintain high-visibility leadership positions.
- Significantly enhanced enrollment and program exposure via high-impact public/community relations.

Special Assignments, Washington, D.C.
1985 to 1996

RESOLUTION TRUST CORPORATION   1992 to 1996
Special-Project Manager to National Director of Marketing

- Produced four national live-action marketing documentaries. Developed and managed $1/4 million budget, crews, and projects through completion to promote sales of RTC assets to the public through national sales seminars: Multi-Family Housing, "Overview," Affordable Housing, "A Dream Realized," Auction, "Where the Market Speaks," and Small Investor, "New Horizons."
- Received "Achievement Award," Resolution Trust Corporation.

(Page 1 of 2)

ACADEMIC ADMINISTRATOR (CONT.)

PROFESSIONAL EMPLOYMENT (Continued)

Special Assignments, Washington, D.C.
1987 to 1996
(Continued)

OFFICE OF THRIFT SUPERVISION   1990 to 1991
Special Assistant to Director of Public Affairs
- Prioritized Director's work flow, researched issues, and presented findings in oral briefings and written reports. Followed up on political, administrative, and operational issues. Arranged special functions affecting public affairs. Prepared weekly reports to the Treasury Department.

OFFICE OF PERSONNEL MANAGEMENT   1988 to 1990
Special Assistant to Deputy Director
- Instrumental in the development of regulations allowing use of private-sector temporary-employment services by the Federal Government for the first time; law enacted in 1989. Represented Deputy Director in public-forum settings and meetings. Led nationwide discussion concerning Combined Federal Campaign.

GENERAL SERVICES ADMINISTRATION   1985 to 1988
Special Assistant to Director of Personnel/National Capital Region
- Conducted needs assessment related to college graduates. Developed on-campus recruiting strategies resulting in the hiring of 40 well-qualified applicants for difficult-to-fill positions in less than 6 months.
- Evaluated and restructured management-training program for managers and line supervisors. Increased attendance and enhanced enthusiasm for the program.

NORRELL SERVICES, Palm Beach County, FL   1980 to 1985
Owner/Manager/Sales
- Established and managed the growth of a temporary-employee national franchise from start-up.
- "Norrell Corporation President's Club," for meeting and exceeding budgeted sales.
- "Special Award," Palm Beach Community College, for participation in the Female Entrepreneurial Program.

EDUCATION

Bachelor of Fine Arts   UNIVERSITY OF ARIZONA, Tucson, AZ
3.75 GPA—President's Honors

PROFESSIONAL/CIVIC AFFILIATIONS (Partial Listing)

- Executive Women of Little Rock Couonty; Former Board Member; Recipient of "Special Award"
- United Way of Little Rock; Former Board Member
- Growing Together, Auxiliary Board Member
- Public Relations Society of America

References Furnished upon Request

SPEECH LANGUAGE PATHOLOGIST

LYNDA A. WHEALAN

99 Green Street
Baldwin, New York 11510
(516) 555-1212/email@email.com

PROFESSIONAL SPEECH LANGUAGE PATHOLOGIST

Enhancing the Quality of Life for Children and Adult Populations
Serving Children with Multiple Handicaps/Adults with Speech & Language Impairments

A dynamic, energetic, empathetic, and motivated Speech Language Pathologist with solid credentials as a Coordinator for Exceptional Student Education. Recognized for inspiring success with students by enriching their lives through inclusive, small-group, and individual teaching techniques. Extraordinary collaborator and team-builder; expert in compliance with legal and regulatory issues, supported by seasoned communications and interpersonal skills.

Experienced as testing coordinator, peer coach, parent liaison, and planning coordinator. Proficiency in strategic planning and implementation, organization, and records management. Effective "Train-The-Trainer" skills.

AREAS OF CONTRIBUTION

Understand the development of articulation, receptive, and expressive language skills
Evaluate speech and language skills through formal and informal procedures
Develop appropriate goals and objectives to meet individual needs of the client
Implement interventions that aid in the acquisition of effective communication skills
Collect data to measure increased/decreased abilities for targeted goals and objectives

HIGHLIGHTS OF EXPERIENCE

- Directly responsible for the speech and language needs of up to 100 students—kindergarten through grade 12—who require special educational needs.
- Disabilities served include: Articulation, expressive and receptive language delays/disorders, fluency, and voice disorders of students enrolled in the following programs: Speech and Language Impaired, Educable Mentally Handicapped, Emotionally Handicapped, Specific Learning Disabilities, Hearing Impaired.
- Evaluate, report, and assess Individual Education Plans while serving on a multidisciplinary treatment team.
- A major contributor to developing/implementing inclusive education at Egret Lake Community Elementary School.
- Presenter (in-service training-the-trainer) to countywide staff.
- Authored proposal for a state-funded pilot program (FEFP) that was adopted and executed throughout Florida.

EDUCATION

NOVA SOUTHEASTERN UNIVERSITY, Fort Lauderdale, Florida
Master of Science: Speech-Language Pathology, (Expected, 8/98)
STATE UNIVERSITY OF NEW YORK AT GENESEO, Geneseo, New York
Bachelor of Science: Speech Pathology and Audiology (1992)

Clinical Practicum

CLINIC LAB AT NOVA SOUTHEASTERN UNIVERSITY (9/97–12/97)
- Provided speech-language therapy to clients presenting with autism, language delay, and aphasia

(Page 1 of 2)

SPEECH LANGUAGE PATHOLOGIST (CONT.)

Clinical Practicum

DIAGNOSTICS II AT NOVA SOUTHEASTERN UNIVERSITY (4/97–8/97)
- Experience with CELF-Preschool, CELF-R, Goldman Fristoe Test of Articulation, Rosetti, SICD, CSBS, Listening Test, and Compton Phonological Assessment of Foreign Accent, to perform diagnostic evaluations.

BOCES 1 PRESCHOOL (3/92–5/92)
- Serviced children presenting with articulation, expressive, and receptive language delays and disorders. Services were provided individually and in small and large-group settings.

CLINIC LAB AT STATE UNIVERSITY OF NEW YORK AT GESESEO (7/91–11/91)
- Provided professional assistance to adult clients presenting with English as a second language and preschoolers presenting with articulation disorders.

PROFESSIONAL EXPERIENCE

EGRET LAKE COMMUNITY ELEMENTARY SCHOOL, Baldwin, New York   1994–Present
Speech Therapist
Exceptional Student Education Coordinator

Presentations While Working At Egret Lake Community Elementary School:

Egret County, Area III Exceptional Student Education Coordinator Meeting (1/94)
- Delivered a speech on Inclusive Education—how it works, its advantages and disadvantages, and specifically those who would most benefit from this model of service.

Egret County School System District Meeting (1/97)
- Delivered a speech to a variety of school personnel on Inclusive Education—how it benefits students with special needs, organizing schedules for regular/ESE teachers, and program implementation.

NORTHWEST ELEMENTARY SCHOOL, Baldwin, New York   1993–1994
Speech Therapist

CALEDONIA-MUMFORD SCHOOLS, Caledonia, New York   1992–1993
Speech Therapist

PROFESSIONAL CERTIFICATES & AFFILIATIONS

Professional-Nonrenewable Certificate to Teach Speech and Language-Impaired Students in Grades K-12 (1993)
New York State Certification of Qualification as a Teacher of Speech and Hearing-Impaired Students, Grades K–12 (1992)
Member: National Student Speech-Language Hearing Association

- References and Supporting Documentation Furnished upon Request -

SOCIAL STUDIES/ENGLISH TEACHER

GINA R. CROWLEY

642 Willow Bend Road
Raleigh, North Carolina 27652
(919) 555-1212/email@email.com

CERTIFIED TEACHER (Social Studies/English), Grades 5–9
Creating an Inspiring Learning Environment
Classroom Management/Meeting Individual & Collective Needs

CORE STRENGTHS

Communication skills—verbal and written
Problem-solving and mediation skills
Community outreach and relations

Higher-level critical-thinking skills
Curriculum development and enhancement
Cultural-diversity awareness and teaching

HIGHLIGHTS OF TEACHING EXPERIENCE

BAIR MIDDLE SCHOOL, Raleigh, North Carolina   1995 to Current
Sixth Grade Social Studies and Reading Teacher (1996–current)
Sixth Grade Study Skills, Social Skills, Reading, and Internal Suspension Teacher (1996)
Eighth Grade Interim Language Arts Teacher (1995–96)

- Initially hired as interim substitute teacher and became a full-time teacher (6th grade) in January of 1996. Create and implement lesson plans using effective reading and study strategies. Evaluate student progress using standard and alternative assessment. Establish and maintain outstanding rapport with students, inspiring them to be challenged by and enjoy the learning process. Encourage the development of positive relationships through cooperative learning.

- Teach sensitivity, kindness, and cultural acceptance from a historical perspective. Maintain close communications with parents, other teachers, guidance counselors, and administration. Sustain consistent/high-energy learning environment and encourage the use of high technology (including the Internet). Developed curriculum and initiated a Study Skills Class.

HIGHLIGHTS OF SUMMER/SUBSTITUTE EMPLOYMENT

BAIR MIDDLE SCHOOL, Raleigh, North Carolina   1997, 1998, 2000
Teacher: Sixth-Grade Reading/Seventh- and Eighth-Grade Language Arts

KOTA COUNTY SCHOOL BOARD, Piper High School, Raleigh, North Carolina   1999
Attended: African and African-American Cultures Workshop

EDUCATION AND DIAGNOSTIC SERVICES, Raleigh, North Carolina   1997
Middle- and High-School Tutor: Reading-Comprehension/Study-Skills Teacher

DAVID SAUL COMMUNITY CENTER, Raleigh, North Carolina   1996
Teen Travel-Camp Director

KOTA COUNTY SCHOOLS, Raleigh, North Carolina   1994, 1995
Elementary/Middle-School Substitute Teacher—All Subjects

EDUCATION

Bachelor of Arts: History, 1992   UNIVERSITY OF SOUTH FLORIDA, and Tampa, Florida

OTHER

For Children's Sake: Former Chairperson of Tutoring Department and Member of Advisory Board/Council; Tutor with concentration on reading comprehension and note-taking skills for ESE/Foster Care Students.

References and Supporting Documentation Furnished upon Request

12

Finance

FINANCIAL/MARKETING RESEARCHER/ANALYST

SCOTT L. RANDALL

125 Coral Drive
Boynton Beach, FL 33435

Telephone: (561) 555-1212
Email: email@email.com

FINANCIAL/MARKETING RESEARCHER/ANALYST

"Voice of the Shareholders"—Designing Programs to Enhance Shareholder Value

**Market Intelligence/Survey Design & Management/Senior-Level Project Management
Strategic Planning & Implementation/Secondary Research & Analysis
Profit-Center Development & Enhancement**

Highly experienced, accomplished, and creative professional with extensive experience in analytical research and assessment to improve products, services, distribution and delivery, labor resources, and accounting methodologies, to positively impact corporate profitability and shareholder value.

CORE PROFESSIONAL STRENGTHS

Survey design/questionnaire development	Goal development/implementation
Long/short-term financial forecasting	Resource estimating and forecasting
Database design for financial tracking	Competitive analysis and positioning
Statistical and quantitative analysis	Cash-flow management/projection

PROFESSIONAL EXPERIENCE

Damond Sound Consulting, West Palm Beach, Florida   1997 to Current
FINANCIAL RESEARCH ANALYST
Direct and manage all financial research and analysis for customer-service database and financial acquisitions for this financial and marketing-consulting organization. Monitor the marketplace for any development relative to past, present, and future trends that will affect income. Profile existing and prospective activities—cost vs. return.

- Improved database efficiency by reducing the number of entries by more than 60%—freeing up $1.2 million in cash outlay.
- Moved database orientation from corporation to the individual, allowing for tracking movement of individuals.
- "Pushing" marketplace information, resulting in meetings with customers for the sales force, and sales increases of 77%.
- Improved shareholder earnings an average of 19% a year—7% above expectation.

Treasure Coast Associates, Inc., Stuart, Florida   1993 to 1997
FINANCIAL AND MARKETING ANALYST
Conducted all financial, market-intelligence, and research activities for this $27 million corporation. Developed financial models to improve profit margins. Developed marketing databases and redesigned sales strategies to optimize sales and marketing efforts. Provided demographic profiles to support models and strategic initiatives.

- Improved bottom-line income by $3.7 million or 23% through increased efficiencies and higher margins.
- Database structure allowed for the creation of potential-customer lists for the sales forces.
- Designed the sales territories that added structure to the sales organization and led to more-efficient sales management.
- Managed direct mail marketing campaign that increased customers both by direct response and product awareness.
- Reengineered financial reporting system to reflect corporate integrity and standard accounting practices.

IBM Corporation, Boca Raton, Florida   1981 to 1993
FINANCIAL ANALYST (1991–93)
Directed all financial and resource activity for $11 million operating budget of Information Development organization. This involved tracking labor resources expended by product each month, in addition to planning future labor expenditures by product. Led all sizing efforts for new products and planned changes.

(Page 1 of 2)

169

Scott L. Randall
Page two

PROFESSIONAL EXPERIENCE

<u>IBM Corporation</u>
(Continued)

- Developed proposal to save $400 thousand a year in contracted labor cost.
- Designed financial model and process to recover revenue for division.
- Devised creative ways to optimize headcount in budget-cutting situation.
- Worked with top management to strategically relocate operations outside of Florida.

STRATEGIC PLANNER (1989–91)
Developed and managed customer/market-requirements strategy for an Information Development organization. Managed customer/developer meetings. Functioned as advisor for the organization on measuring performance (six-sigma).

- Moved documentation evaluations up to par with other product attributes.
- Customer strategy was singled out as organizational high point during independent reviews.
- Led first-ever customer review of unannounced information products.
- Developed metrics for use in quality control and product improvement.
- Managed research project designed to explore product issues.

MARKET RESEARCH ANALYST (1985–89)
Assumed lead role in getting monthly customer survey up and running. Survey measured customer attitudes and tracked product quality on a monthly basis. Worked with multiple internal areas (service, sales, manufacturing) and external vendors.

- Set new standards for IBM survey methodology by probing customer responses.
- Utilized customer feedback as quality control by helping to drive engineering changes in products with repair issues.
- Structured survey to allow for "question of the month" capability, which aided product planners in determining future product specifications.

PROCUREMENT ANALYST (1981–85)
Purchased semiconductors for personal computer manufacturing. Managed worldwide supply/demand forecast.

- Supervised supplier interaction with IBM Engineering.
- Constructed database of personnel information.

EDUCATION & SOFTWARE SKILLS

Memphis State University, Memphis, TN
Master of Business Administration, (Concentration on Quantitative Management), 1980
Bachelor of Business Administration (Major: Management—Quantitative Analysis), 1979

SOFTWARE SKILLS

Lotus 1-2-3	MS Access	MS Word
Lotus Freelance	MS Excel	BusinessMap Pro
Lotus Approach	MS PowerPoint	MarketPlace
Lotus Notes	MS Publisher	Maximizer

References and Supporting Documentation Furnished upon Request

CASH-FLOW MANAGER

LORI ANNE DRASHER

275 Second Avenue
New York, New York 10001
Phone: (212) 555-1212/Cell: (212) 555-7272
email@email.com

CASH-FLOW MANAGER
Maintaining Corporate Financial Vitality and Integrity

Cash-Flow Management/Slashing Bad Debt—A/R Management
Organizational Leadership/Policy & Procedure Development
Integrating High Technology with Traditional Methodologies

A well-organized and highly motivated Credit, Collections, and Accounts Receivable Manager with more than 19 years of verifiable success—thriving in fast-paced environments.

Recognized for outstanding personnel leadership skills and for optimizing both physical and labor resources to improve credit and collections efforts. Experienced in developing comprehensive policies/procedures to improve efficiency.

CORE STRENGTHS

Personnel training and empowerment	Long/short-term strategic planning
Cash management and control	Negotiation and mediation
Problem solving and troubleshooting	Research and analysis
Account reconciliations	Vendor relations and negotiations
Customer service/client relations	Reporting and documentation

■ Computer Skills: Excel, Word, Lotus 123, Accpac Accounting Systems, ADP, and Ceridian

HIGHLIGHTS OF PROFESSIONAL EXPERIENCE

WIN STUFF, Headquartered in Long Island City, New York   1990 to Current
(Good Stuff Corporation/Cool Stuff Corporation/Fantasma, LLC)
Credit, Collection, & Accounts Receivable (A/R) Manager

Good Stuff: Manufacturer/distributor of licensed toys to retail, crane, amusement, and sports customers, with sales of $12 million; Cool Stuff: Manufacturer/distributor of license logo coolers, mouse pads, and wrist pads, with revenues of $3 million; Fantasma: Manufacturer of licensed and private label watches and clocks, with sales of $15million.

Managed Good Stuff Corporation from 1990–2000, Cool Stuff Corporation from 1992–1996, and Fantasma LLC, 1993–1998. Organized an A/R department, supervised/trained a staff of two in A/R and four in the Order Entry department, and organized/facilitated weekly staff meetings with subordinates. Developed and enforced credit-department policy and procedures with sales personnel and customers. Negotiated collection schedules with delinquent accounts, reviewed sale orders, and developed/maintained solid relationship with clients (leading to faster collection efforts).

Prioritized workload for A/R and reconciled retail mass merchant accounts (Ex: Target, Wal-Mart, K-Mart, Toys-R-Us) as well as with smaller customers. Developed and implemented a highly effective credit-application and collection process that eliminated unknown credit risks. Evaluated credit applications and established customer credit lines. Communicated with international customers (Euro Disney, Disney Japan, and Warner Brothers) relative to purchase orders and collections. Responsible for administration of employee medical insurance.

- Saved in excess of $1 million in charge backs by reviewing customer purchase orders for freight terms, quantity changes, and delivery dates. Also analyzed charge-back issues, saving $100,000 in duplicated charge backs.
- Reduced accounts-receivable aging to below 20–25% in 90 days.
- Decreased bad debt to below $1/2$%.

(Page 1 of 2)

HIGHLIGHTS OF PROFESSIONAL EXPERIENCE

WIN STUFF (Continued)

Summary of Accounting Responsibilities:

Weekly Responsibilities:
Approval of customer credits, accounts-receivable closings (Postings—cash, letters of credit, wire transfers, and adjustment entries), and prepared-cash-forecast spreadsheets.

Monthly Responsibilities:
Month-end closings and journal entries.

Yearly Responsibilities:
Year-end closings (write-offs, bad debt). Worked with the auditors to verify year-end A/R (verification of A/R balances with customers and review of posting journals).

Additional Responsibilities/Titles Concurrent with Above:
Director of Human Resources (1999–2000—Win Stuff LLC, Corporate Office—nationwide distributor of crane machines). Managed and supervised department of two, responsible for 500 employees reporting to branch offices nationwide. Oversaw payroll for 500+ employees, nationwide. Converted payroll system from ADP to Ceridian. Administered and was company fiduciary for self-insured medical and dental benefits, LTD, STD, Life Insurance, 401K, flex benefits. Handled Workman's Compensation issues. FMLA. Cobra and new enrollments.

- Saved approximately $500,000 avoiding a potentially costly lawsuit (Alabama).
- Rewrote company policy and involved with negotiating employee disputes.

RIS PAPER COMPANY, INC., Long Island City, New York   1986 to1990
Assistant Controller

Scope: RIS is a paper merchant with annual revenues exceeding $95 million.

Reorganized the accounting department and worked closely with the Controller in establishing necessary administrative-accounting systems and controls. Interviewed and played a contributing role in personnel selection, training, and supervision—with particular emphasis on accounts payable and billing. Personally responsible for New York State sales tax audit, bank audits, sales tax, and commercial rent tax returns. Served as liaison between sales personnel and corporate officers, responsible for making adjustments to invoices and journal entries required to accurately compute sales commissions.

- Saved over $100,000 in Accounts Payable by instituting a creative and effective system of payment.
- Restructured the method for A/P according to revised and more-accurate cash-flow analysis.

EDUCATION

QUEENSBORO COMMUNITY COLLEGE, Bayside, New York
Bachelor of Arts: Accounting, 1985

THE WOOD BUSINESS SCHOOL, New York, New York
Certificate of Completion—Cash Management Strategies, 1995

References and Supporting Documentation Furnished upon Request

CERTIFIED PUBLIC ACCOUNTANT/CERTIFIED MANAGEMENT ACCOUNTANT

CURT A. HENDERSON, CPA, CMA
2963 Hike Canyon Road, Apt. 157
Houston, Texas 77081

email@email.com
(713) 555-1212

CERTIFIED PUBLIC ACCOUNTANT
CERTIFIED MANAGEMENT ACCOUNTANT
Corporate Accounting Positions Contributing to Financial Growth

Professional qualifications include experience as senior and staff accountant for "Big Five" international accounting firm and world's seventh-largest accounting firm, successfully working with key, high-technology national/international clients.

AREAS OF STRENGTH

Substantive testing	Financial reporting	Time management/deadline oriented
Variance analysis	Client interviewing	Customer-service management
Financial statement analysis	Cost allocation	Research, evaluation, interpretation
Controls evaluation	Budgeting knowledge	Teaching/Training

HIGHLIGHTS OF PROFESSIONAL EXPERIENCE

BECKERCONVISER CPA REVIEW
- Specifically selected to teach course based on CPA exam results
- Teach audit and cost CPA sections to over 100 students with highly successful exam results

ARTHUR ANDERSEN LLP
- Recipient of *"Green Sheet"* Award for excellence in customer service—Arthur Andersen
- Selected to work with key national/international accounts in diversified industries (specifics provided on request)
- Field work: Traveled nationwide performing due diligence for international client (NY, CA, AZ, IN, MS, NH)

PROFESSIONAL EXPERIENCE

ARTHUR ANDERSEN LLP, Houston, Texas 1998 to Current
Accountant
- ❑ Traveled extensively throughout United States performing due diligence work
- ❑ Recipient of "Green Sheet" Award for excellence in customer service

BECKERCONVISER CPA REVIEW, Houston, Texas 1994 to 1998
Instructor for world's largest CPA review company
- ❑ Provided students with real-world accounting examples
- ❑ Provided CPA candidates live instruction on how to pass exam
- ❑ Tutored students/provided feedback for all students

INTERNSHIPS

HEALTH & POLICY RESEARCH GROUP, Chicago, Illinois Summer, 1993 & 1994
Internship—Accounting

EDUCATION

Master in Public Policy	UNIVERSITY OF CHICAGO	1994
Bachelor of Science: Psychology	VILLANOVA UNIVERSITY	1992

AFFILIATIONS

Member: American Institute of Certified Public Accountants (AICPA)
Member: Institute of Management Accountants (IMA)

References Furnished upon Request

ELECTRICITY TRADER

RENEE L. JABLONSKI

12104 Cove Road
Monterey, California 92056
(760) 555-1212/email@email.com

Seeking Position as...

ELECTRICITY TRADER
Specializing in Real-Time Scheduling Operations
Utilizing Four Years of Exceptional Brokering Experience

Contributing Team Member in Enhancing Growth & Profits By ...

* Utilizing Established Network of Industry Contacts
* Negotiating and Closing Sales in Hourly Markets
* Scheduling and Tagging Transactions

A dynamic, team-spirited, bottom-line-oriented professional offering four years of successful brokering experience in physical power, options, derivatives, lumber, and retail commodities.

CORE STRENGTHS

Building strategic industry alliances and partnerships
New-business development, sales, and marketing
Communications and interpersonal skills
Multitasking; coordinating multiple tasks concurrently

Strategic planning and market analysis
Solid analytical skills
High-impact decision making
Customer-service and quality relations

HIGHLIGHTS OF EXPERIENCE

- Executed 400+ trades of varying duration/structure, resulting in $60,000 in revenues in three-month period
- Develop and maintain a strong network of contacts with power marketers, traders, brokers, and the financial community
- Passionate and knowledgeable about the power industry—proven record for working effectively in fast-paced environment
- Experienced at identifying and capitalizing on new and emerging market opportunities

PROFESSIONAL EXPERIENCE

BTU ENERGY BROKERS, Monterey, California   1998 to Current
OTC Power Broker
Brokered physical power between Utilities and Power-marketers in Cinergy, TVA, Entergy, and Com-Ed hubs. Responsible for new-customer development while servicing existing base. Trained new employees with emphasis on brokering fundamentals and trading techniques—enhancing overall productivity and output.

- Significantly enhanced short-term trading—ranging up to 30 short-term trades daily
- Researched, developed, and executed trades in areas not covered by BTU, including
    - Amaren - NSP - AEP - Off-peak Markets
- Successfully worked and coordinated activities in four or more hubs simultaneously
- Brokered physical-power and option derivatives—focused on short-term markets, as noted above

BUCKEYE PACIFIC, Portland, Oregon   1992 to 1998
Lumber Trader
Member of the Forest City Trading Group involved with trading all types of softwood lumber products. Sold truckloads and railcars of lumber to lumber yards around the country. Cold-canvassed and marketed for new business opportunities.

- Developed local market in bottom-line profits—from $0 to more than $2500 per week
- Worked the California market and developed key clients in a short time span

(Page 1 of 2)

RENEE L. JABLONSKI
Page Two

PROFESSIONAL EXPERIENCE (Continued)

NATSOURCE, New York, New York   1990 to 1992
OTC Electricity Broker
Brokered physical-power and option derivatives and executed trades of varying duration and structure for this institutional brokerage firm specializing in electricity, natural gas, and weather derivatives.

- Brokered the mid-continent region and moved to PJM for the duration
- Developed 12 key working relationships with traders from power-marketers and utilities to enhance growth/profits
- Used "Black Scholes" model to determine option values

INFINITY TRADING GROUP, New York, New York   1986 to 1990
Commodities Broker
Brokered commodities with emphasis on "the energies," including crude oil, natural gas, heating oil, and unleaded gas. Diversified into currencies, grains, financials, and softs. Generated and closed new business opportunities.

- Met or exceeded all business-development goals and objectives
- Utilized both fundamental and technical analysis techniques and recommended futures and options strategies—assisting customers in the management of their positions
- Obtained "Series 3" certification

EDUCATION

UCLA, Los Angeles
Bachelor of Science Degree: International Business (Finance Concentration), 1985

WEST COAST COMMUNITY COLLEGE, Los Angeles, California
Associate Degree, Business Administration, 1994

- Computer Skills:
Windows, Word, Excel, and Internet Applications

ACTIVITIES

Certified Stunt Woman
Enjoy Golf, Skiing, Skydiving, and Hiking
Community Service—Humane Society

References and Supporting Documentation Furnished upon Request

FINANCIAL ANALYST/PLANNER

JACQUELINE CORTEZ

Residence
3313 SW Logger Drive
Port St. Lucie, Florida 34953

Mailing Address
PO Box 5555
PSL, Florida 34985-5555

Phone/Fax: (561) 555-1212/Cell: (561) 555-3232
email@email.com

> *Seeking Entry-level Position as...*
>
> ## FINANCIAL ANALYST/PLANNER
> **Utilizing Outstanding Analytical, Accounting, and Financial-Leadership Skills**
>
> *High-tech/Computer Integration—Software and Hardware*
> *A Team Player with Excellent Communications and Interpersonal Skills*

A highly astute, energetic, and team-spirited Financial Analyst/Planner seeking entry-level opportunity while attending FAU. Accurate, precise, and highly ethical in all work-related assignments—**seeking to contribute to financial goals and objectives.**

CORE STRENGTHS

Strategic financial planning and analysis
Expense control; cash-flow analysis
Staff training and supervision
Customer service/client management

Bookkeeping and budget management
Regulatory compliance assurance
Asset management and control
Quality control

Computer Skills: Excel, Lotus, Word, WordPerfect, QuickBooks, PowerPoint, and Internet Applications

EDUCATION

FLORIDA ATLANTIC UNIVERSITY, Boca Raton, Florida
Bachelor of Business Administration: Finance, Summer, 2001 (Present GPA: 3.56)
(Selected Curriculum: Advanced Managerial Finance, International Finance, Operations Management)

INDIAN RIVER COMMUNITY COLLEGE, Fort Pierce, Florida
Associate of Arts: Business and Accounting, 1996

WEBSTER COLLEGE, Fort Pierce, Florida
Diploma, Paralegal/Legal Assistant, 1991

EMPLOYMENT HIGHLIGHTS

BEALL'S OUTLET, Port St. Lucie, Florida   1997–Current
Supervisor
Supervise sales associates in various areas, including scheduling, training, productivity enhancement, and overall day-to-day management. Train sales associates, supervisors, and management trainees. Work to improve sales, reduce shrink, control/reduce expenses, and enhance efficiencies—all in an effort to contribute in a positive way to the bottom line. Particular emphasis on maintaining and improving levels of customer service.

- Introduced new, efficient approach to daily cash-summary reconciliation, without compromising accuracy or quality.
- Trained key staff members in preparation for management positions.
- Assisted in the conversion/introduction of new computer software that significantly improved profitability.

PROFESSIONAL AFFILIATIONS

Financial Management Association

References and Supporting Documentation Furnished upon Request

FINANCIAL SALES EXECUTIVE

ELIZABETH BRADLEY

15730 Cedar Grove Lane
Nyack, New York, 10960
(914) 555-1212

FINANCIAL SALES EXECUTIVE
Expert in Developing Multimillion-Dollar Accounts with High-Net-Worth Individuals

Pension Strategies/Investment Markets/Compliance Issues
Outstanding Networking Skills and Key Contact Development—Nationally

---

Dynamic, top-performing, and disciplined financial sales and marketing executive, recognized for inspiring people and organizations to act through educational approach—delivered with sincerity and high integrity. Experienced in introducing and successfully promoting new products and services. Professionally aggressive and persistent in pursuit of company/client goals and objectives.

Visionary leadership in assessing client needs, and strategically positioning financial programs to achieve specific objectives. Solid interpersonal and communications skills in building key alliances and partnerships to ignite sales performance and enhance corporate visibility.

AREAS OF EXPERTISE

* Asset management and wealth-building
* Break down and simplify complex financial issues
* Territorial development and case management
* Complex project planning and coordination
* Detailed problem-solving ability

* Presentation and closing skills
* Spearheading new market initiatives
* Personnel management
* Productivity and performance enhancement
* Delivering "Five-Star" customer service

HIGHLIGHTS OF EMPLOYMENT

MUTUAL OF AMERICA LIFE INSURANCE COMPANY OF NEW YORK, NEW YORK, NY   1990–Present

Field Vice President, New York   (1997–Present)
Vice President, Indianapolis, IN   (1993–1997)
Associate Regional Manager   (1990–1992)

Field Vice President: Responsible for sales and service of pension plans throughout New York, including 401(a) Money Purchase, Profit Sharing, 401(k), 403(b) Thrift, 457, Defined Benefit Plans, and 457(f) Deferred Compensation for not-for-profit executives. Involved in financial planning for executive-level participants and the sale of individual nonqualified annuities, IRAs, and Variable Universal Life, on a payroll deduct basis. Administrative duties include assistance with ADP and ACP testing, 5500 preparation, 5300 and 5307 filings, Form 500 preparation for Defined Benefit terminations, compliance and voluntary amendments, plan installations, online administrative installations, changeovers from Defined Benefit to Defined Contribution approach, thorough actuarial analysis and cost projections, and contract interpretation.

Vice President: Directed all operations in the state of Indiana, responsible for all sales-related functions (see listing above), and overall management of the service department. Region included approximately 220 client organizations with approximately $150 million under management.

- Ranked #1 in overall new-business production, 1994–1996; ranked in top five in 1991, 1992
- Ranked #1 in Corporate Pensions, 1994–1996
- Ranked # 1 in Voluntary Plans, 1994–1996
- Increased region's revenues 400% over six-year period
- Personally managed 20 Defined Benefit plans while directing high-volume region
- Oversaw large cases with over 2,000 participants and assets of up to $30 million

(Page 1 of 2)

ELIZABETH BRADLEY
Page Two

HIGHLIGHTS OF EMPLOYMENT

MUTUAL OF AMERICA (Continued)

- Developed one of the largest 457(f) plans in the country—over 100 physicians and hospital executives
- Consistently had 401(k) enrollments that far exceeded company averages for participation and percentage of pay deferred
- Took Indiana territory from last in regional rankings a year prior to my arrival, to #1 region, over 3-year period (1994–1996)
- Trained and developed two service correspondents into top-producing sales consultants

METLIFE RESOURCES (A Division of Metropolitan Life Insurance Company of New York)   1987–1990

Senior Financial Advisor, Indianapolis, IN and Cincinnati, OH

Sold 403(b) plans as well as mutual funds and nonqualified annuities primarily to hospitals.

- Member of the "Golden Circle" (top 5% in sales production); consistently in top 20 out of 300+ sales professionals
- Won national sales contest in 1988
- Selected as Senior Financial Advisor to handle one of the firm's largest endorsements, Sisters of Charity Healthcare Systems—25,000 employees in the system
- Instrumental in developing the healthcare market for the company

SYNOPSIS OF EMPLOYMENT PRIOR TO 1987

Claims Adjuster, Economy Fire and Casualty, Lebanon, IN
Insurance Broker, Pulliam Insurance Agency, Newton, IL
Agent, Northwestern Mutual Life, Tyler, TX

EDUCATION, TRAINING & LICENSES

GREENVILLE COLLEGE, Greenville, IL
Bachelor of Arts, Cum Laude, 1983

Seminars/Workshops/Personal Development
* Completed Northwestern Mutual's "Sales Cycle," by Al Grannum
* Completed estate planning courses presented by Eagle and Fein
* Passed eight exams for the Certified Employee Benefits Specialist (CEBS) designation
* Licensed in Life, Health, Series 6, series 63 (since 1984)
* Attended numerous pension-related seminars

AFFILIATIONS & ACTIVITIES

Member: Mutual of America's Sales Contest Committee, 1996–Present
Member: Sales Panel—2000–2001 Sales Conference
Team Leader: 1998–2001 United Way Day of Caring
Campaign Organizer: United Way Campaign, 1995–99 (Member of Key Club)
Member: Board of Directors: Fort Benjamin Harrison YMCA
Presenter/Speaker: Frequent speaker on pension and retirement planning for employee groups and boards of director
Member: St. Vincent Hospital Seton Society

- References and Supporting Documentation Furnished upon Request -

INTERN—FINANCIAL SERVICES

MICHAEL JOSEPH

1815 South Willow Avenue
West Palm Beach, Florida 33401
(561) 555-2233/email@email.com

Seeking position as...

INTERN
With Financial Services/Asset-Management Firm
Utilizing Outstanding Analytical and Organizational Proficiency
Solid Communications and Interpersonal Skills

A dynamic, hard-working, and results-oriented individual seeking a challenging Intern position where academic training and former work experience **can contribute to organizational goals and objectives**.

Recognized as a team player, a quick study (able to grasp complex issues/concepts quickly and effectively), and a creative/capable problem solver. **An excellent work ethic, consistently going the "extra mile"** to exceed customer expectations. Also skilled in assisting company in new-business development.

Familiar with **financial analysis, statistical analysis, and evaluating balance sheets and financial statements**. Also familiar with forecasting, budgeting, investment analysis, and documentation/reporting.

AREAS OF STRENGTH

Research and financial analysis
Communication skills—verbal and written
Organization, prioritization, and time management
Quality control and assurance

Building strategic partnerships and alliances
Multiple-task management/coordination
Personnel training and supervision
Customer service/relations

■ Computer Skills: Windows, Word, Excel, PowerPoint, and Internet Applications

EDUCATION/TRAINING

FLORIDA ATLANTIC UNIVERSITY, Boca Raton, Florida
Bachelor of Business Administration Candidate, 2001

PALM BEACH COMMUNITY COLLEGE, Lake Worth, Florida
Associate of Arts: Business, 1997–99

PROFESSIONAL EXPERIENCE (While Attending School)

Charley's Crab/Muer Corporation, Palm Beach, Florida   1995 to Current
Floor Supervisor/Server (Fast-paced, 320-seat Up-scale, Specialized Palm Beach Restaurant)
- ❑ Track and monitor all activities of servers, ensuring 100% satisfaction of sophisticated Palm Beach clientele.
- ❑ Assumed supervisory position based on outstanding performance, in addition to server's responsibilities.
- ❑ Chosen to train staff each year for approaching "season" and to sit on Advisory Committee to enhance productivity.

Hunters Run Country Club, Boynton Beach, Florida   1998 to 1999
Member/Guest Service—Cart/Bag-Room Attendant (Exclusive, Up-scale Country Club; 54-holes)
- ❑ Assisted members (1500) and guests with golf-club repair and maintenance. Cleaned and maintained 150 golf carts.
- ❑ Worked this job concurrently with Charley's Crab (above) while attending college full time.

Martell's, Pt. Pleasant, New Jersey   1993 to 1995
Barback/Bartender
- ❑ Food and beverage server for high-volume Tiki Bar. Responsible for openings and closings.
- ❑ Responsible for inventory management—requisitioning, supplying, and replenishing stock.

References, Transcripts, and Professor recommendations Furnished on Request

ASSOCIATE—MERGERS AND ACQUISITIONS

Donald C. Stringini

1374 Themes Road
Arlington, Massachusetts 01652
Phone: (617) 555-1212/Cell: (508) 555-7979
Email: email@email.com

Seeking Position as...

Associate in Mergers & Acquisitions with Investment Banking Division
MBA Graduate with Concentration in International Business

Quantitative & Analytical Proficiency/Organization & Time-Management Skills
215 Insurance, Series 6, 7, and 63 Licenses/3 Years' Finance Experience
PROFIT AND GROWTH ORIENTED

Highly motivated, intellectually strong, and results-oriented MBA graduate recognized for working effectively in entrepreneurial and client/team-based environments. Self-composed, work well in fast-track, high-pressure settings, innovative ("out-of-the-box" thinker), and strong leadership skills.

CORE AREAS OF STRENGTH

Communication skills—verbal and written	Strategic planning—a global thinker
Integrating high/new technologies with traditional methodologies	Finance and accounting expertise
Problem solving and complex troubleshooting	Venture-capital work experience
Interpersonal and relationship-building skills	Presentation and public speaking
Quality customer/client service and relations	Business development/sales

EDUCATION

UNIVERSITY OF MIAMI SCHOOL OF BUSINESS ADMINISTRATION, Coral Gables, Florida
MBA—Degree of Master's in Business Administration, 2001
  • Concentration in International Business; ranked top 6% of class

UNIVERSITY OF PHOENIX, Phoenix, Arizona
Bachelor of Science in Business Administration (3.81 GPA), 1999
  • Emphasis in Finance, Accounting, Economics, and Statistics

SHERIDAN COLLEGE, Sheridan, Wyoming
Advanced Spanish (During senior year of high school for college credits, Spring, 1990)

WORK EXPERIENCE

COLLIER ENTERPRISES, Cambridge, Massachusetts   Summers, 1999/2000
Summer Internship/Associate
  • Financial analysis with emphasis on venture capital—including real estate and development. Enabled improvements in membership for The Collier Reserve Country Club. Collier is a $1.8 billion corporation (as declared by Forbes... with an additional $2.8 billion within company's Private Capital Management group). Collier's involvement within Florida includes real estate/development, agriculture, and venture capitalism (Merger with the King Ranch of Kingsville, Texas established the largest citrus-producing company in the nation in 1999).

  • An active participant in making improvements within The Collier Reserve Country Club, including enhanced accounting and real-estate practices from previous mishaps within the organization.

  • Venture capital efforts included analysis of startup companies for minimal investments (that would eventually be sold/merged for profit) and key decision-making/recommendations (including in-depth statistical analysis) used to assist upper management in making decisive evaluations and decisions on initial capital layout.

(Page 1 of 2)

Donald C. Stringini
Page two

WORK EXPERIENCE

MASS MUTUAL/DBS FINANCIAL GROUP, Boston, Massachusetts   Summers 1997 and 1998
Financial Services Professional/Insurance Agent
- Trained for and obtained Series 6, 7, and 63 securities licenses and a 215 insurance license for the State of Florida. Sold financial services, including life, health, mutual funds, retirement planning, and variable annuities.

- Utilized and refined sales, marketing, and closing skills, and enhanced sales and new-business development. This atmosphere required using entrepreneurial, time-management, and strategic planning/implementing skills. Incorporated strong communication skills to improve closing ratios and customer service and retention.

KING'S SADDLERY AND ROPES, Sheridan, Wyoming   Summer 1994 to 1996
Marketing Agent
- A family business since 1946, King's specializes in western tack and lariat rope, selling nationally and internationally. Market products and services at numerous trade shows nationally.
- Designed and created high-impact Internet Web page and produced company catalog.
- Attended world's largest leather show yearly (Miami) to develop new-business clientele and vendor sources.
- Expanded company into larger markets to include Canada, Argentina, Germany, Australia, and New Zealand.

PROFESIONAL AFFILIATIONS

American Finance Federation
Pi Kappa Alpha International Alumni Association
Big Sky Alumni Association

INTERESTS

Certified Divemaster (PADI); enjoy racquetball, golf, tennis, jogging, and travel.

References and Supporting Documentation Furnished upon Request

FINANCIAL SERVICES—TRADER

JUSTIN GOBRERRA

708 7th Lane
Grand Rapids, Michigan 45632
(467) 555-1212/email@email.com

Recent College Graduate Seeking Position in...

FINANCIAL SERVICES—TRADER

Sales, Busines-Development, and Customer-Service Positions in Fast-track Environments

Lead Generation/Presentation & Closing Skills/Retention & Referral Management
Building Strategic Relations and Alliances/Up-selling/Delivering Value-added Service

A highly motivated, energetic, and team-spirited individual **seeking to contribute in the Financial Services industry** in sales, business development, and customer relations, combining outstanding finance, analytical, and strategic-planning skills.

CORE STRENGTHS

Prospecting, networking, and market development
Relationship and consultative sales techniques
Training and development; organizational leadership
New-product introduction
Goal setting and implementation planning

Presentation and public-speaking skills
Research and analysis; financial planning
Regulatory compliance and adherence
Problem solving and conflict resolution
Customer-service/retention management

■ Computer Skills: Windows, Word, Excel, and Internet Applications

EDUCATION

MICHIGAN STATE UNIVERSITY
Bachelor of Arts: Finance, 2000
- GPA: 3.42
- Member: Finance Club (Junior/Senior Years)
- Financed 100% of Education

CHRONOLOGY OF EMPLOYMENT

Waiter/Customer-Service Positions while Financing Education, & Summer Work

TOO BIZARRE, Belmont, Michigan	1996–2000
BIG CITY TAVERN, Belmont, Michigan	1998–2000
PANAMA HATTIES, Miami, Florida	Summers, 1998–2000
BASIL'S, West Palm Beach, Florida	Summer, 1997
NAVIGATOR'S, Martha's Vineyard, Massachusetts	Summer 1996

HIGHLIGHTS OF EMPLOYMENT

- Recognized for going the extra mile—tips averaging 11% above industry standard.
- Promoted to Floor Trainer; maintained excellent relations with all employees in a team-spirited manner.
- Performed well in high-stress, high-volume operation—five tables/20 customers at a time.

References and Supporting Documentation Furnished upon Request

13
Government

CIVIL AVIATION SECURITY INVESTIGATIVE OFFICER

BENJAMIN HARDING

7759 Ace Drive • Baltimore, Maryland 21203
(410) 555-1212/email@email.com
SS#: 000-00-0000/Veteran Status: N/A/U.S. Citizen

Department of Transportation—Federal Aviation Administration
Applying For: Civil Aviation Security Investigative Officer
Investigative Specialist—Maintenance Expert
GD-111-222-33/4

Licenses/Credentials

Top Secret Security Clearance
Private Pilot's License
Level 4 Investigative Grade

U.S. Army Maintenance Certification—L12
Advanced Navigational Training
Aviation Regulations 76, 88, FR6, and RR52

Education

GEORGE WASHINGTON UNIVERSITY, Washington, D.C.
Bachelor of Technical Science: Aviation Management, 2000
Aviation Planning
Aviation Technology
Aviation Disaster Investigation I, II, III

Aviation Safety and Security
Aviation Crisis Management
Aviation for Future Generations

Internship: Dulles Airport—Security Officer/Investigator, Small Aircraft
- Inspections
- Evidence Gathering
- General Security

◼ Computer Skills: SourceBook, AviatePro, NavSystems 6.0, Simmod, Office, and Internet

Professional Experience

AVIATION CONSULTANTS INTERNATIONAL, Baltimore, Maryland   1995 to Current
Aviation Investigator/Assistant to Lead Investigator

- Hired on a part-time basis while attending school to assist and support Lead Investigator in aviation and aviation-related accidents/incidents. Utilized extensive technical and mechanical experience to fit the pieces of the aviation puzzle back together, including crashes, near misses, callbacks, and airline mechanical records and reports. Most assignments are requested by the FAA through Aviation Consultants International.

- Advanced to Aviation Investigator upon completion of BTS degree in Aviation Management in 2000. In the past eight months, successfully investigated six private-aircraft crashes, nationwide, and developed three comprehensive reports for FAA regarding maintenance records of two major airlines for an eight-month period.

- Trainer of new recruits hired on as Assistants to Lead Investigators. Developed comprehensive orientation program that significantly reduced overall "break in time."

Affiliations/Activities

American Pilots Association
National Aviation Association of America

National Association of Aviation Investigators
Aviation Mechanics Association

References Furnished upon Request

DOREEN SCHLADERER
Am Gries 1287
R-85935 Regensburg, Germany
Telephone: (49) 555-23456/Mobil: (49) 555-7654321
Email: EMAIL@EMAIL.COM

GOVERNMENTAL/CORPORATE INTERFACE

Vacancy Announcement: A-0687-77-TRT

20 Years of Successful Entrepreneurial Business Experience in Europe

Enhancing Revenues and Profits in Global Markets
Multilingual Marketing Expert/MBA

High-profile career spanning 20+ years—enhancing growth and profitability in international arenas. Fluent in English, German, and French, with a strong working knowledge of Spanish. Highly competitive and driven in exceeding organizational growth and profit objectives via governmental interface and influence.

CORE PROFESSIONAL STRENGTHS

Strategic Visioning/Planning	Brand Development and Management
Corporate/Business Development	Product and Service Development/Enhancement
Resources Management—Physical and Labor	Senior-Level Project Management/Leadership
Building Key Strategic Alliances and Partnerships	Training—Curriculum Development/Enhancement

CAREER HIGHLIGHTS

- Grew business from start-up position to a thriving enterprise employing 80 people with DM 8,000,000 in sales
- Leadership role in developing/expanding the lucrative German fitness market (Germany, Austria, Switzerland)
- Trained over 3,000 woman and men as health trainers/instructors—enabling them to make their hobby their career
- Special Awards: *Business Person of the Year* for the German Fitness Industry
- Successfully introduced Evian Mineral Water to the German fitness market —penetrated more than 600 new clubs
- Spearheaded successful development of high-impact program—*Personal Performance Center*—for Life Fitness
- Coproduced with 20th Century Fox Germany 7 Fitness Videos

PROFESSIONAL EXPERIENCE

Foliatec Gmbh—a Publicly Traded German Company, Nürnberg Germany   1992 to Current
Marketing and Sales Consultant

- Worked closely with the owner/managing director in developing new "branding" strategies for automotive retailers, internationally. Successfully created new product names as well as the packaging and accompanying displays. Formulated the concept and led production team in developing a high-impact marketing campaign to promote one of the main product lines—Auto Glass Films—to U.S. government and state agencies.

- Established a new sales tool, creating a 90-page Website to enhance prospect's decision-making and eventual ordering techniques for over 300 products. Worked closely with the graphic artist for the final conception, and directed the photo shoots. Produced several different (in size and shape) complete "Shop-in-Shop" concepts for the site. Included in this project was the complete ad campaign presentation for this program.

- Results were sensational. Travel to Washington, D.C. and work closely with U.S. governmental officials—for past five years. Improved company sales and revenue stream by 22%.

Adrienne Schladerer Group, Regensburg, Germany   1982 to 1992
Managing Director/General Manager/Business Development

- Conceptualized an idea and created the business concept—active in day-to-day activities in leadership roles. The first company was involved in high-end fitness wear—having developed and managed the brand "*Forever Fit by Doreen Schladerer.*"

- Designed the completed product line, sourced and contracted with key manufacturers in France, Portugal, and the Czech Republic. Developed "catalog distribution concept," as well as the "new" wholesale distribution channel of fitness clubs. During the second stage, expanded sales to a retail mail-order business.

(Page 1 of 2)

DOREEN SCHLADERER
(Page 2 of 2)

PROFESSIONAL EXPERIENCE

Doreen Schladerer Group, Regensburg Germany (Continued)

- Founded Fitness School Division that initially offered courses in basic and advanced education/training to aerobic instructors. Developed the concept and the "brand" name, ***Training for Trainers by Adrienne Schladerer.***" Created course programs, accompanying manuals, and all marketing and collateral materials.

- Grew business at "double digit" rate in the midst of tremendous competition. Maintained industry-leadership role—expanding programs to include specialized training using state of the art fitness equipment for select target markets, and offered management and marketing seminars for fitness club personnel.

- Created the next growth component the distribution of "small" aerobic fitness equipment. Identified emerging trends—for example, **"The Step,"** and hence acquiring exclusive distribution rights for Germany, Austria, and Switzerland. Sourced other fitness products in the Far East and marketed them under the **"Forever Fit"** brand. When no feasible deal could be consummated with reputable U.S. spinning-bike manufactures, developed own superior product in Taiwan.

- Rounded out the fitness group with the opening of the club ***"Forever Fit Performance"*** in 1989. Catering to the high-end fitness member, offering cutting edge in fitness equipment/programs to 1500 prominent members.

- Developed fitness-evaluation and training programs for the "Baby Boomer" market segment specifically designed to employ a cutting-edge product line for **Life Fitness**. Instrumental in assisting Life Fitness launch successfully and to sell new fitness product line.

Sport Insel, Regensburg Germany   1981 to 1989
Aerobic Director and Fitness Boutique Owner

- An Aerobic Director on a consulting basis. Responsible for developing an aerobic program that soon became the largest in Germany. Personally trained all instructors, developed class curriculum/formats, and taught classes. Responsible for all advertising and marketing for the club over an eight-year period.

- Started a fitness boutique within the club, offering fashionable and fast-selling products that were unavailable at that time in Europe. Initially did the buying in the United States from the top brands. Became an exclusive distributor for Germany, Austria, and Switzerland, for the leading American brand at the time, ***Dance France***.

PROFESSIONAL EXPERIENCE (1973–1981)

Pilot, Flight instructor and Aerobic Instructor
Free-Lance Flight Instructor, Freiburg, Germany
Free-Lance College Instructor
Part-Time Language Instructor

EDUCATION/TRAINING

MBA, 1975   BOSTON UNIVERSITY, Boston, Massachusetts
(Completed in Europe)

Bachelor of Arts: International relations, 1973   SCHILLER UNIVERSITY, Germany and France

Licenses/Certifications

Commercial Pilot SEL and MEL; Certified Flight Instructor (CFIAII) SEL, MEL, Instrument

PERSONAL

SS#: 000-00-0000
Citizenship: Dual: American/German

- References and Supporting Documentation Furnished upon Request -

DATA-PROCESSING SPECIALIST

WALLACE SWAN

775 Tenth Street, Northwest • Washington, D.C. 20016
(740) 555-1233/email@email.com

Social Security Number: 000-00-0000
Citizenship: United States
Federal Status: Office of the Secretary, U.S. Department of State
Veteran's Preference: N/A

Objective:
DATA-PROCESSING SPECIALIST—HT29-0
Office of the Secretary, U.S. Department of State

"Utilizing State-of-the-Art Technology to Advance Goals and Objectives of the U.S. Department of State"

SUMMARY

- Six years as Lead Data-Processing Specialist with solid track record of high achievement supported by departmental commendations, awards, and recognitions in all past positions held.

- Areas of expertise:
  - Install, configure, and update major hardware and software applications
  - Technical problem-solving and troubleshooting existing projects ((LAN/e-mail)
  - Monitor/analyze system accuracy, speed, and overall performance to meet high system demands
  - Update information and data to ensure timely and accurate intelligence information
  - Analyze interrelationships of relevant system components, and optimize capacity and output
  - Write, install, and constantly upgrade department's security-data-processing systems
    - Java, C/C++, Perl, SQL, HTML, EJBs, RMI, XML, JMS, JavaScript,
    - Oracle, Sybase, Postgress, JDBC
    - AS/400, SYS/36, SYS 38, IBM 3270/5250 Emulation, VAX, TPX , Novell Software

EXPERIENCE

UNITED STATES DEPARTMENT OF STATE
Washington, D.C.
1990 to Current

Lead Computer Operator: SGS-4   **1997–Current**
Office of the Assistant to the Secretary (202) 555-1212, ($29,400), 40 Hours/Week

- Oversea Grade 3–6 IS and technical operations, directing a staff of nine technical employees. Supply and ensure IS and technical support for more than 1200 users at mid and upper departments, require a TS-1 security clearance.

- Ensure quick and timely reporting programs to ensure that all secretaries and officials receive daily data and information reports. Review and evaluate software programs relative to present and future needs—and develop new programs to meet/exceed those requirements.

- Provide advanced data-processing and computer-software-application courses for the Department as an SGS-3 Trainer. Reinforce programming and security programming skills required to maintain integrity of classified data and information.

- Recipient of 12 letters of commendation—1997–Current

(Page 1 of 2)

DATA-PROCESSING SPECIALIST (CONT.)

EXPERIENCE (Continued)

E-mail Supervisor: GS-8   **1990–1997**
Office of the Assistant to the IS Secretary (202) 555-2323, ($23,400), 40 Hours/Week

- Directed and managed all electronic mail system, imaging, and Local Area Networks (LANs). Provided technical and logistical support, troubleshooting expertise, and new-application set-up/implementation assistance for users throughout the entire Department of State.

- Provided technical support for key "strategic" electronic mail system: Principal Officer's EMS (POEMS) and POEMS Security Virus and Detection Software.

- Installed Novell Netware 4.13 on LANs throughout the Department. Installed DCD200 PC computers for administrative assistants and executive secretaries to interface with main system. Installed an e-mail micro system for locations outside Washington, D.C.

COMPUGRAPHIC INTERNATIONAL
Washington, D.C.
1988 to 1990

Programmer—Corporate Accounts

- Worked with Fortune 500 clientele to program IS software to meet specific applications. Main programs used include: Java, C/C++, Perl, SQL, HTML, EJBs, RMI, XML, JMS, JavaScript.

A Selection of Clients Include:

General Electric	Boeing
General Motors	Johnson and Johnson
Delta Airlines	Wall Street

EDUCATION

DARTMOUTH COLLEGE, Hanover, New Hampshire
Master in Computer Programming Technology, 1989
- President's List (GPA 3.56)
- Vice Chair—Information and Technology Club, 1980/1981

TUFTS UNIVERSITY, Boston, Massachusetts
Bachelor of Science: Management Information Systems/Programming, 1987
- GPA: 3.5
- Active Member: Dartmouth Undergraduate Computer Group

CORPORATE/GOVERNMENT LIAISON

T.J. ZEKE

610 DeVosta Grade Road
Upperville, Virginia 20184
Phone/Fax: (540) 555-1212/email@email.com

HIGH-LEVEL CORPORATE /GOVERNMENT RELATIONS
State and Federal Congressional/White House Liaison

Increasing Corporate Growth & Exposures Through Governmental Access and Influence

High-Level Government Access/Strong Media Alliances
Incorporating Strong Private-Sector Partnerships

A well-connected, achievement-driven Public Relations/Communications Executive with outstanding qualifications in all phases of corporate/governmental communications, with particular emphasis on strategic crisis management. Spearheaded the public-relations efforts for national and international crises including:

- **Tylenol Crisis**
- **Three-Mile Island Crisis**
- **Teamsters/Government Takeover**

HIGHLIGHTS OF EXPERIENCE

- Spokesperson for International Union representing more than 2 million members and affiliate members
- Director of Public Relations and Congressional Liaison for the American Revolution Bicentennial Administration
- Presidential Appointment, Vice Chairman, National Parks Advisory Board, 1991 to 1995
- Appointed Vice Chairman, Presidential Inaugural Committees, 1969, 1981, and 1989
- Nominee, National Mediation Board, 1995
- Featured guest on *Nightline*, *The Today Show*, *Dateline*, and all network news, including CNN
- Speechwriter (White House and three U.S. Senators).; best-selling author of *Devil's Pact: Inside the Teamsters*

PROFESSIONAL EXPERIENCE

VIRGINIA THOROUGHBRED ASSOCIATION, Warrenton, Virginia   1995 to 2000
Executive Director

- Developed programs to enhance breeding of native thoroughbred industry while promoting racing in Virginia. Created and implemented high-impact programs and interfaced closely with industry leaders, breeders, government officials and the legislature to meet association goals and mandates.

- Oversaw budget processes, administered state breeder's fund, directed educational seminars, spearheaded fundraising activities, and serviced association members—all in an effort to enhance Virginia's stature as a nationally recognized center for thoroughbred nurseries.

- Coordinated and initiated activities with the Virginia Racing Commission—writing newsletters, brochures, and press releases; developing high-impact advertising, marketing, and promotional programs, including the Virginia Derby and the annual Thoroughbred Hall of Fame Awards Banquet.

WASHINGTON ASSOCIATES INTERNATIONAL, LTD., Washington, D.C.   1992 to 1997
Vice President/Government and Public Relations

- Directed marketing, economic development, public relations, and communications-consulting services to international and national clientele—from both the public and private sectors. Assisted clients in seeking joint-venture or strategic-alliance partners, and provided economic planning and marketing counsel for new ventures.

- Created coalitions for large, grass-roots advocacy campaigns and supervised media strategies to support objectives. Contracts included economic planning audits, communications and special-events management, lobbying, and community-relations efforts. Wrote speeches, produced promotional films/videos, and managed fundraisers.

(Page 1 of 2)

CORPORATE/GOVERNMENT LIAISON (CONT.)

T.J. Zeke
Page two

PROFESSIONAL EXPERIENCE

INTERNATIONAL BROTHERHOOD OF TEAMSTERS, Washington, D.C. 1978 to 1992
Director of Communications/Executive Assistant to the President

- Served as international spokesman and was fully responsible for all communications and media-relations efforts for the two-million-member union and its affiliates. Managed a staff of 20 in producing all publications, educational and policy material, and other pertinent collateral information for the membership.

- Spearheaded logistical efforts for national conventions. PR responsibilities included developing retiree programs, international trade, media relations, and economic development programs. Served as Executive Assistant to the President and Director of Government Relations, including White House Liaison for international union activities.

AMERICAN CAUSE, Washington, D.C. 1976 to 1978
Assistant Director/Vice President

- Established efforts to promote U.S. international policies, commerce, and trade to enhance targeted causes with government, industry, and business leaders. Wrote speeches and directed press/communications efforts.

- Directed policy development and communications on domestic and international policy for national think-tank organization founded by Senators George Murphy, John Stennis, and others, including the late John Wayne.

AMERICAN REVOLUTION BICENTENNIAL ADMINISTRATION, Washington, D.C. 1971 to 1976
Director of Public Relations/Congressional Liaison

- Contributing leadership role in developing and implementing all aspects of communications and public relations, including promotional planning, for the National Bicentennial Celebration. Liaison with Congressional members relative to administration and federal development and planning for national observance.

- Chief of the News Bureau, responsible for all press relations, publications and media development, marketing, and high-level speech writing.

HILL AND KNOWLTON PUBLIC RELATIONS, INC., Washington, D.C. 1967 to 1971
Vice President/Account Executive

- Directed government-liaison activities and public-relations campaigns for several major accounts, including Ernest & Ernest, American Airlines, The Wine Institute, Gillette, Owens Illinois, Miles Laboratories, Procter and Gamble, Continental Can, Zenith Radio Corp., and *The New York Times*.

- Developed crisis-management strategies for the Tylenol Crisis and the Three-Mile Island Crisis.

ASSISTANT TO MINORITY SECRETARY OF THE U.S. SENATE, Washington, D.C. 1962 to 1967
Administrative/Executive Assistant

Served as personal liaison to then Minority Leader of the U.S. Senate, following four years as a U.S. Senate Page.

EDUCATION

Bachelor of Arts: Communications, Journalism	George Washington University	1966
Associate's Degree: Political Science	Dartmouth College	1962
International Law and Foreign Relations Studies	Georgetown/Catholic University	1966 to 1967

AFFILIATIONS

Virginia Society of Association Executives	Public Relations Society of America
National Press Club	Who's Who in American Politics

REFERENCES

Senator John W. Warner (202) 555-1212	Congressman Tom Davis (202) 555-1212
Lawrence J. Brady (603) 555-1212	Richard Quinn (714) 555-1212

LEAD OFFICER—OPERATIONS AND LOGISTICS

KAREN BENJAMIN

7759 Eisenhower Drive • Naval Air Station #123455-BT • Madrid, Spain TF-10523
555-122-1233/email@email.com
SS#: 000-00-0000/Veteran Status: Active—Military Police Team Leader/U.S. Citizen

---

Objective:
Lead Officer—Operations & Logistics
Department of Military Affairs, U.S. Navy Command 201—Spain
MP-111-222-33/4

"Protecting and Serving Military Personnel, Guests, and Dignitaries"

SUMMARY

- Five years as senior law-enforcement officer III; Naval Police Team; Madrid, Spain—responsible for 33 officers and a staff of five. Ensure total safety and security for an air station comprising 3,000 people.

- Three years as military police officer I, II, and III—in charge of access control and escort, and emergency-response team member in enforcing U.S. Navy/Military codes/standards.

- Awarded seven commendation medals, including three Silver Stars for significantly exceeding job standards. Recognized for strong organization, administration, and time-management skills. Recipient of eight consecutive Merit Awards from superior offers for top job performance.

U.S. MILITARY SERVICE

UNITED STATES NAVY
Naval Air Station, Madrid, Spain
1994 to Current

Senior Law Enforcement Officer III	1999 to Current
Military Police Officer III	1997 to 1999
Military Police Officer II	1996 to 1997
Military Police Officer I	1994 to 1996

Top Secret Security Clearance (Level Six)
Expert/Certified Weapons Specialist—Trainer IV
Private Pilot's License

EDUCATION

AMERICAN UNIVERSITY, Madrid, Spain
Bachelor of Science: Criminal Justice and Law-Enforcement Management, 2000
GPA: 3.73

Key Course Work:

Law and the Judicial Process in the Military	Leadership in a Global Community
Terrorist Detection and Prevention	Access-Control Management
Facilities Safety and Protection Management	Crisis and Emergency Planning

Computer Skills:
Windows, PC, Mac, Office, QuickBooks, PhotoShop, and Internet Applications

MARKETING RESEARCHER/CUSTOMER ANALYST

JANICE RANDALL

12A Ridgepointe Drive
Bedford, Pennsylvania 32343
Telephone: (717) 555-1212
Email: email@email.com

Position: Marketing Researcher Grade 9
Department of Consumer Affairs
SS #: 000-00-0000
Citizenship: U.S.
Federal Status: N/A

MARKETING RESEARCHER/CUSTOMER ANALYST
"Voice of the Consumer"—Designing Programs to Enhance Customer Satisfaction

*Market Intelligence/Survey Design & Management/Senior-Level Project Management
Strategic Planning & Implementation/Secondary Research & Analysis*

Highly experienced, accomplished, and creative professional with extensive experience in analytical research and assessment. Recognized for developing high-impact programs aligned with customer and market needs/projections. Bottom-line oriented strategist with a verifiable record for igniting sales, improving productivity of sales staff, and maximizing available resources—physical and labor.

CORE PROFESSIONAL STRENGTHS

Survey design/questionnaire development	Database design
Direct-mail marketing	Competitive analysis
Resource estimating	Vendor management
Customer-service and retention management	Quality-control management

PROFESSIONAL EXPERIENCE

Horowitz Consulting Group, Ltd., Bedford Falls, Pennsylvania   1999 to Current
MARKET RESEARCH ANALYST
Directed the complete overhaul and manage customer-service database and data acquisition for this sales-and-marketing organization. Monitor the marketplace for any development relative to past, present, and future customers. Profile existing and prospective customers and industries. Conduct ad hoc research on people, places, and things.

- Improved database efficiency by reducing the number of entries by more than 60%.
- Moved database orientation from corporation to the individual, allowing for tracking movement of individuals.
- "Pushing" marketplace information, resulting in meetings with customers for the sales force.
- Customer and industry profiles provided a clear roadmap for targeted-marketing campaigns.

BellTower Marketing, Bedford, Pennsylvania   1994 to 1999
MARKETING ANALYST
Conducted all market-intelligence and research activities for corporation. Developed marketing databases and designed sales territories. Provided demographic profiles of prospective markets.

- Database structure allowed for the creation of potential-customer lists for the sales forces.
- Designed the sales territories that added structure to the sales organization and led to more-efficient sales management.
- Managed direct-mail marketing campaign that increased customers both by direct response and product awareness.
- Created customized presentations integrating both company and potential-customer information that paved the way for securing national accounts.
- Recommended the most-efficient locations for depots.

(Page 1 of 2)

MARKETING RESEARCHER/CUSTOMER ANALYST (CONT.)

PROFESSIONAL EXPERIENCE

IBM Corporation, Springfield, Pennsylvania   1988 to 1994
FINANCIAL ANALYST (1992–94)
Directed all financial and resource activity for $11 million operating budget of Information Development organization. This involved tracking labor resources expended by product each month, in addition to planning future labor expenditures by product. Led all sizing efforts for new products and planned changes.

- Developed proposal to save $400 thousand a year in contracted labor cost.
- Designed financial model and process to recover revenue for division.
- Devised creative ways to optimize headcount in budget-cutting situation.

STRATEGIC PLANNER (1990–1992)
Developed and managed customer/market-requirements strategy for an Information development organization. Managed customer/developer meetings. Functioned as advisor for the organization on measuring performance (six-sigma).

- Moved documentation evaluations up to par with other product attributes.
- Customer strategy was singled out as organizational high point during independent reviews.
- Led first-ever customer review of unannounced information products.
- Developed metrics for use in quality control and product improvement.
- Managed research project designed to explore product issues.

MARKET RESEARCH ANALYST (1985–1990)
Assumed lead role in getting monthly customer survey up and running. Survey measured customer attitudes and tracked product quality on a monthly basis. Worked with multiple internal areas (service, sales, manufacturing) and external vendors.

- Set new standards for IBM-survey methodology by probing customer responses.
- Utilized customer feedback as quality control by helping to drive engineering changes in products with repair issues.
- Structured survey to allow for "question of the month" capability, which aided product planners in determining future product specifications.

PROCUREMENT ANALYST (1988–1985)
Purchased semiconductors for personal computer manufacturing. Managed worldwide supply/demand forecast.

- Supervised supplier interaction with IBM Engineering.
- Constructed database of personnel information.

EDUCATION & SOFTWARE SKILLS

University of Pennsylvania, Philadelphia, Pennsylvania Campus
Master of Business Administration, (Concentration on Quantitative Management), 1987
Bachelor of Business Administration (Major: Management—Quantitative Analysis), 1985

SOFTWARE SKILLS

Lotus 1-2-3	MS Access	MS Word
Lotus Freelance	MS Excel	BusinessMap Pro
Lotus Approach	MS PowerPoint	MarketPlace
Lotus Notes	MS Publisher	Maximizer

References and Supporting Documentation Furnished upon Request

PARALEGAL SPECIALIST

CLAUDIA KING
272 Commonwealth Avenue #201
Boston, Massachusetts 10923
(617) 555-1234/Cell: (718) 555-1222
email@mail.com

Social Security Number:	**000-00-0000**
Citizenship:	**United States**
Veteran Status:	**N/A**
Federal Civilian Status:	**N/A**
Objective:	**Paralegal Specialist IV (Ann. #GS-1021)**
	Civil Division: State of Massachusetts—Dept. of Justice

"Combining Solid Education and Legal Training with Two Years of High-Visibility Experience"
Fluent in English, Spanish, & French

A personable, highly detail-oriented, and results-focused Paralegal seeking position as Paralegal Specialist IV with the State of Massachusetts. Presently employed by C.D. Hanna, working on high-exposure civil cases. Excellent references available.

Education

Endicott College, Beverly, Massachusetts
Graduate—Two-Year Paralegal Certification (with Honors), 2000

Salem State College, Salem, Massachusetts
Bachelor of Arts: Political Science, 1998 (with Honors)

Computer Skills:
Windows, PC, Mac, Office, QuickBooks, PhotoShop, and Internet Applications

Legal Applications:
NEXIS/LEXIS/BASYS/Dbase LegalPro/PARALEGAL QX

Experience

Hanna and Walter, Ltd., Boston, Massachusetts   1999 to Present
Legal Assistant—Full time, $28,600/Yr./Supervisor: C.D. Hanna

- Provide support services assisting attorney, prepare for and conduct civil-litigation activities for this major Boston law firm. Review depositions of witnesses/experts providing testimony.

- Prepare written summaries highlighting key points of testimony and identifying potential issues of relevance. Schedule meetings and brainstorming sessions, generate statistics and charts for crucial points of evidence, and compile necessary material in preparing witnesses for trial.

- Work with foreign clients utilizing fluency in three languages. Good working knowledge of international law to complement national certification, enhancing value to the firm.

Recognitions

Who's Who Among Boston Paralegals, 2000 and 2001
Red, White, and Blue Achievement Award for Paralegal Excellence
Provided three pay raises due to outstanding performance exceeding expectations
Named International Liaison for the Firm, 2000

U.S. POSTAL SERVICE COMMUNICATIONS CLERK

GLORIA JEAN WILLIAMS
7759 Coral Way • Miami, Florida 33340
(305) 555-1234/email@mail.com

Social security Number:	**000-00-0000**
Citizenship:	**United States**
Veteran Status:	**N/A**
Federal Civilian Status:	**N/A**

Objective:

Communications Clerk III
U.S. Postal Service—92-388

"Seeking to Contribute to U.S. Postal Operations, Offering 10 Years of Communications Expertise"

Profile

A highly experienced Communications and Customer-Service Specialist with 10 years' experience with AT&T (six years) and Office Depot (last four years) at a corporate level. Positions held include: Assistant Communications Director, Customer-Service Supervisor, and Customer-Service Clerk.

Expertise

- Managing key accounts—with outstanding track record of success
- Exceeding customer expectations and needs in a highly professional manner
- Research and analyze simple-to-complex problems in a win-win manner
- Develop high-impact written correspondences to achieve high-impact results
- Develop and implement new programs and systems to enhance productivity, efficiency, and quality

Experience

OFFICE DEPOT, Deerfield Beach, Florida   1998 to Present
Communications Technician—Key National Accounts
Responsible for maintaining close contact with 138 key national accounts, including Ford, Microsoft, U.S. Department of Defense, General Foods, Honeywell, and the McArthur Foundation.

- Improved relations and revenues as a result of providing consistent professional service.
- Began with 35 key accounts and given increasing responsibility—now at top level of 138 accounts.
- Recipient of "President's Award," past three years—1999, 2000, and 2001.

AT&T, Miami, Florida   1992 to 1998
Customer-Service Supervisor/Customer-Service Clerk
Responsible for overall customer service and for maintaining high service ratings. Research and resolve any and all customer problems relating to service, billing, and other communications problems.

- Turned around a network region where service levels were 89%, and within four weeks, achieved 98% rating.
- Consistently averaged a 98.2% CS rating—some 2% above outstanding level recognized by AT&T.
- Promoted from Customer-Service Clerk to Supervisor after two years—responsible for up to 30 CS Clerks.

Education

UNIVERSITY OF MIAMI, Miami, Florida
Bachelor of Arts: Sociology, 1991 (with Honors)

Computer Skills:
Windows, PC, Mac, Office, QuickBooks, PhotoShop, and Internet Applications

14
Health Care

CERTIFIED MEDICAL TECHNOLOGIST

MICHAEL J. HARDING

1858 Sterling Road
Jupiter, FL 33478
(561) 555-1212/email@email.com

NATIONALLY CERTIFIED MEDICAL TECHNOLOGIST
Instrumentation Specialist/Outstanding Mechanical & Maintenance Expertise

Troubleshooting Laboratory Instruments/Management and Personnel-Training Experience
Florida License in Immunohematology, Serology, Chemistry, Hematology, and Microbiology

---

OVERVIEW

Successfully blending scientific, laboratory proficiency with mechanical, maintenance, and outstanding interpersonal and "people" skills. Detail-oriented and precision-focused, recognized for adhering to stringent turnaround times in a cost-effective manner with attention to quality control. A resourceful professional with excellent problem-solving and troubleshooting skills.

INSTRUMENT EXPERTISE (Selected)

Chemistry Analyzers
- Technicon DAX and RAXT
- Vitros 250

- Ektachem 500, 700, and 950
- IL 1640 Blood Gas Analyzer & 682 CO-

Oximeter
- Abbott TDX, IMX, and AXSYM
- Syva 30R
- Clinitek 200

- Beckman ELISE
- Baxter Stratus II

Hematology Analyzers
- Coulter STKS, STKR

- MaxM, Onyx, and Sysmex E500

Coagulation Analyzers
- MLA 900 and 1000

- Sysmex CA6000

Microbiology
- Organon Teknika BacTalert

- Gen-Probe Leader 450i

EDUCATION

FLORIDA INTERNATIONAL UNIVERSITY, Miami, FL
Bachelor of Science: Medical Technology; Chemistry Minor, 1995
- Treasurer: Medical Laboratory Students Club
- Recipient of Full Scholarship from Memorial Regional Hospital

PROFESSIONAL WORK HISTORY

ST. MARY'S MEDICAL CENTER (Intracoastal Health Systems, Inc.), West Palm Beach, FL   1998–Present
Medical Technologist/Generalist
A 460-bed facility with a Level-1 Adult and Pediatric Trauma Center.
- Worked primarily in Microbiology but assisted in Hematology and Chemistry.
- Set up specimens for culture, performed rapid tests (Group A and B Strep., Rotavirus, RSV, and C. Diff.)
- Performed Gen-Probe gonorrhea and chlamydia tests, as well as ova and parasite screening/identification.
- Read/report gram-stained smears.

MEMORIAL HOSPITAL WEST, (South Broward Hospital District), Pembroke Pines, FL   1992–1998
Medical Technologist/Generalist
A 110-bed acute-care facility with a Level-2 Newborn Intensive-Care Unit.
- Resource Technologist recognized for troubleshooting/resolving challenging issues and problems.
- Performed and implemented generalist duties and tracked ER blood bank and chemistry turnaround times.
- Scheduled and trained a staff of 40+ laboratory employees.

(Page 1 of 2)

MICHAEL J. HARDING
Page 2

PROFESSIONAL WORK HISTORY

JOHN H. HARLAND COMPANY, St. Petersburg, Sunrise, and Miami, FL/Chicago, IL   1985–1992
Production Supervisor
The second-largest check printers in the United States—other products/services include printing of financial documents and providing of marketing software to financial institutions.
- Promoted from mailroom clerk to Mechanic, then to Supervisor of maintenance, and finally to Production Supervisor.
- Facilitated staff meetings, managed established budgets, and hired, trained, and directed a team of 15–25 employees.
- Rebuilt high-priced printing equipment; in charge of maintenance of 41,350 sq. ft facility.
- Set up production facilities and trained maintenance staff in St. Petersburg, St. Louis, Chicago, Miami, Jacksonville, and Puerto Rico, in the operation, maintenance, and repair of printing equipment.
- Implemented successful preventive-maintenance programs.
- Decreased downtime and improved productivity.
- Successfully passed all formal inspections by the maintenance and engineering department and the research and development department (for equipment, inventory, and documentation and record keeping).

ADDITIONAL SKILLS AND QUALIFICATIONS

Communications skills—verbal and written
Time management—deadline sensitive
Personnel training and development
Quality assurance

Organizational leadership and managerial skills
Detail oriented—thorough and accurate
Budget management (cost containment)
Resource utilization

BROWARD COMMUNITY COLLEGE, Fort Lauderdale, FL
Associate of Arts, 1985   Education funded by the John H. Harland Company

CERTIFICATION

Associate Member of the American Society of Clinical Pathologists

References and Supporting Documentation Furnished upon Request

HEALTH-CARE/NURSING-HOME ADMINISTRATOR

LESTER E. BRANDON
5706 Grand Circle * Golden Bridge, New York 10526 * (914) 555-1212 * email@email.com

---

HEALTH-CARE/NURSING-HOME ADMINISTRATOR
Driving Growth & Profits in Competitive/Fluctuating Markets

**Multisite & Single-Facilities Management/Organizational Leadership &Empowerment
Start-up & Turnaround Management Expertise**

Dynamic operating/management professional offering 15-plus years of successful leadership positions in health-care environments. Expertise in Medicare administration and protocol. Outstanding business-development skills.

AREAS OF EXPERTISE

Personnel team-building; union avoidance	Customer service/quality control management
Regulatory compliance management	Building strategic partnerships and alliances
Public speaking; community relations	Cross-cultural new-business development
Finance management, budgeting, expense control	Profit-center realignment/reorganization

PROFESSIONAL EXPERIENCE

INTEGRATED HEALTH GROUP, Westin, New York   1993 to Current
Administrator—Directed total operations for 120-bed skilled nursing facility, managing 130 employees for health-care center specializing in both short-term rehabilitation and long-term care for managed care, Medicare, Medicaid, private pay, and insurance residents. Developed and administered a $9.7 million annual operating budget. Accountable for regulatory compliance, business development/retention, quality customer service, and bottom-line/profit attainment.

- Increased average daily census from 71% to 96% in six months via aggressive, high-impact marketing techniques
- Enhanced contribution margin from 5% to 19% by controlling costs and improving management team
- Developed new profit center—a highly successful outpatient therapy program

NORTH CENTRAL MANOR NURSING CENTER, Boynton Bridge, New York   1987 to 1993
Administrator—Managed total operations for 167-bed skilled nursing facility directing more than 145 employees for health-care center specializing in both short-term rehabilitation and long-term care for managed care, Medicare, Medicaid, private pay, and insurance residents. Develop and administer annual operating budget of $10.2 million. Accountable for regulatory compliance, business development/retention, quality customer service, and bottom-line/profit attainment.

- Received two Superior Ratings—JCAHO Accreditation
- Significantly reduced turnover and lowered Worker's Compensation cases
- Proactively blocked union signing and campaign while dramatically improving employee morale and productivity
- Negotiated and implemented new managed-care contracts

EDUCATION & LICENSES

Bachelor of Science: Biology, GPA: 3.58 (Top 25%)   ELIZABETHTOWN COLLEGE
- New York Nursing Home Administrator License

PROFESSIONAL AFFILIATIONS

Member: American Health Care Association (Former Voting Delegate)
Member: American College of Health Care Administrators

References and Supporting Documentation Furnished upon Request

CLINICAL-INFORMATION SPECIALIST/DIRECTOR

CATHERINE G. LOPEZ, R.N., M.S.N.

130 Meadow Breeze Drive
Williamette, Oregon 97345
(503) 555-2121
email@email.com

CLINICAL-INFORMATION SPECIALIST/DIRECTOR

**Solid Contributor to Organizational Growth and Profitability
Combining Nursing, Health Policy, Clinical Informatics, and Management Expertise**

*Efficiency and Productivity Management/Organizational Leadership
Cost Containment and Expense Control/Process and Technology Specialist
Fluent—English and Spanish*

A dynamic, market-driven Clinical Information Professional offering nine years of successful experience in nursing, health policy, clinical informatics, and management environments. Recognized for outstanding regulatory-compliance management relative to HCFA, JCAHO, AHCA and related issues.

CORE STRENGTHS

Balance quality patient care with budget constraints
Strategic planning—clinical information technology
Personnel/staff training, development, and team building
Develop quality-improvement processes/monitors
Customer-service and quality-control management

Design process and introduce new technology
Clinical-informatics curriculum development
Time/priority management
Maximize physical and labor resources
Senior-level project management

EDUCATION/TRAINING/LICENSURE

UNIVERSITY OF MARYLAND, Baltimore, Maryland
Master of Science: Nursing/Health Policy, 1987

BARRY UNIVERSITY, Baltimore, Maryland
Bachelor of Science and Nursing, 1984

- Registered Nurse, State of Oregon

- Computer Skills: Word, Excel, Proprietary Software, and Internet Applications

PROFESSIONAL EXPERIENCE

BETHESDA HEALTHCARE SYSTEMS, Springfield, Oregon   1996 to Current
Director of Clinical Information/Nursing Resources

- Provide strategic leadership in the area of clinical-information systems and nursing-resources management for Patient Services Division. Develop, implement, and manage the Patient Services' clinical information strategic plan, in addition to operationalizing the automated patient record for the entire health-care system.

- Coach and empower Staffing Office personnel and operate as a key resource to departments regarding quality-improvement activities. Launch new and modified quality-improvement initiatives for the division. Provide comprehensive consultative services to other departments and staff vis-à-vis federal and state regulatory standards. Spearhead multiple clinical-information-system enhancements concurrently.

Catherine G. Lopez, R.R., M.S.N.
Page two of two

PROFESSIONAL EXPERIENCE

NATIONAL INSTITUTES OF HEALTH, Springfield, Oregon   1990 to 1996
(NATIONAL INSTITUTES OF NEUROLOGICAL DISEASES AND STROKES)
Nurse Consultant/Research Nurse Coordinator

- Maintained quality health care by (1) Staff empowerment and development, (2) maintaining strict compliance with clinical center and federal policies and regulations, (3) optimizing the utilization of appropriate resources and services, and (4) the coordination of interdepartmental services to meet rapidly changing patient needs.

- Directed care of adult and pediatric patients in numerous research protocols. Directed clinical activities of the Neurological Diseases section. Responsible for staffing, scheduling, and efficiency management for the section. Successfully marketed services to hospitals, physicians, patients, and state and federal agencies.

- Developed continuing educational programs for staff and patient populations. Introduced a computerized database system to facilitate the data collection and to improve assessment quality. Identified and analyzed trends in care within the clinical center.

- Consulted with physicians, nurses, and the FDA, in addition to outside collaborative research centers and primary-health-care providers, in managing research protocols. Collaborated in writing research protocols.

NATIONAL INSTITUTES OF HEALTH, Hope, Oregon   1988 to 1990
(CLINICAL CENTER NURSING DEPARTMENT)
Charge Nurse

- Full Charge Nurse supervising a staff on a 40-bed Neuro-Surgical and Neuro-Medical Care Unit for both adult and pediatric patients. Designed and directed implementation of nursing protocol abridgements for the Nursing department. Representative on Quality Improvement and Nursing Informatics Committees.

PROFESSIONAL AFFILIATIONS

American Association of Neuroscience Nurses
Oregon Nurses Association

SELECTED PRESENTATIONS

"The Role of the Nurse in Health Policy," Florida Atlantic University, 1999
"Healthcare Technology Assessment: A Necessary Toll in Health Care Delivery," University of Maryland, 1996
"Dysphasia in Inclusion Body Myositis," Poster Presentation, American Academy of Neurology Conference, 1996
"Inclusion Body Myositis: Nursing Management," National Institutes of Health, 1995–1996
"Managed Care and Its Impact on the Nursing Profession," University of Maryland, 1995–1996
"Post-Polio Syndrome: Nursing Management, National Institutes of Health, 1994–1996
"Nursing Management of the Patient After Liver Biopsy," National Institutes of Health, 1994–1996
"Domestic Violence: Social and Policy Issues," University of Maryland, 1993, 1999

References and Supporting Documentation Furnished upon Request

SOCIAL SERVICES PROFESSIONAL

VIVIENNE L. PETTRICELLI

34844 Tangerine Boulevard
Kansas City, Missouri 63221
(616) 555-1212/email@email.com

SOCIAL SERVICES PROFESSIONAL
Counseling/Case Worker/Administration

"Making A Difference"

Patient Relations/Community Outreach/Program Development & Implementation
Organizational Leadership/Quality-Control& Risk Management

A highly dynamic, team-spirited, and results-oriented professional seeking to combine outstanding academic training with excellent work experience to make a significant contribution in a social-services environment-supported by credible and verifiable references.

AREAS OF EXPERTISE

Patient assessment/intake
Advocacy and support
Teaching and training
Problem solving and conflict resolution

Crisis intervention
Documentation/regulatory compliance
Policy development and enforcement
Budget and finance management

Computer Skills: Word, Excel, One-Write Plus, Quicken, and Internet Applications

EDUCATION

CALIFORNIA STATE UNIVERSITY, Long Beach, California
Master of Arts: Applied Anthropology (Geriatrics/Applied Anthropology), 1995

CALIFORNIA STATE UNIVERSITY, Dominquez Hills, California
Bachelor of Arts: Social Behavioral Science (Sociology, Psychology, and Anthropology), 1992

LOS ANGELES CITY COLLEGE, Los Angeles, California
Associate of Arts: Business Administration, 1986

PROFESSIONAL EXPERIENCE

ELDERCARE AND HOME MANAGEMENT AGENCY, Kansas City, Missouri   1995 to 2000
Operations Manager/Case Worker/Counselor

- Founded and directed the successful start-up of a company specializing in home care for the elderly.
- Worked with more than 50 clients throughout the Los Angeles area.
- Provided and ensured quality custodial care, health, personal hygiene, nutrition, and home management.
- Assessed clients' needs (medical, economic, and social) and developed plans to meet those needs.
- Balanced quality care with budgetary management, ensuring growth/profitability.
- Recruited, trained, and directed up to 150 employees in 5-year period.
- Managed master operations calendar.
- Involved with marketing, promotion, public relations, customer service, and retention management.

References and Supporting Documentation Furnished upon Request

MEDICAL BILLING PROFESSIONAL

IDA R. PAGUAGA
402 Hope Sound Lane
West Palm Beach, Florida 33415

(561) 555-1212
email@email.com

MEDICAL BILLING PROFESSIONAL
Electronic Claims Specialist
Expert in Accurate Claims Submission, Coding and Updates, & Collections
FAST, ACCURATE COLLECTIONS

INTRODUCTION

Highly experienced in all phases of medical billing—Medicare, Medicaid, Champus, HMOs, PPOs, and private insurance carriers, including secondary insurance claims. Outstanding record with Worker's Compensation, auto, and personal-injury claims. A professional who respects the fact that *"accurate billing and prompt collections are paramount to the physician."* A verifiable record of success in managing billing operations—leading to enhanced collections and cash flow in ever-changing environments.

Trained in computer hardware/software, electronic data transmission, and health-care-claim reimbursement. A resourceful, solution-focused individual recognized for lowering receivables, troubleshooting billing problems, and addressing challenges due to a lack of payment for insurance claims. Verify that billing codes are current and accurate. Additional areas of strength include:

* **Business start-up and expansion**	* **Telephone communication skills**
* **Skilled negotiator**	* **Patient relations—professional/courteous**
* **Research and analysis**	* **Powerful writing skills**
* **Employee management and supervision**	* **Training and development**
* **Follow up; detail oriented**	* **Integrity; maintain high ethical standards**

PROFESSIONAL EXPERIENCE

GTR Medical Billing Service, West Palm Beach, FL   1995–Present
Billing & Collection Agent/Manager—Start-up management and supervision for new billing office. Marketed services to local physicians and medical practices—preparing oral/written presentations. Directed all phases of billing service. Implemented a successful system for intensive and comprehensive follow-up for all nonresponsive insurance companies approaching the 30-day limit for payment. Improved practice's collections/cash flow; organized record keeping and aging reporting, and significantly reduced bad-debt write-offs.

- Significantly reduced outstanding accounts receivable over 90 days by 77%—wrote off the balance
- Reduced returned claims from Medicare/Medicaid by nearly 95%
- Collected $49,000 of monies scheduled to be written off
- Maintained an above-average billing ratio of 73/27

PROFESSIONAL EXPERIENCE (Prior to 1995)

Glendale Federal Savings & Loan Association, Delray Beach, FL   1985–1995
Loan Officer

Nationwide Insurance Companies, Palm Beach Gardens, FL   1983–1985
General Insurance Agent

EDUCATION

Associate's Degree: Business Administration	Palm Beach Community College, Lake Worth, Florida, 1982
Insurance Billing for 3d-Party Billing	Palm Beach Community College, Lake Worth, Florida, 1992–1994
Medicare Guidelines	Medicare Guidelines & Billing Seminar, Tampa, Florida, 1996
Advanced Electronic Billing	Synaps Introduction to Insurance Billing, St. Petersburg, Florida, 1999

References and Supporting Documentation Furnished upon Request

LICENSED/CERTIFIED CONSULTANT PHARMACIST

MARGARITA GRIGORIO

2021 West Drive
Orono, Maine 17461
(261) 555-1212
email@email.com

LICENSED/CERTIFIED CONSULTANT PHARMACIST
Solid Contributor to Organizational Goals and Objectives
Combining Nursing, Health Policy, Clinical Information, and Management Expertise

Efficiency and Productivity Management/Organizational Leadership
Cost Containment and Expense Control/Process and Technology Specialist
Fluent—English and Spanish

A dynamic, customer-service-oriented Licensed Pharmacist/Certified Consultant Pharmacist offering six years of successful experience in fast-track, high-volume environments.

CORE STRENGTHS

Regulatory-compliance management
Personnel training, development and empowerment
Customer-service management

Communication skills
Problem solving/conflict resolution
Quality-control management

EDUCATION/TRAINING/LICENSURE

Bachelor of Science: Pharmacy, 1994
Licensed Pharmacist—PS 0029548
Pharmacy Internship: Jacobi Hospital

LONG ISLAND UNIVERSITY, Brooklyn, New York
Consultant Pharmacist—PU 0004605
Pharmacy Internship: Pathmark Supermarket

PROFESSIONAL EXPERIENCE

PHARMERICA (Formerly Pharmacy Corporation of America), Bangor, Maine   1985 to Current
Staff Pharmacist

- Process/dispense prescription orders for high-volume pharmacy (filling up to 1200 prescriptions daily). Manage pharmacy staff of up to 14, including pharmacists, pharmacy technicians, and data entry personnel.
- Communicate with nursing-home staff/management relative to drug-related issues and concerns, including order clarifications, drug interactions, and therapeutic recommendations.
- Assist in the training and evaluations of newly recruited pharmacists and pharmacy technicians.
- Specialist in pharmacokinetcs, IVs, and TPN prescription orders.
- Increased company's gross revenues by more than $98,000 through a special project.
- Contributor in the development and implementation of a system to handle narcotic CII prescriptions.
- Expertise in online Medicaid billing.

Consultant Pharmacist for Pharmerica

- Supervise narcotic and medication utilization for local medical facilities. Inspect and supervise all procedures and counts concerning controlled and noncontrolled drugs. Ensure all medical records for accuracy and compliance. Review Adverse Drug Reaction reports.

PROFESSIONAL AFFILIATIONS/COMMUNITY SERVICE

Member: Florida Pharmacy Association
Member: Palm Beach Pharmacy Association
Volunteer: Landmark Education Corporation

References and Supporting Documentation Furnished upon Request

PSYCHIATRIST/TEACHER/LECTURER/RECRUITER

MICHAEL BERNARD WILSON, M.D., Ph.D.

2748 Kittbuck Way
Falls Church, Virginia 22132
(703) 555-1212/email@email.com

Nonpracticing...

PSYCHIATRIST/TEACHER/LECTURER/RECRUITER

Combining more than 25 years of medical expertise with outstanding sales, marketing, managerial, and communications skills. Seeking position where qualifications and experience can enhance organizational recruitment, growth, profits, efficiency, resource utilization, and employee satisfaction.

Patient-Treatment Evaluation/Hospital-Stay Cost Analysis/Pharmaceutical Drug Management
Physician-Patient Consultation/Education & Research/Article Writer & Editor
Insurance Evaluations/Medical Advertisement Writer & Consultant

---

Highly experienced and accomplished retired physician successfully combining medical expertise with organizational-leadership, growth-management, and productivity-enhancement experience. Able to assist contemporary organizations navigate through a dramatically changing medical environment on all fronts and facilitate reorganization, training, and staff education and updating.

CORE PROFESSIONAL STRENGTHS

Team-building and problem solving	Proactive strategic planning
Presentation/public-speaking skills	Research and development
Active treatment expertise	Preventative treatment protocols
Expert in drugs (efficacy/side effects)	Advertisement compilation
Project management/coordination	Medical history expert
Working with diverse cultures	Resource utilization (physical/labor)
Patient-relations management	Quality-control management

Languages: Fluent in English, German, Yiddish; G

EDUCATION/BOARD CERTIFICAT

Columbia University, New York, New York   52–1956
Bachelor of Arts: Humanities & Science (Geolo
Harvard University and the University of Chicago,   56–1959
Ph.D.: Geology and Archeology
Chicago Medical School, Chicago, Illinois   59–1962
Medical Doctor (MD)
New Rochelle Hospital, New Rochelle, New York   62–1963
Internship
Kings Park State Hospital, Kings Park, New York   64–1967
Psychiatry Residency
New York School of Psychiatry, New York, New   67–1969
Q.P. (Qualified Psychiatrist)—NY State

* Board Eligibility: American Board of Psychiatry   )71
* Board Certified, American Board of Psychiatry   )81
* Medical Licenses: NJ, NM, NY, SC, VT (Currently Expired)   964–1976

(Handwritten note overlaid: 95384 SCCF IL ell / PO Box 3 / Pueblo Co / 81002)

MICHAEL BERNARD WILSON, M.D., Ph.D.
Page two

HIGHLIGHTS OF PROFESSIONAL EXPERIENCE

❑ General Practitioner—private practice for 8 years.
❑ 10 years as a Staff Psychiatrist in Kings Park State Hospital, Kings Park, Virginia.
❑ 10 years as a practicing and well-respected private psychiatrist.
❑ Division Psychiatrist in the United States Army Medical Corps (Major), Republic of Vietnam.
❑ Medical Treatment Director for Suffolk County Mental Health Board, Narcotic Clinic, Hauppauge, NY.
❑ Recruited and worked as Senior Associate Medical Director for Sandoz Pharmaceutical in East Hanover, NJ.
❑ National/international lecturer, speaker, consultant, and presenter at conferences, conventions, symposiums, and meetings.
❑ A published author on various topics for numerous publications (specifics provided upon request).
❑ Expert medical consultant/witness on various subjects, including drugs, treatment, preventative medicine, and advertising.
❑ Proven experience in the area of change management, new-business development, and overall strategic planning.
❑ Experience in psychiatric/neurologic drug research and development.

CHRONOLOGY OF PROFESSIONAL EXPERIENCE

Sandoz Pharmaceuticals, East Hanover, Virginia   1986–Current
Senior Associate Medical Director

Private Practice—in association with Dr. Fredrick Apowitz, Smithtown, Virginia   1975–1986
Psychiatry (For Suffolk County Mental Health Boards)

Northeast Nassau Psychiatric Hospital, Kings Park, New York   1971–1975
Psychiatrist II and III

United States Army Medical Corps (Rep. of Vietnam)   1967–1971
Division Psychiatrist

SELECTED MEDICAL ARTICLES/REPORTS

"Brain Chemistry," *C&EN Magazine*, pp. 79–93, June, 1999
"Diet and Brain Function," *Nutrition Reviews/Supplement*, pp.12–15, May 1996
"Management of Adverse Events," a 21-page booklet, Sandoz Pharm. Corp., 1995

PROFESSIONAL AFFILIATIONS

American Medical Association
American Psychiatric Association
Association of Pharmaceutical Research Physicians
State Medical Societies—NJ, NM, NY, SC, VT
Chicago Medical School Alumni Association
Far Eastern Study Group of Archeological Association of Long Island, NY (Past President)
Stoney Brook Museum (Curator of Oriental Art)
Metropolitan Museum of Art (Consultant—Oriental Art)
Drew University, NJ (Curator of Ancient Art)
Archeological Institute of America (Lecturer)
Gemological Institute of America (Certified Gemologist)

References and Supporting Documentation Furnished upon Request

HOME COMPANION/HOME HEALTH AIDE/HOME MANAGMENT

MARY ROSE BUCKLEY

2300 Rollings Avenue • Baltimore, Maryland 21228 • (410) 555-1212 • email@email.com

---

HOME COMPANION/HOME HEALTH AIDE/HOME MANAGEMENT
Patient Advocate—Senior Populations

Unparalleled Quality Patient Care—Senior Populations

Housekeeping/Meal & Nutrition Management/Financial Management
Medication & Healthcare Oversight/Transportation Coordination
Personal Care & Activity Organization
Family& Social Liaison

Education/Training/Certifications

University of Maryland, Baltimore, Maryland
Bachelor of Arts: Education, 1985

Post-Graduate Studies and Professional Training

Business Curriculum—College of Business, University of Maryland, Baltimore, Maryland	1985 to 1987
Financial Accounting—College of Business, University of Maryland, Baltimore, Maryland	1988 to 1990
Life-Support Skill Training—Baltimore Emergency Medical Group, Baltimore, Maryland	1998 & 1999

Certification

Home Healthcare Companion Specialist—(HHCS)	Current
CPR and Advanced First Aid	Current
Advanced Cardiac Specialist	Current

■ Strong Computer Skills: MS Office

Work Experience

Confident Companions, Inc., Baltimore, Maryland   1994 to Current
Lead Companion
Home companion and health aide for well-respected couple in the D.C. area. Responsible for staff recruiting and management (cooking staff, lawn-maintenance crew, and transportation team). Major emphasis on medical care, including physical therapy, medication and nutrition management, and physician visitations and follow-up.

* Exceeded all household financial budget projection while exceeding quality of care
* Received two letters of appreciation from client's physician for exceptional medical attention in emergency situation
* Significantly improved staff morale and teamwork, resulting in higher productivity and overall production

Military Service

Healthcare Specialist, United States Navy, U.S. and Germany   1986 to 1994

* Achieved rank of Major—directing healthcare operations, central division (serving 17 bases and 40,000 soldiers)
* Received seven letters of commendation for outstanding work performance

References Furnished upon Request

STAFF NURSE—OPERATING ROOM

GRACE JENKINS, R.N., B.S.N.

736 Palm Aire Drive
Wellington, Florida 33414
(561) 555-1212

Seeking Position as...

STAFF NURSE—OPERATING ROOM
More than 5 Years' O.R./Critical-Care Experience—17 Years of Total Nursing Experience

Patient Advocate/Healthcare Advocate

**General/Vascular/Neuro/Orthopedic/Ophthalmology/Hand/Outpatient/Ambulatory Surgery
Fluent: English/Spanish**

Proven record of success as O.R. Nurse, able to excel in a high-intensive-care environment in a highly professional, cohesive, and compassionate manner. Independently initiate advanced perioperative care to patients, in conjunction with a team of other medical/health professionals. Recognized for sound clinical judgment in assessing, planning, implementing, documenting, and evaluating the perioperative process of nursing care.

CORE STRENGTHS

Communication skills (verbal & written)
Training, coaching, motivating, & supervising personnel
Problem solving in high-stress working conditions
Team player with other healthcare professionals

Organization, scheduling, & time-management skills
Up-to-date with latest healthcare technologies
Flexible & adaptable to changing environments
Client/patient relations and quality control

PROFESSIONAL EXPERIENCE

THE VETERANS ADMINISTRATION MEDICAL CENTER
West Palm Beach, Florida—1986 to Current

Staff Nurse/OR Nurse — 1989 to Current

- Full-time Staff Nurse in 6A—Acute Care—Medical/Surgical/Oncology/Hematology/Infectious-Disease Unit. Assess, plan, implement, and evaluate nursing care. Educate patients and family members relative to nursing protocol—policies/procedures, diet, medication (including Chemotherapy), and pre/postoperative procedures.
- Initiate, monitor and inform patient and family members about Chemotherapy. Document and communicate to appropriate personnel patient condition, treatment, progress, and other pertinent information relative to patient health.
- Work and train new staff members, serve as Unit Facilitator, and act as grief counselor for patients/family members.

Intermittent Registered Nurse — 1985 to 1989
West Palm Beach Veterans Administration Medical Center
West Palm Beach, Florida (Nurse Manager: Donna Echardt, RN)

- Same responsibilities as above, except Chemotherapy.

EDUCATION/QUALIFICATIONS

METROPLITAN COLLEGE, Rio Piedras, Puerto Rico
Bachelor of Science in Nursing, 1985

License: Professional Nursing License #015945/registration #95-025772
Current BCLS & ACLS, Recertification scheduled for April, 2005
HIV Counselor/Trained for Chemotherapy

PROFESSIONAL AFFILIATIONS (Past and Present)

Association of Operating Nurses, Florida/New York
Association of Critical Care Nurses, Florida

15

Nonprofit

GRANTS-MANAGEMENT SPECIALIST

LONNIE H. FRANKLIN
142 Glendale Court
Palm Beach Gardens, Florida 33418
Phone: (561) 555-1212/Email: email@email.com

Seeking Position as...

ASSOCIATE DIRECTOR, FLORIDA PHILANTHROPY
John D. & Catherine T. MacArthur Foundation

Grants-Management Specialist
* Foundation Resource * Community Resource * Fundraising

A highly organized, results-driven individual with professional qualifications in strategic planning, long/short-term goal setting, finance and budget management, program development, and personnel team-building and leadership. Equally effective in needs evaluation and identification, implementation, and outcome assessment. Recognized for outstanding lobbying skills, fundraising expertise, and resource utilization. Successfully blend experience in the private sector with nonprofit and volunteer service. Solid writing and presentation/public-speaking skills.

AREAS OF EXPERTISE

* Creative, visionary thinking and strategic planning
* Program/grant evaluation and enhancement
* Research, analysis, and assessment
* Intra-department/agency cooperation
* Policy and procedure development
* Networking—building key alliances/partnerships

* Grant making on contemporary issues
* Performance review and improvement
* Organizational leadership
* Cross-cultural training/supervision experience
* Volunteer recruitment, training, and supervision
* Integrity—maintaining high ethical standards

PROFESSIONAL EXPERIENCE

FLORIDA MEDICAL ASSOCIATION ALLIANCE, INC., Palm Beach Gardens, Florida   1994–Present
First Vice President/Member, Board of Directors

- Supervise and direct vice presidents in provision of resources, training, and support, to enhance operations of county medical alliance on a statewide basis. Served as District Vice President, Health Projects Chair, Annual Convention Chair/Co-chair, Coordinator of Idea Fair, Membership Summit, and S. District Workshop.
- Promoted optimal functioning of alliances in areas of public relations, fundraising, health-project administration, membership, and leadership development. Developed guidelines for implementation of Action Resource Team program to consult with alliances throughout the State of Florida. Developed/implemented $29,000 convention budget. Member of Finance Committee.
- Write in-depth, comprehensive reports. Developed state membership brochure, Health Projects Guide, and written guidelines for implementation of A.R.T. Program. Oral presentations.
- Selected as Grassroots Lobbyist to represent FMA/Alliance on key legislative health/safety issues. Spearheaded fundraising efforts for County Alliance, resulting in raising $80,000 in 1999 and $105,000 in 2001.
- Recipient of "Presidential Service Award," 1997–2001. Appointed to represent alliance on critical FMA committees.

EDUCATION

Bachelor of Arts in Social Work, 1985   DAMON   UNIVERSITY, Orlando, Florida
Leadership Conference, 1998   AMERICAN MEDICAL ASSOCIATION ALLIANCE, INC.

SELECTED VOLUNTEER AND COMMUNITY-SERVICE WORK

PALM BEACH COUNTY MEDICAL SOCIETY AUXILIARY, West Palm Beach, FL   1990–Present
Parliamentarian/Member, Board of Directors
- Former President, Treasurer, Assistant Treasurer
- Chaired Charity Review, Finance, Legislation, and Long-Range Planning Committees
- Recipient of Palm Beach County Medical Society Outstanding Service Award, 1995
- Recipient of FMA Alliance Membership Award, 1994, 1995, 1996, 1997, 1998, 1999, 2000, 2001

ASSOCIATION MANAGEMENT/DIRECTOR

SCOTT DAVID COOPERSMITH

6682 Blue Bay Circle • Chicago, Illinois 60662
(212) 555-1212 • Cell: (561) 555-4321 • email@email.com

ASSOCIATION MANAGEMENT/DIRECTOR
Increasing Membership, Profit Centers, and Members Services

**Educational-Program Development/Profit-Center Development & Enhancement
15 Years' Successful, Verifiable Experience in Building & Directing Trade Associations**

A dynamic, respected, and energetic professional-association management professional with 15+ years of growth-driven, bottom-line-oriented, membership-oriented expertise—integrating outstanding operations-management experience with new-member development.

Core Professional Strengths

Program and special-events development	Educational-program development
High-tech integration; Internet-driven programming	Operations and logistics control and coordination
Committee and volunteer coordination	Start-up management
Strategic planning and tactical implementation	Building key strategic partnerships and alliances

Professional Experience

AMERICAN ASSOCIATION OF CAREER COACHES   1985 to Current
Founder/Executive Director
Conceptualized and orchestrated the start-up and management of a new association targeting an up-and-coming niche market not previously served—career/employment coaches. Developed all marketing and collateral materials, policies and procedures, mission statements, and member programs, to successfully launch this organization. AACC has annual revenues in excess of $920,000.

- Took organization from start-up position to 1800 members in less than 36 months, with annual dues totaling $405,000.
- Developed, through committee participation, the first international certification program for career coaches.
- Initiated product sales (books, videos, and audiocassettes) adding $30,000 in gross revenues.
- Organized and executed annual conventions for 400–600 attendees—generating $295,000 in convention revenues.
- Developed 14 top-rated educational programs (in-person and Internet) contributing $48,000 in income to the association.
- Took advantage of the international market by building key international strategic alliances (300+ international members).
- Work with government agencies, including the Bureau of Labor Statistics, to enhance image and exposure of the association.
- Initiate and Coordinate a bi-annual employment conference involving six other employment-related organizations.
- Work with key national authors to endorse their works (when appropriate) to improve AACC exposure.

Education

St. Bonaventure University, St. Bonaventure, New York
Master's Degree: Public Administration, 1984

Hofstra University, Uniondale, New York
Bachelor of Arts: Public Administration, 1982

Activities

Member: American Association of Association Directors
Member: Association Training Institute of America
Volunteer: Junior Achievement

Additional Information, Documentation, and References Furnished upon Request

FOUNDATION DEVELOPMENT/DIRECTOR OF COMMUNITY RELATIONS

WAYNE JOHNSON

236 Seville Road
Denver, Colorado 80526
(310) 555-1212/email@email.com

FOUNDATION DEVELOPMENT/DIRECTOR OF COMMUNITY RELATIONS
Fundraising Expertise/Board Training & Development/Building Strategic Alliances

Organizational Leadership/Increasing Community Awareness & Giving
"Building Strength in Numbers"

A dynamic, creative, and top-performing foundation-development and community-relations specialist offering more than eight years of solid achievement in nonprofit environments.

CORE STRENGTHS

Strategic planning and implementation	Build and maintain key alliances/partnerships
Organizational leadership and empowerment	Identify/capitalize on emerging opportunities
Presentation and persuasion skills	Board relations and management
Fundraising management	Volunteer recruitment and supervision

PROFESSIONAL EXPERIENCE

AMERICAN HEART ASSOCIATION, Denver, Colorado   1989 to Current
Area Director/New-Business Development
Direct marketing and growth-oriented activities for a unique program, "Together for Life" (TFL), a partnership program between the American Heart Association and the American Cancer Society. Primary responsibilities include expanding the program by bringing in new participating organizations, and increasing the level of financial support from existing campaigns.

Provide volunteer speakers for company presentations, develop and train members of volunteer speakers' bureau, and manage/direct volunteer board of directors. Coordinate volunteer activities with company executives, make public presentations at community/organizational meetings/events, and raise the level of community awareness. Full-charge budgeting/finance responsibility for the entire program ($2.3 million annually).

- Directed 9-person fundraising team that raised $21.4 million over past three years.
- More than doubled the number of TFL partners, and achieved double-digit growth for past nine years.
- Nominated and selected for the prestigious "Leadership Seattle Award," 1998–2001.
- Spearheaded community-relations efforts that resulted in four major new sponsors ($3.5 million in pledge support).
- Orchestrated annual gala-event auction that raised more than $300,000 for five years running.

EDUCATION/TRAINING

FLORIDA STATE UNIVERSITY, Tallahassee, Florida
Bachelor of Science: Public Affairs Communication; Minor in Psychology, 1990

Dale Carnegie	• How to Win Friends, 2000
	• Salesmanship Skills, 1999
Computer Skills:	• Word, Excel, PowerPoint, QuickBooks, Access, PhotoShop, and Internet Applications
Member:	Toastmasters International
	American Association of Philanthropic Leaders
	National Association of Community Development Directors
	Seattle Chamber of Commerce (Former Membership Director)

References and Supporting Documentation Furnished upon Request

215

NONPROFIT FUND DEVELOPMENT EXECUTIVE

RICHARD P. ANDERSON	
1701 Village Boulevard, #112	email@email.com
Sarasota, Florida 38742	(812) 555-1212

NONPROFIT FUND DEVELOPMENT EXECUTIVE
31-Plus Years' Contribution to The Salvation Army
Raised $63+ million for The Salvation Army Over Past Twelve Years

OVERVIEW:

A dynamic, highly effective Development Director with a verifiable record of raising $63+ million for The Salvation Army between 1985 and 1997 (directly or indirectly). Successfully develop and implement sophisticated long and short-term fundraising strategies.

Recognized for analyzing and identifying highly targeted donor profiles for solicitation. Pursue funding sources through direct mail, special events, United Way, government sources, annual giving, "do-it-yourself," program fees, capital campaigns, and special grants.

Coordinate and direct high/low-dollar special events, maintain comprehensive prospect research database program, recruit and train volunteers, plan and create appropriate fundraising material, and evaluate and implement sweeping strategies to ignite fundraising efforts for individual, corporate, and foundation giving.

* Administration, organization, and management	* Senior-level decision making
* Major-gifts cultivation	* Effective board development
* Cause-related fundraising	* Corporate-giving cultivation
* Public/community relations	* Cultivate foundation support
* Prospect management	* Multiple-project management
* Finance management	* Verbal and written communications

HIGHLIGHTS OF EXPERIENCE:

♦ Directly/indirectly raised $63+ million for The Salvation Army over past twelve years.
♦ Project Share: Statewide Emergency Assistance Program providing assistance to 1000+ people.
♦ Cultivated Georgia Power to match dollar-for-dollar with Project Share. Raised $3.75 million annually.
♦ Secured $3 million foundation grant to build 13 service centers in rural Georgia (annual budget of $350,000/center).
♦ Raised $1.3 million to build Corps Community Center (capital campaign) in Griffin, GA (75,000 population).
♦ Secured $1 million endowment for Georgia Division.
♦ Secured foundation grant to enlarge dining-room/kitchen facilities at camp Grandview ($600,000).
♦ Designed the Georgia Development Program that included the following departments: Direct Mail—Division & Metro, Planned Giving Division, Project Share, Service Units and Centers, Volunteer Department, Public Relations.
♦ Directed program awarded *The Salvation Army's National Social Services Award* (Project Share).
♦ Designed Georgia Division Advisory Board Training & Development Program.

EMPLOYMENT:

THE SALVATION ARMY—Tennessee, Georgia, Florida
1963–1994/1997–Present

Development Director	West Palm Beach, FL 1997–Present
Divisional Development Director	Atlanta, GA 1990–1994
Social Services Director	Atlanta, GA 1984–1990
Business Administrator	Orlando, FL 1983–1984
Executive Director—Community Center	Orlando, FL 1982–1983
Executive Director—Community Center	Chattanooga, TN 1963–1982

(Page 1 of 3)

EMPLOYMENT:
(Continued)

Development Director, Sarasota, Florida   1997–Present
Florida Division

- Budget: $5 million; direct staff of five
- Created a Development Department responsible for all fundraising
- Coordinate public relations and direct mail campaigns; manage all special events
- Supervise Capital Campaign Phase II, major gift solicitations, and grant proposals

Divisional Development Director, Atlanta, GA   1990–1994
Georgia Division

- Budget: $8–$12 million; directed staff of 40
- Direct-Mail Division/Metro Atlanta—$5 million
- Planned Giving—$3 million
- Project Share—$4 million
- Service Unit/Service Centers—$3 million
- Grant Proposals—$1.5 million
- Special-Events Fundraising—$1 million
- Major Gifts—$200,000
- Oversaw Volunteer Department and Public Relations
- Initiated direct-mail marketing plan, increasing direct-mail contributions over 100%—$1.6 million to $3.4 million

Social Services Director—Metro Atlanta/Project Share Consultant, Atlanta, GA   1984–1990
Georgia Division

- Capital company raised $3 million
- Extensive consultations relative to Project Share

Social Services Director—Metro Atlanta/Project Share Director, Atlanta, GA   1985–1989
Georgia Division

- Budget for Project Share: $250,000; directed staff of four
- Raised $4 million annually

PROJECT SHARE:

- Provided assistance statewide—159 counties—100,000 annually
- Cultivated matching gifts from Georgia Power—dollar for dollar
- 2500 billboards posted annually—cost of printing only
- Secured TV and radio spots featuring the Governor and Lt. Governor annually
- Awarded The Salvation Army's national Social Services Award—first time in Southern Territory
- National Fuel Fund highlighted Project Share as model for Fuel Funds; largest Fuel Fund in United States

Social Services Director—Metro Atlanta, GA   1984–1985
Georgia Division

- Budget: $1 million; directed staff of 66
- Emergency Assistance Casework
- Directed Christmas Intake, Youth Shelter, Woman's Shelter, Family Shelter, Men's Shelter
- Supervised Job Training & Placement, G.E.D. Program, and How to Read Program
- Turned around program that was $300,000 in debt to $500,000+ in reserve

Richard P. Anderson
Page three

EMPLOYMENT:
(Continued)

Business Administrator, Orlando, FL   **1983–1984**
Florida Division

- Budget: $3.5 million; directed staff of 45
- Managed all Corps Programs; directed all fundraising activities
- Managed Social Service, Day Camp, and before/after School Programs
- Senior (HUD) High-Rise Housing; Adult Day Programming

Executive Director—Community Center, Orlando, FL   **1982–1983**
Florida Division

- Budget: $800,000; directed staff of 21, serving 600 members
- Secured grant for Before-School—After-School Program

Executive Director—Community Center, Chattanooga, TN   **1963–1982**
Kentucky/Tennessee Division

- Budget: $600,000; directed staff of 12, serving 1200 members
- Recipient of Tennessee Department Recreation Award for best recreation program in the state

---

EDUCATION & TRAINING:

University of Tennessee at Chattanooga, Chattanooga, TN
Bachelor of Science: Human Services Management, 1975
Emory University, Atlanta, GA
Certificate for Nonprofit Management, 1986
* Continuing Education: including graduate-level credits toward MBA
* Computer Skills: Windows 3.1/95, Excel, Word, PowerPoint, Quicken, QuickBooks, WordPerfect, Lotus 1-2-3, and Corel Draw.

AFFILIATIONS:

National Association of Fundraising Executives   American Correctional Association
National Fuel Fund Association   American Jail Association
*(Presenter and speaker at all the above mentioned conferences)

- References, Supporting Documentation, and Success Portfolios Furnished upon Request -

FUNDRAISING PROFESSIONAL

MARY BELLE JACKSON

8310 Sands Point Boulevard, Bldg. L #308
Seattle, Washington 98376
Cell Phone: (941) 555-1212/Home: (941) 555-4343
Email: email@email.com

FUNDRAISING PROFESSIONAL

Raising Money in a Philanthropic Spirit of Community Giving

**Volunteer Management/Event Planning and Execution/Corporate-Giving Management
Organizational Leadership/Team Building**

A highly competitive, self-motivated, and accomplished professional with a proven, verifiable track record for raising money for worthy causes.

CORE STRENGTHS

Strategic planning and implementation	Building and maintaining key alliances/partnerships
Prospecting, cold-canvassing, and networking	Key-project/event management
Presentation/public-speaking skills	Negotiation, persuasion and solid closing expertise
Office-management and administrative skills	Public/community relations
Fundraising and committee leadership	Budget management and expense control
Mail-order and direct marketing	Newspaper, radio, and television advertising

HIGHLIGHTS OF EXPERIENCE

SEATTLE CHAMBER OF COMMERCE, Seattle, Washington   1994 to Current
Director of Membership Services

<u>Fundraising responsibilities:</u> Solicit donations and coordinate silent auctions and special programs for various Chamber fundraising events. Target and recruit members to participate in all such activities. Schedule all personnel for fundraising events. Act as liaison between chamber members and community organizations. Invoice all participants and ensure collections of monies owed.

<u>Membership-services responsibilities:</u> Direct new-member-recruiting efforts via cold-canvassing, networking, building community and business alliances, and following up on in-house leads. Encourage members to become actively engaged with chamber committees and to take best advantage of chamber membership. Organize, coordinate, and attend monthly membership breakfasts and business-after-hours networking events. Generate and review reports for preparation of invoicing monthly membership-renewal billing.

<u>Office-management responsibilities:</u> Ensure that all new members are entered into computer database, receive welcome phone call upon joining, and that they receive new-member information packets. Prepare and attend monthly Board of Director's Meetings, taking and transcribing Board minutes. Provide input and proof/edit monthly newsletter. Notarize and seal Certificates of Origin for export companies. Supervise daily office procedures.

- Ignited new Chamber of Commerce memberships from 2200 to more than 5000.
- Raised more than $2.3 million for key fundraising events over 7-year period.
- Significantly increased membership participation in the various chamber committees.
- Played a pivotal role to dramatically enhance membership retention through aggressive/creative communications methods.
- Personally sit on two committees and have increased membership on the Ambassador Committee from 10 to 40 people.
- A major contributor to fundraising and revenue-generating events (silent auctions, corporate events, and special programs).
- Coordinated "Signature Awards Dinner," Business Expo, and Business/Community Holiday Fest fundraising events.
- Gave speech representing the Chamber on Veteran's Day at a ceremony honoring Wal-Mart for their fundraising program.

(Page 1 of 2)

MARY BELLE JACKSON
Page two

HIGHLIGHTS OF EXPERIENCE (Continued)

MACY'S, Seattle, Washington   1992 to 1994
Sales/Customer-Service Representative
Responsible for sales and service of Macy's customers in the shoe department as well as fine jewelry department.

- Consistently met and/or exceeded all sales and service goals.

THOMAS M. DACHELET, P.A., Seattle, Washington   1989 to 1992
WASHINGTON STATE ATTORNEY'S OFFICE, Seattle, Washington   1987 to 1989
Legal Secretary
Worked as a legal secretary at various stages throughout career, including one year with the State Attorney's Office.

- Worked in many areas of law, including real estate, wills and estate planning, theatrical, and matrimonial law.
- Efficiently prepared court documents and submitted them to the courts.
- Prepared proposed prospectus for theatrical plays—representing known television and movie personalities.

BOOT AND SHOE FACTORY CLEARANCE OUTLET, New York, New York   1979 to 1987
Owner/General Manager/Business Development
Owned and operated three (3) retail shoe stores and mail order business. Sourced new products; purchased and managed inventory; hired, trained and supervised personnel; and directed all sales and marketing efforts. Ensured customer satisfaction.

- Oversaw start-up operations and grossed $100,000 after first year in business.
- Increased sales over 100% in second year with revenues exceeding $224,000.
- Opened second retail store and improved sales annual to over half-a-million dollars.
- Saw opportunity to open third store and attained $1.1 million in revenues maintaining solid profit margins.

EDUCATION/TRAINING

Associates degree: Barry University, Seattle, Washington, 1978

Heffley & Browne, Brooklyn, Seattle, Washington
Court Reporting Course, Legal Terminology, Bookkeeping, Office Management

Workshops/Continuing Education:
- Fundamentals of Fundraising, National Association of Fundraising Executives, 2000
- Understanding Yourself and Others, Educational Systems, 1999
- Housing & Development Workshop (Sun Trust Bank), 1999

Additional Skills:
- Computer Skills: Windows, Word, Excel, WordPerfect, Lotus, and Internet Applications
- Notary Public, Seattle

PROFESSIONAL AFFILIATIONS

Member: National Society of Fund Raising Executives
Member: Educational Systems
Fundraiser: Numerous Community and Civic Organizations

References Furnished upon Request

PROGRAM COORDINATOR

JEANNIE M. HOBAN, MSW

201 Monceaux Road * Dallas, Texas 75201 * (214) 555-1212 * email@email.com

---

PROGRAM COORDINATOR
New-Program Coordination/Fundraising/Resource Utilization/Collaborative Management
- Eleven Years' Successful Experience in Nonprofit Environments -

* Program/event coordination
* Strategic planning and implementation
* Research and evaluation expertise
* Total-quality management
* Highly effective grant writing

* Individual and group counseling
* Facilitation of volunteer training sessions
* Networking—key contact development
* Business development, sales and marketing
* Organizing and coordinating fundraising events

PROFESSIONAL EXPERIENCE

15TH JUDICIAL CIRCUIT, COURT ADMINISTRATION, Dallas, Texas   1992 to Current
Domestic Violence Program Coordinator—Nonprofit Organization

- Coordinate all Domestic Violence Services through Court Administration. Wrote court proposal for Chief Judge (mentioned in *Dallas Tribune*). Produce and distribute a Resource Guide for the community and made information available on the Internet. Supervise staff and visitation program. Assisted in the coordination of the International Supervised Network Conference.

- Currently establishing a staffed childcare program for parents and caregivers who are in court. Wrote State Justice Institute grant for South County Internet Project. Successfully procured grants and coordinated large-scale fundraising events—$28,000 SJI (1997) and $35,000 VOCA (1996). Continuously network and interface with affiliated programs for funding and referrals. Serve as liaison with community groups and the judiciary. Created innovative programs for women and children.

SOUTHWESTERN COMMUNITY COLLEGE, Dallas, Texas   1990 to Current
Adjunct Professor (Part-time)

- Prepared syllabus, lesson plans, and exams for social science course. Maintained attendance and academic records. Assisted students after class or by appointment.

PARENT-CHILD CENTER, INC., Dallas, Texas   1988 to 1992
Family Services Specialist—Nonprofit Organization

- Established program for victims of domestic violence. Supervised four contract therapists, two interns, and eight volunteers for victim-services component. Facilitated women's support group (VOICES), planned community activities, maintained involvement with affiliated groups and coalitions, and provided case management. Developed and managed Project Debby. Also provided training and in-services to the community. Organized major fundraising events.

- Facilitated victims' support group, performed individual/group therapy, and provided case management and in-home visits. Taught violence-prevention curriculum in schools and conducted workshops for community groups.

EDUCATION AND TRAINING

FLORIDA INTERNATIONAL UNIVERSITY, Miami, Florida
Master of Social Work, 1994

BARRY UNIVERSITY, Miami, Florida
Bachelor of Science: Liberal Studies, 1992

* Certified Children's Case Manager
* Certified Victim Services Practitioner

* Trained in Love and Logic Parenting Facilitation
* Certified Facilitator of Batterer's Intervention Programs

COMMUNITY AFFILIATIONS

* Domestic Violence Council, Executive Committee   1994–Present
* Texas Coalition Against Domestic Violence   1996–Present
* Rebecca's House Transitional Living Shelter, Board Member   1998–Present

References Furnished upon Request.

PUBLIC RELATIONS/MARKETING/CORPORATE COMMUNICATIONS EXPERT

MARY ELLEN JOHNSTON, APR
1705-2 Sea Oats Lane
Juno Beach, FL 33408
Phone: (561) 555-1212/Email: email@email.com

PUBLIC RELATIONS/MARKETING/CORPORATE COMMUNICATIONS
ENHANCING EXPOSURE FOR NONPROFIT ENVIRONMENTS
Nationally Accredited by the Public Relations Society of America

A highly creative and proactive communications expert with qualifications in competitive market analysis, strategic positioning, and implementing effective programs to meet business-development goals for **NON-PROFIT** organizations.

AREAS OF STRENGTH

Networking—forming key collaborative alliances	Conceptual strategist—creative thinker
Key-project management (small–large)	Market research and analysis
Public-speaking/speech-writing skills	Advertising (print media, radio, TV, Internet)
Fundraising and community service	Finance and budgeting ($500,000+) skills
Staff/volunteer training and management	Customer-service management/retention
New-business development	Crisis communications

PROFESSIONAL EXPERIENCE

GROWING TOGETHER, INC. (A Community Chest/United Way Agency), Lake Worth, FL   1994–Present
Director of Development—Public Relations
Direct all aspects of fundraising for this nonprofit residential substance-abuse treatment facility serving adolescents. Program assists clients and their entire families. Treatment fees are subsidized 50% or more through fundraising efforts. As Director of Development, direct all fundraising (corporate/individual), special fundraising programs and events, grant writing, and long/short-term strategic planning. As Director of Public Relations, establish high-visibility contact with all media sources, the community, and collaborative agencies and support resources.

- Spearheaded fundraising programs and efforts accounting for 1/3–1/2 of the annual $900,000 budget.
- Wrote, delivered oral presentation for, and awarded $100,000 grant for much-needed computer system.
- Conceptualized and manage new volunteer auxiliary unit, which raised $12,000 during initial fundraising program.
- Successfully gained needed public exposure through aggressive media relations and communications efforts.

PALM BEACH COUNTY PRIVATE INDUSTRY COUNCIL, West Palm Beach, FL   1989–1994
Director of Marketing
Responsible for all public relations and marketing programs for $12 million organization charged with training, retraining, and job placement of unemployed and underemployed individuals. Worked closely with community and employers to enhance program visibility and success. Developed newsletters and promotional materials.

- Played leadership role in developing numerous community alliances with key supporting agencies and organizations.
- Successfully involved tourism officials in collaborative plan to attract new business and jobs to western communities.
- Collaborated with the Palm Beach Post to produce and distribute summer youth-employment tab section.

EDUCATION

Bachelor of Arts: Mass Communication   UNIVERSITY OF MIAMI
Public Administration (Marketing Fellowship)   UNIVERSITY OF SOUTHERN CALIFORNIA

- Computer Skills: Windows, WordPerfect, Microsoft Word, Aldus, PageMaker, and Internet Applications

- References Furnished Immediately upon Request -

RESEARCH PROFESSIONAL

NANCY G. GILBERT, Ph.D.
2 Diamond Back Road
North Reading, Massachusetts 01864
(985) 555-1212/email@email.com

RESEARCH PROFESSIONAL
Theoretical & Applied Research/Laboratory & Field Experience

Providing Vital Information for Nonprofit Organizations

A dynamic, highly enthusiastic and motivated individual offering outstanding analytical, strategic-development/implementation, organizational, and problem-solving/troubleshooting skills supported by a solid, successful 15-year track record having worked ...

* **On NASA, U.S. Army, and Florida Legislative Education Grants**
* **As a Research Associate—Columbia University and Nova Southeastern University**
* **As a Statistical Analyst, Tufts University Engineering & Design Research Department (Funded by E.I. DuPont Corporation)**

AREAS OF EXPERTISE

Research Design & Implementation	Market-Research & Survey Methods
Product Engineering & Design	Information-Systems Management
Complex Problem Solving & Troubleshooting	Multivariate-Data Analysis
Project/Personnel Management	Task Analysis
Grant Writing & Technical-Report Development	Human-Performance Management
Public-Speaking/Professional-Presentation Skills	Technical Engineering
Mathematical Modeling & Scaling	Psychophysics

EDUCATION

Ph.D. Experimental Psychology, 1983   COLUMBIA UNIVERSITY
M.Phil. Psychology, 1982
M.A. Psychology, 1976
B.Sc. Mathematics/Psychology, 1975   TUFTS UNIVERSITY

PROFESSIONAL EXPERIENCE

1998–Present

RESEARCH ASSOCIATE: Design and conduct research projects evaluating intervention programs (early-learning program for children with autism and other related disorders)   **- Peter J. Baudhuin Foundation**

PRINCIPLE INVESTIGATOR: A task-analytic approach to teaching practical life skills to children with autism. Designed and conducted research project to evaluate various task-analytic approaches to teaching tooth brushing to preschool children with autism and other related disorders.   **- Peter J. Baudhuin Foundations**

BOIDOIN RESEARCH: Independent research on Attention Deficit Disorder and curriculum planning. Fundraising options and feasibility for University School, Boston University.   **- Boston University, Nonprofit & Funding Division**

1985–1998

NASA CONTRACT: "Acoustically Induced Visualization Interrupts Visual Information Acquisition." Designed and conducted experiments investigating behavioral breakdown due to cognitive overload in an applied setting. Subjects were monitored dials on an instrument panel, viewing a video recording of an approach to an airport recorded from the cockpit of a small airplane. The experiment evaluated varying technologies that use eye movement to rack cognitive overload, and resulted in an alternative and less-expensive equipment design to the Gulf and Western Eye Tracker.   **- Psychophysics Laboratory, Columbia University**

U.S. ARMY CONTRACT: "Human Performance at Night and in Darkness." Designed and conducted experiments that investigated the psychophysical responses of subjects to acoustic noise (annoyance and loudness) presented in the dark and in the light.   **- Psychophysics Laboratory, Columbia University**

(page 1 of 2)

NANCY G. GILBERT, Ph.D.
Page two

PROFESSIONAL EXPERIENCE (Continued)

NASA CONTRACT: "A New Scaling Method to Quantify Individual Attitudes During Social Surveys." Analyzed data generated from a survey in which 120 residents of communities near JFK Airport were interviewed. Coauthored technical reports and a paper presented at the Eastern Psychological Association Meetings, Washington, D.C., 3/78.

- Psychophysics Laboratory, Columbia University

RESEARCH ASSOCIATE: For professors whose research interests include human factors, psychoacoustics, visual-form perception, mathematical modeling, and scaling. Duties included the design, execution, analysis, and presentation of data from these experiments. **- Columbia University**

TEACHING ASSISTANT: For one graduate and three undergraduate-level courses (Introduction to Mathematical and Statistical Methods, Introductory Psychology, and Experimental Psychology) **- Columbia University**

HONORS

Faculty Fellowship in Psychology, Columbia University, 1975–1979
Honorary Fellow to New England Psychological Association, 1975
Scholarship, United Aircraft, 1971–1975

PUBLICATIONS/WRITINGS/ THESES

* Graham, N., Kramer, P., and Gilbert, N. Attending to the Spatial Position of Near-Threshold Visual Patterns. In M.I. Posner & O.S.M. Marin (Eds.), Attention and Performance (pp. 269–284). Hillsdale, NJ. Lawrence Erlbaum Associates. (1985)
* Gilbert, N. Correlation of Noise Sources and Bandwidth Estimates: "An Analysis of a Multiple-Channels Model of Visual-Form Perception." Unpublished Master's Thesis, Columbia University.
* Gilbert, N. "Temporal Characteristics of Emotional Response. A Decay Model of Annoyance Response to Acoustic Noise." Unpublished Doctoral Dissertation, Columbia University.

References on Request

COMMUNITY-RELATIONS MANAGER/
NONPROFIT VOLUNTEER-CENTER DIRECTOR

LESLIE L. JOHNSTON

2629 East Way, #1
Newton, New Jersey 07860
(973) 555-1212
email@email.com

COMMUNITY-RELATIONS MANAGER/NONPROFIT VOLUNTEER-CENTER DIRECTOR
Combining Outstanding Social Services Experience with Solid Leadership Skills

Volunteer Management/Organizational Leadership/Logistics Management
Community & Media Relations/Program Development & Enhancement
Business Development, Marketing, & Growth Leadership

A dynamic, team-spirited, and results-oriented individual with more than five years' successful experience blending seasoned social work experience with proven administrative and business-development skills. Recognized for creating strategic business/community alliances, and for creative, high-impact marketing and business-development proficiency.

AREAS OF STRENGTH

Recruiting, training, and team-building	Program development and enrichment
Community, media, and public relations	New-business development and expansion
Counseling, coaching, and conflict resolution	Volunteer management and empowerment
Internal career pathing and mentoring coordination	Manage multiple complex tasks effectively
Change management—long/short-term strategic planning	Finance and budget management

FORMAL EDUCATION

Master of Social Work, 1995   FLORIDA STATE UNIVERSITY, Tallahassee, Florida
Bachelor of Science, Sociology, 1993   FLORIDA STATE UNIVERSITY, Tallahassee, Florida

* Licensed Clinical Social Worker, State of New Jersey

PROFESSIONAL EXPERIENCE

MENTOR CENTER OF MARTIN COUNTY, Springfield, New Jersey   1995 to Current
Executive Director
(Mentor Center is a nonprofit countywide initiative to promote youth mentoring)

Community/Media Relations:
- Created highly successful advertisement/mentor-recruitment campaign utilizing diverse strategic efforts
- Developed and presently maintain solid media relations with television, radio, and print-media contacts
- Generated high-visibility exposure in all media—TV, radio, and print media
- Created media kits for the organization and special press kits for specific events

Business Development/Marketing:
- Developed strategic plan and annual budget ($200K) for communitywide resource, serving community of 2 million
- Established Quality Assurance standards for mentoring programs to use as benchmark for future program development
- Received grant award of $100,000 to develop one of two pilot mentor-training institutes in the nation
- Generated more than $300,000 in donated services in first year of operations, contributing to program success

Training & Development:
- Developed "professional development series" for nonprofit mentoring programs on a quarterly basis
- Conducted specialized training for School District of Martin County staff—in support of 21,000 public-school volunteers
- Provided consultation and technical assistance to over 30 nonprofit and corporate organizations
- Initiated training seminars to organizations interested in developing youth-mentoring programs

(Page 1 of 2)

Leslie L. Johnston
Page two

PROFESSIONAL EXPERIENCE

MENTOR CENTER OF MARTIN COUNTY
(Continued):

Volunteer Management:
- Recruited and conducted orientation for more than 200 mentors within first six months of recruitment campaign
- Provide ongoing training sessions to mentors in preparing them for mentoring relationships
- Developed and maintain up-to-date database of mentors recruited, trained, and matched
- Assist volunteers in selecting volunteer opportunities from 15 organizations

Team Building and Relationship Development:
- Created strategic partnerships with local corporations and professional associations to increase mentor-recruitment efforts
- Served as liaison between mentoring organizations and corporations to ensure success of the alliance
- Developed collaborative nonprofit network (15 organizations) previously competing for volunteer base

NEW JERSEY COMMUNITY COLLEGE, Worthington, New Jersey   1996 to Current
Adjunct Faculty Instructor—Center for Personalized Education

- Internal Career Pathing/Mentoring; Program/curriculum development; classroom facilitation (30+ students)

PROFESSIONAL EXPERIENCE (Prior to 1995)

ST. MARY'S MEDICAL CENTER (Dept. of Child Development), Trenton, New Jersey   1990 to 1995
Family Services Coordinator

- Provided in-home therapy and case management services for 60 families in Suffolk County (women/children)
- Responsible for program development, team building, administrative oversight, reporting, and community outreach
- Developed and nurtured strong partnerships internally and with other network organizations

WESTERN COUNTY MENTAL HEALTH CLINIC, Hanover, New Jersey   1984 to 1990
Family Therapist—Family Strengthening Program

- Constructed family-assessment instrument and additional clinical-documentation forms for new program
- Functioned as lead therapist for a team comprising of three staff professionals
- Conducted individual and family assessments and psychotherapy in school, clinic, and home environments
- Served as Spokesperson for the Family Strengthening Program—created/distributed PR/marketing materials

BIG BROTHERS/BIG SISTERS OF PB COUNTY, Trenton, New Jersey   1980 to 1984
Social Worker II

- Trained and supervised a caseload of 35 active volunteer mentors—conducted orientation for 100+ volunteers/year
- Interviewed and matched more than 50 children per year with mentors, supervising 30+ volunteers
- Coordinated activities of 45 additional volunteers in four after-school mentoring programs
- Prepared and coached volunteers and youths for media interviews and public speaking

AFFILIATIONS/ACTIVITIES

Member, Directors of Volunteer Services of Martin County
Member, Habitat for Humanity (Family Selection and Nurturing Committee)

References and Supporting Documentation Furnished upon Request

16
Professional

ACCREDITED AIRPORT EXECUTIVE

JAY L. GREENMAN, A.A.E.
112 Southeast Cobra Cove Terrace
Hobe Sound, Florida 33455

email@email.com
(561) 555-1212

ACCREDITED AIRPORT EXECUTIVE
10 Years as Director of Planning & Development at Medium-Hub Airport
AIRPORT SECURITY EXPERT
Aviation Development/Environmental Permitting/Visionary Leadership/Team Building

✈ Sixteen years' aviation experience and ten exemplary years of service as Director of Planning and Development for the Palm Beach County Department of Airports, representing the Director of Airports in all matters relating to strategic planning (short/long-term); project management; facility replacement, rehabilitation, and development; intergovernmental coordination; site selection and acquisition; environmental permitting/compliance; tenant relations/leasehold modifications; finance management/capital-improvement budgeting; consultant and construction/ design management; media relations; and grant management.

✈ Outstanding qualifications in personnel management, team building, and optimizing individual and group productivity. An excellent track record of working extraordinarily well with boards of directors, airlines, concessionaires, government agencies, and the public at large.

HIGHLIGHTS OF ACHIEVEMENT

- Coordinated planning and development of new "Reliever Airport" (North County General Aviation Airport)—site selection, land acquisition, environmental permitting, design, construction, and selection/hiring of management firm (Only airport built in Florida over the past 20 years). Recipient of "Airport Project of the Year Award."

- Recipient of "FAA Southeast Region Environmental Award."

- Developed Master Plan and revised antiquated plans for Palm Beach International Airport and three reliever airports.

- Coordinated integration project of a new U.S. Customs facility with main terminal at PBI Airport. Managed project from design through completion. Increased passenger processing capability from 50 to 250 per hour.

- Spearheaded the design, development, and construction of a 50,000 square-foot air-cargo facility at PBI Airport. Facility included an aircraft apron for three wide-body aircraft.

- Sought/received approval for a Passenger Facility Charge through the FAA. This resulted in the funding of $47 million to be applied to capital improvement projects.

- Purchased over 500 parcels (190+ acres) of land adjacent to PBI Airport for noise abatement and proposed future development. Negotiated win-win agreements with all parties.

- Obtained approval for a Foreign Trade Zone with sites at North County and PBI Airports.

PROFESSIONAL EXPERIENCE

PALM BEACH COUNTY DEPARTMENT OF AIRPORTS, Florida   1985–Present
Director of Planning and Development (1987–Present)
Planning Manager/Noise Abatement Officer (1985–1987)

Planning: Administrator of short/long-term planning efforts for PBI Airport and three general-aviation airports. Responsible for preparation of Aviation Element of County's Comprehensive Plan and Airport Zoning Ordinance. Direct Airport Cargo Development Plan and Foreign Trade Zone approval process. Managed four Airport Master Plans, four Environmental Assessments, one Terminal Area Plan, one Cargo Development Study, and one Noise Compatibility Plan.

(Experience Continued on Page Two)

JAY L. GREENMAN, A.A.E.
Page two

PROFESSIONAL EXPERIENCE *(Continued)*

Environmental Issues: Prepared one of the nation's first FAR Part 150 Noise Compatibility Programs, establishing groundbreaking noise-abatement and mitigation activities, including the creation of noise-based operating fees. Conceived and managed 500-parcel noise-and-land acquisition program. Initiated residential sound insulation program—sound insulated large middle school. Obtained environmental permits for new airport—working closely with the Army Corps of Engineers and the FAA. Prepare and submit annual environmental impact reports for the airports.

Finance & Budget Management: Prepare and administer Planning & Development Division's operating budget. Responsible for airport system capital improvement budget—fiscal 1997, totaling $40 million. The CIP budget has increased over the past several years in response to customer demand and business development efforts.

Management: Responsible for recruiting and managing airport staff, including planners, engineers, construction supervisors, contract managers, and clerical staff personnel. Key department liaison to other county departments, including County Attorney; Employee Relations; Minority Business Development; Planning, Zoning and Building; Purchasing; Risk Management; and County Administration—to ensure that common goals are met.

Design, Construction, Permitting: Manage the design and construction of small to large-size capital improvement projects, including new runways, taxiways, aprons, passenger terminal improvements, Federal Inspection Stations, air cargo facilities, airfield signage and lighting, Part 107 security improvements, airside and landside roadways, fuel farms, and aircraft maintenance hangers. Complete all permitting necessary for airport development and redevelopment.

Properties: Prepare Minimum Standards documents for tenant improvements on airport property. Review and carry out approval responsibility for all tenant leasehold modifications and improvements. Review and comment on nonstandard leases prepared by properties section. Coordinate with tenants on construction projects.

Communications-Media/Public Relations: Represent the department in public meetings—ranging in size from simple presentations for small civic and community organizations to well-attended "spirited" public hearings on complex issues. Frequently interviewed by television, radio, and print media with highly favorable results.

Federal and State Grants: Secure and administer federal and state grants for four separate airports. During fiscal year 1997, successfully managed AIP grants and State of Florida Grants for these airports. Obtained approval to collect Passenger Facility Charges.

BROWN & ASSOCIATES, St. Louis, Missouri   1982–1985
Contract Employee to St. Louis Airport Authority

Served as project Planner for Airport Environs Plan. The Plan's purpose was to develop strategies for reducing the number of people exposed to aircraft noise.

EDUCATION

SOUTHWEST MISSISSIPPI STATE UNIVERSITY, Springfield, Mississippi
Bachelor of Science: Urban and Regional Planning, 1979
Geographic Honor Society

AFFILIATIONS & RECOGNITIONS

- American Association of Airport Executives—Accredited Executive
- Florida Airport Managers Association
- Chairman: Florida Aviation System Plan for Palm Beach, Fort Lauderdale, Miami, and the Florida Keys
- Resolution of Appreciation—Florida Aviation System Plan Steering Committee, for efforts to modify state statutes

CERTIFIED EXECUTIVE CHEF/CHEF INSTRUCTOR

ANDREW J. OFFERHAUS, C.C.C., C.E.C.

4823 Via Palm Lake Suite 1316
Beverly Hills, California 93422
(650) 555-1212/email@email.com

CERTIFIED EXECUTIVE CHEF/CHEF INSTRUCTOR
Five-Star Chef for Top-Ranked Culinary Organizations
Maintain Highest Quality Standards/Achieve Budget Numbers

Professional qualifications in Fine, Five-Star Dining, as Executive Chef and Chef Instructor. Recognized for team-oriented, regimented management style resulting in consistent, five-star service.

EDUCATION AND CREDENTIALS

THE CULINARY INSTITUTE OF AMERICA, Hyde Park, New York
* **Bachelor of Science: Culinary Arts, 1978**
* **Externship, Ritz Carlton, New York, 1976–78**

ORWELL COOKING INSTITUTE, London, England
* **Certified Master Chef, 1979**

AMERICAN CULINARY FEDERATION, St. Augustine, Florida
* **Certified Executive Chef; Certified Chef de Cuisine, 1979**

CULINARY AWARDS AND SELECTED RECOGNITIONS

Gold Medal, Awarded 1st Place, Hilton Head Island, South Carolina, Seafood Cook-Off, 2000
Gold Medal, Awarded 1st Place, Boston Seafood Extravaganza, 2000
Gold Medal, Awarded Hot Food Competition, Orlando Food Expo, 2000
Gold Medal, Awarded S.E. Food Service Expo—Hot Food Mystery Box Competition, 1999
Silver Medal, Awarded S.E. Food Service Expo—Hot Food Mystery Box Competition, 1999
Silver Medal, Seafood Cook-Off of Florida, St. Augustine, FL, 1998
Silver Medal, Awarded nationally to compete in NAFEM Culinary Competition, 1997
Featured in *Chef Magazine* (11/97, p.70): Article entitled "Char grilled Sea Bass," 1999 and 2000

HIGHLIGHTS OF PROFESSIONAL EXPERIENCE

* Performed exclusive catering for U.S. government officials, royalty, and international guests.
* As Chef Instructor, taught international cuisine, coached student team to Gold Medal.
* As Banquet Chef, planned and executed functions ranging in size from 20 to 15,000 people, managing 62 chefs.
* As Garde Manger Chef, responsible for cold food preparation, menu planning, and alterations.
* Coordinated costing & banquet planning, purchasing/inventory control, and projected/maintained food and labor costs.
* Current Advertising Chairman/Vice President: Northern California Chef's Association (NCCA).

CHRONOLOGY OF PROFESSIONAL EXPERIENCE

Executive Chef, Palm Springs Polo Club, Palm Springs, California	1997 to Current
Chef Instructor, California Culinary Institute, Los Angeles, California (Weekends)	1992 to Current
Executive Chef, Grand Hilton, Beverly Hills, California	1985 to 1997
Executive Chef, Eastpointe Country Club, Palm Springs, California	1982 to 1985
Executive Sous Chef, Mariner Sands Hotel & Club, San Diego, California	1980 to 1982

References on Request

ASSOCIATE/CORPORATE COUNSEL

BERNARD BUCKLAND

285 Eagle Trace • Sudbury, Ontario, Canada P3B 4K1 • Phone: (705) 555-1212 • email@email.com

---

ASSOCIATE/CORPORATE COUNSEL
20 Years of Legal Experience in United States and Canada

Tax-Reduction Expertise/Consultant

A dynamic and enterprising individual with 20 years of successful legal experience with emphasis on tax law, business and contract law, insurance law, real-estate law, and jury and nonjury litigation.

HIGHLIGHTS OF EMPLOYMENT

- Developed regional reputation in corporate world for significantly reducing tax liabilities and legal expenses.
- Integrated analytical and strategic planning in attaining success in trials and board hearings on behalf of company.
- Selected as Board President for three Sudbury organizations—sit on four corporate boards.

CHRONOLOGY OF EMPLOYMENT

THE CHAMPEANNE COMPANY, Sudbury, Ontario, Canada   1993 to Current
Lead Corporate Counsel

- Reduced tax liability by more than $12 million between 1993 and 2002 through corporate-status restructure.
- Reviewed four major long-term contracts and renegotiated them—earning the company an additional $8.7 million.
- Successfully negotiated four union agreements in a professional and win-win manner with no work stoppage.
- Work closely with president and top vice presidents on all legal and contractual activities.
- Represent the company in community, volunteer, and civic work, to give back to the community.

PARISE & HENNESSY FOODS, Sudbury, Ontario, Canada/New York, New York   1985 to 1993
Corporate Attorney

- Worked on all vendor and subcontractor legal agreements/documents for this $124 million food manufacturer.
- Negotiated long and short-term agreements for partnership relationships for food products.
- Contributing team member in working with top executives to reduce legal costs and liabilities as a food manufacturer.
- Spent 60% of time in Canada and 40% in New York—incorporating and optimizing both legal systems.

EDUCATION/BAR ADMITTANCE

UNIVERSITY OF WINDSOR, Windsor, Ontario, Canada
L.L.B. Degree. (Juris Doctor), 1984

LAURENTIAN UNIVERSITY, Sudbury, Ontario, Canada
Bachelor of Arts: Economics, 1981

MEMBER: Ontario Bar, 1980 to Current

BOARD EXPERIENCE

Idylwylde Golf Club, 1993–97 (Board President 1995–1997)
Ontario Association of Family Services Agencies, 1985–1993 (President 1989–1991)
Service Familial de la Region de Sudbury, Inc., Sudbury Family Services, 1984–1991
Centre Franco-Ontarien de Folklore, 1984–88 (President 1987–1988)
Children's Aid Society, 1985–1990 (Board Member)

References and Supporting Documentation Furnished upon Request

FLIGHT ATTENDANT

janice f. brooks

108 Paradise Harbour Boulevard, Apt. 405
Fallbrook, California 92028
Phone: (760) 555-1212/Cell: (760) 555-2323
email@email.com

FLIGHT ATTENDANT—FOR A MAJOR AIRLINE
Customer Service/Problem Solving/Organizational Expertise
10 Years of Impeccable Flying Experience

Outstanding Interpersonal and Rapport-building Skills
Recognized as a Team Player/Leader

A hard-working, service-oriented professional recognized as an enthusiastic team player dedicated to enhancing organizational goals and objectives. More than 15 successful years in fast-track service environments.

CORE STRENGTHS

Policy and procedure enforcement
Crisis management
First Aid and CPR training
Training and development
Creative and innovative

Regulatory compliance
Organizational leadership/team building
Communication skills (verbal/written)
Flexible and adaptable
Quality control

PROFESSIONAL EXPERIENCE

WINGS OF MAN EXECUTIVE TRANSPORT, San Diego, California   1992 to Current
Lead Flight Attendant

- Ensure outstanding customer service and that all guests safely enjoy their flying experience.
- Train and develop new hires over the 3½ years as senior employee with the airline.
- Developed policy and procedures manual leading to improved efficiency and substantial cost savings.
- Successfully maintained calm and order during two emergency landings.

IBIS GOLF & COUNTRY CLUB, La Jolla, California   1988 to 1992
Assistant Manager

- Consistently meet/exceed club-member expectations while managing main dining room.
- Hired, trained, and supervised a staff of 34 people, including eight chefs and four supervisors.
- Managed and coordinated banquets ranging in size from 15 to 650 people.

EDUCATION

University of Maine, Portland, Maine
Bachelor of Science: Psychology and Pre-Med, 1982–1986

Johnson & Wales College, Providence, Rhode Island
Food & Beverage Management, 1986–1988

ACTIVITIES

Volunteer: Make a Wish Foundation
Volunteer: Special Olympics
Marathon Runner and Fitness Instructor

References Furnished upon Request

ENTRY-LEVEL FLIGHT ENGINEER

EDWARD DONAVAN
1922 North West 134 Terrace
Pembroke Pines, Florida 33029

Email: email@email.com
Telephone: (954) 555-1212

Seeking position as...

ENTRY-LEVEL FLIGHT ENGINEER
FAA-Certified Multiengine Commercial Pilot

Good Judgment/Highly Dependable/Seasoned Communications Skills
Perfect Safety Record

A Certified Multiengine Commercial Pilot seeking entry-level position as Flight Engineer. Combine both academic background (Bachelor of Science in Economics and an Associate of Arts in Aeronautical Science/Aviation) and piloting credentials/proficiency with more than 15 years' successful experience in corporate America—the past 13 with Federal Express.

AREAS OF STRENGTH

Strategic planning and implementation	Organizational and team leadership
Safety management	Crisis management
Problem solving/troubleshooting; resourceful	Training and development
Scheduling and deadline management	Interfacing with culturally diverse people
Quality control and assurance	Customer-service management

BUSINESS EXPERIENCE

FEDERAL EXPRESS
Miami, Florida
1987 to Present

International Coordinator/Trainer
- A contributing member of Quality Action teams; a liaison between management and staff.
- Served as International Coordinator and Corporate Trainer—prepared presentations, recruited sales, planned account strategies, organized employee training, and coordinated client needs in Germany, Brussels, Belgium, France, and Great Britain.
- Awarded *Bravo Zulu* award for outstanding job performance for 12 consecutive years (1987–1999).
- Helped implement new route structure, controlled costs, and maximized resources through enhancing efficiency.

PROFESSIONAL EXPERIENCE (Other)

Warehouse Manager	ABACO Industrial Supplies, Miami, Florida	1986 to 1987
Mail Clerk Supervisor	DWG Corporation, Miami Beach, Florida	1984 to 1986

EDUCATION/TRAINING

FAA Certified: Commercial Multiengine Land Instrument Airplane — 1999

Florida International University, Miami, Florida
Bachelor of Science Degree: Economics (Emphasis on Engineering) — 1994

Miami-Dade Community College, Miami, Florida
A.A. Degree: Aeronautical Science/Aviation — 1988

- Computer Literate—Comprehensive

References and Verifying Documentation Furnished upon Request

PGA GOLF PROFESSIONAL

RICHARD F. STRONG, PGA GOLF PROFESSIONAL

2344 Wallace Way
Palm Beach, Florida 33418
Phone: (561) 555-1211/Email: email@email.com

A strong, high-energy and proven **PGA Golf Professional** offering twelve-plus years of successful, verifiable experience for a number of America's most prestigious clubs. **A bottom-line focused professional** with outstanding interpersonal skills. Recognized as a top instructor.

CAREER HIGHLIGHTS—*Old Marsh Golf Club*

OLD MARSH GOLF CLUB, Palm Beach Gardens, Florida   1990 to Current
Director of Golf
Director of Golf for prestigious 18-hole facility (rated one of top private golf clubs in country by *Golf Digest*) designed by Pete Dye. The club boasts 255 members playing 20,000 rounds annually. Direct and manage entire golf operations.
- Prepare and administer $390,000+ annual budget—meeting/exceeding all financial goals.
- Recruit, train, and manage a professional staff of 14—to ensure delivery of premiere service.
- Reorganized and direct a caddie program of 30 professional caddies—rated top 50 in United States (*Links Magazine*).
- Incorporate state-of-the-art video/computer technologies to enhance the quality of member instruction.
- Ignited golf-shop sales from $387,000 to $479,000 through improved operational and sales efficiencies.
- Increased golf-shop profit margins 12% by improving staff productivity and customer service.
- Assist with membership sales and conduct new-member orientations.
- Plan and conduct seven major golf tournaments per year—(concept through awards presentations).
- Personally facilitate 340+ private lessons (in season).
- More than 50 of my students either won or placed in club tournaments.
- Work closely with Director of Instruction (1996–97), Todd Anderson (*Golf Digest* Instructor).
- Organized and conducted Mark Calcavecchia Golf Exhibition.
- Utilize Event Man Software for premiere tournament presentation.
- Conduct four-day men's invitational, including a skills contest and shootout.
- Manage inventory in excess of $150,000 with sales of $479,000 annually.
- Expert club fitter—leading to a 30% increase in golf-club sales.
- Increased dollars-per-round from $19.83 in 1996 to $23.95 in 2000/2001.

CAREER HIGHLIGHTS—Prior to 1990

Head Professional   HATHERLY GOLF CLUB, North Scituate, Massachusetts
First Assistant Professional   JUPITER HILLS CLUB, Tequesta, Florida
Assistant Golf Professional   PEMBROKE GOLF CLUB, Pembroke, Massachusetts

FORMAL EDUCATION/TRAINING

SALEM STATE COLLEGE, Salem Massachusetts
Bachelor of Science: Sports Fitness, 1987

PGA Business School I, II, III; David Leadbetter Retreat; Chuck Hogan Expert School; PGA Advanced Teaching and Playing Seminar; Jim McLean Training School; Rick Smith Golf School; Florida State Golf Association Rules Seminar

PLAYING ACHIEVEMENTS

Contestant, Anhueser Busch Classic PGA Tour; Southeast Chapter Assistant's Champion; Placed 3d on South Florida Section PGA Money List; Inducted into Salem State College Athletic Hall of Fame, 1993; Low Last Round South Florida Open (66); Hogan Tour and Mini Tour Participant 1991–1995; Placed 2d in the Rhode Island Open

References and Supporting Documentation Furnished on Request

INTERIOR-DESIGN PROFESSIONAL

DANIELLE SWANSON

3761 SW Coquina Cove Way, #108 • Phoenix, Arizona 85023
(480) 555-6262 • email@email.com

INTERIOR-DESIGN PROFESSIONAL
Highly Experienced in Sales & Marketing/Concept Development/Project Management

Consistent Track Record of Completing Multifaceted Projects on Time and on Budget
Commercial/Residential/Hospitality

"Strong Command of Period Architecture and Details"

An interior-design professional with extensive background and in-depth industry knowledge in diversified environments, including commercial, residential, and hospitality. Outstanding skills in concept development, space planning, color and materials, drafting, custom fabrication and millwork detailing, specifications and procurement, inventory control, and project installation.

Core Professional Strengths

New-business development, marketing, and sales
Budget and project forecasting—expense management
Product expertise—fabrics, furniture, accessories, etc.
Customer-service excellence/quality control

Assessment—design-concept development
Total-project management/scheduling
Regulatory compliance—code enforcement
Computer literate, including Internet

Professional Experience

SAM TUCKER DESIGN, Phoenix, Arizona   1989 to Current
Technical Research Designer
Work closely with owner and business manager in the research, analysis, and development of technical specifications for interior furnishings and finishes for design company specializing in high-end hospitality, residential, and commercial projects. Coordinate custom fabrication and/or installation with manufacturers. Provide recommendations of custom details and manufacturers to translate ideas of project designer into a cost and time-effective product. Utilize extensive product knowledge of furniture construction, and material treatments for contract and residential use, including state-code compliance.

- Planned, drafted, specified, and coordinated installation and construction of a 40,000 sq. ft. office space.
- Orchestrated the design for 7000 sq. ft. bank—including millwork and interior architectural details.
- Bank project—one of the most extensive in bank history—was completed in less than 120 days.
- Designed and developed specifications for executive cafeteria for major communications company.
- Designed specifications for administrative offices and the chapel for Diocese/Catholic of Wilkinson County.
- Coordinated City Hall development project, 1996 for City of Phoenix.
- Successfully turned around projects for two key clients experiencing conflicts/challenges with previous contact.

Professional Experience (Prior to 1989)

Senior Project Designer and Manager   CORPORATE DESIGN INTERIORS, Scottsdale, Arizona
Senior Designer—Hospitality   JACKSON HEIGHTS MANAGEMENT, INC., Phoenix, Arizona
Architectural Draftsperson   BARTLETT AND ASSOCIATES, Phoenix, Arizona

Education

UNIVERSITY OF CINCINNATI, Cincinnati, Ohio
Bachelor of Science: Design, 1976
- Emphasis on Architectural Interiors/Space Planning

Continuing Education: Feng Shui

References, Supporting Documentation, and Design Portfolio Available upon Request

INVESTIGATOR/SECURITY AND LOSS-PREVENTION-MANAGEMENT PROFESSIONAL

CARL CONKLIN
215 Castlewood Drive
Lancaster, Pennsylvania 17972
(561) 555-1234/email@email.com

> **INVESTIGATOR/SECURITY & LOSS-PREVENTION-MANAGEMENT PROFESSIONAL**
> **10 Years' Service as Police Officer/14 Years' Security-Management Experience**
>
> *Asset-Protection Specialist/Highly Professional*

AREAS OF STRENGTH

investigative
Intelligence gathering/collecting evidence
Nonlitigation negotiation (out-of-court-settlements)

Pretrial preparation/presenting testimony
Interviewing and interrogation

security/loss prevention
Access control; asset, personnel and VIP protection
Emergency-planning and crisis-response management

Community outreach and education
Electronic/high-tech security integration

managerial/supervision
Staff training and supervision
Customer service; public and media relations

Communication skills (verbal & written)
Problem solving/conflict resolution

PROFESSIONAL EXPERIENCE

HILTON NATIONAL RESORT, Lancaster, Pennsylvania   1999 to Current
Director of Security

- ❑ Directed safety and security operations for 2340 acre, 300+ room resort.
- ❑ Trained and empowered staff of 14 professionals.
- ❑ Conducted internal investigations; uncovered and took successful action on six serious incidents.

SAKS FIFTH AVENUE, Lancaster, Pennsylvania   1995 to 1999
Loss-Prevention Manager ($20 million, 75,000 sq. ft. location)

- ❑ Trained and directed detectives, conducted internal investigations/audits, and installed/monitored surveillance cameras.
- ❑ Significantly reduced shrinkage/waste (1 full percentage point) through aggressive apprehensions of shoplifters.
- ❑ Successfully trained and prepared key personnel for advancement and managerial positions.

PROFESSIONAL EXPERIENCE—POLICE OFFICER

TOWN OF LANCASTER, Lancaster, Pennsylvania   1983 to 1995
Law Enforcement Police Officer

- ❑ Criminal investigations, including: White-collar investigations; Drug investigations; Internal investigations; Background/credit checks; Crime-scene investigations; Theft investigations; Missing-persons investigations

TRAINING/CERTIFICATIONS

INDIAN RIVER COMMUNITY COLLEGE, Fort Pierce, Florida
Certified Law Enforcement Officer (State of Florida), 1971

Special Training:
Certified Nunchaku Weapon Trained	Certified Advanced First Aid	Certified CPR
Drug Identification	Arson & Bomb Recognition	Administration (DEA) Academy
Fire Arms Expert	S.W.A.T. Member	Pennsylvania

ACTIVITIES

Paint Your Heart Out Volunteer
Fresh and salt-water fishing

References and Supporting Documentation Furnished upon Request

KRISTINE FORDHAM

10680 Avenue of Americas • Miami Lakes, FL 33356
(305) 555-1212 • Cell: (305) 555-9393
email@email.com

INTERNATIONAL MODEL

Recipient of 12 International Awards, Including *The Randall Award*, Milan, Italy, 2001
12 Years' National & International Experience as a Successful Fashion Model

---

Highly disciplined, results-driven, and outgoing professional seeking magazine and print media assignments in Miami and South Florida area.

PERSONAL

Height: 5'9"	Eyes: Blue	Hair: Blonde, Natural
Size: Six	Weight: 123	Complexion: Fair
Hips: 36	Waist: 25	Bust: 36

EDUCATION/TRAINING

MIAMI SCHOOL OF MODELING, Coral Gables, Florida
4 Years of Study with World-Renowned Trainer, Madame Bubois Liliac, 1996–2000

FLORIDA ATLANTIC UNIVERSITY, Boca Raton, Florida
Bachelor of Arts — Dual Degrees: English and Communications, (Cum Laude/Honors), 1994

PROFESSIONAL EXPERIENCE

International Fashion Model, Based out of Seattle, Washington   1987 to Current
Worked: *Milan, Paris, Vienna, London, Barcelona, Madrid, Tokyo, New York City, Seattle, and Miami*. Developed key strategic relationships with agencies in each city and utilized their contacts to land jobs and establish client relationships for future business.   Assignments included:

Estee Lauder Campaign	Gelati Ice Cream	Polaroid
Camera Calendar	Honda	Nike
PepsiCo	Procter & Gamble	Élan Skies
Ferrari of Italy	Sports Illustrated	TWA

SELECTED AWARDS

The Randall Award, Milan	2001
The Green Diamond, Madrid	2000
The Edgar Snelling Award, London	1999
Model of the Year Award, *Fashion Trend Magazine*	1999
Jacque Denefe Recipient, Paris	1998
The Manhattan Award, New York	1998

AFFILIATIONS

International Modeling Association
Mothers' Connection — Editor for 15-page newsletter, with 350-person circulation

References Furnished upon Request

DIPLOMATE, AMERICAN BOARD OF ANESTHESIOLOGY

DONALD PHILLIPS, M.D.

3300 Port Royale Drive, #816 • Fort Lauderdale, Florida 33308
(954) 555-1212 • email@email.com

Diplomate, American Board of Anesthesiology
Ten Years of Impeccable Professional Experience

Areas of Specialization

- Cardiothoracic Anesthesia
- Growth of Anesthesia Services
- Anesthesia for Super-Morbidly-Obese Patients

- Pediatric Anesthesia
- High-risk Obstetrical Anesthesia
- Ambulatory Anesthesia

Appointments

Attending Anesthesiologist	Florida Medical Center, Fort Lauderdale, Florida	1998 to Current
Attending Anesthesiologist	Wellington Medical Center, Wellington, Florida	1997 to 1998
Attending Anesthesiologist	Westchester County Medical Center, Valhalla, New York	1990 to 1997
Assistant Clinical Professor	New York Medical College, Valhalla, New York	1990 to 1997

Residency

New York Medical College, Valhalla, New York   1987 to 1990
Department of Anesthesiology

CA—3 Years	Cardiothoracic Anesthesia	Six Months
	Pediatric Anesthesia	Six Months

Internship

Metropolitan Hospital Center, New York, New York   1986 to 1987
Department of Internal Medicine

Medical School/Premedical Studies

M.D., 1982	Autonomous University of Guadalajara, Mexico
B.Sc. (Chem)	Dalhousie University, Halifax, NS, Canada

Licensure & Certifications

Licensure: Florida, New Jersey, New York, California
Certification: Diplomate, American Board of Anesthesiology

Publications

- Kubal K, Pasricha S, Bhargava M: Spinal Anesthesia in a Patient with Friedreich's Ataxia. *Anesth. Analg* 1991; 72: 257–8
- Bhargava M, Pothula S: Improvement of Pulse Oximetry Signal by EMLA® Cream. *Anesth. Analg* 1998; 86:915
- Bhargava M, Pothula S, Joshi S: The Obstruction of an Endotracheal Tube by the Plastic Coating Sheared from a Stylet: A Revisit. *Anesthesiology* 1998; 88:548–9

Interests

Computers, Tennis, Travel

References and Supporting Documentation Furnished upon Request

SONGWRITER/ARRANGER/MUSIC INSTRUCTOR

LISA A. DAVIS
31529 Village Boulevard, #706 * West Palm Beach, FL 33409 * (561) 555-1212 * email@email.com

SONGWRITER/ARRANGER/MUSIC INSTRUCTOR
Pianist/Guitarist/Vocalist
Offering Outstanding Teaching, Training, Motivating & Empowering Skills

"Sharing the Gift"

OVERVIEW

A dynamic, highly skilled, and talented musician/entertainer/instructor with professional qualifications as a Songwriter (music and lyrics), Arranger with knowledge of midi-music-software recording equipment, Pianist, Guitarist, and Vocalist. A creative, artistic, self-motivated teaching professional, with a solid reputation for effectively providing instruction in any subject to people at all ages.   Additional areas of skill include:

* Organization and administration	* Communication skills (verbal/written)
* Sales and marketing experience	* Entrepreneurial experience
* Program/event planning and coordination	* Performer and entertainer
* Computer and technical aptitude	* Management and supervision

Home Recording Studio Equipment Includes:

Kurzweil K-2000	Tascam MSR 16 Track Recorder	Seck 18 Channel Mixing Board
Roland TD-7 Percussion Sounds	Panasonic DAT Deck Sv3500	SPX 90 Digital Effects Unit
Boss 8 Channel Mixing Board	AKG 414 Microphone	Midiverb Reverb Unit
Proformance—1+ Piano Module	Sure SM57 Microphone	Tascam 112 B Cassette Deck
Midi: Time Piece II (Interface)	Visions Software	Steinberger Guitar
Macintosh 2 ci Computer	Performer Software	Roland A-80 Midi Board

EDUCATION & TRAINING

BERKLEE COLLEGE OF MUSIC, Boston, MA
Bachelor of Music Degree in Songwriting, May, 1990

Piano Lessons: Craig Najjar (Berklee College of Music—4 years); Gene Favatella (4 years); Judy Mikalenic (4 years)
Guitar Lessons: Tony Scally (4 years); John Van Wre (1 year)
Voice Lessons: Merril Shea (6 months); June Fiske (6 months)

MUSIC EXPERIENCE

- Developed and operated piano teaching/recording center for the past ten+ years
- Created new approach to teaching, utilizing advanced software technology—*Music International Magazine* 7/01
- Wrote, arranged, recorded, and produced theme music to local radio show—assisted with dialogue and show concept
- Empowered clients to reach their full creative potential

Music Teacher	Music 1, Chelmsford, FL
Music Teacher	Shepard Music Education Center, Palm Harbor, FL

ACTIVITIES

- Television appearance on the Evan Korey Variety Show
- Songwriters forum: Student-run organization at Berklee—student- critique/review organization
- Performed in jazz ensembles playing piano at Berklee College of Music
- Producing, songwriting, arranging, recording, singing, and sequencing from home recording studio

Portfolio and References Furnished on Request

STAGE DESIGNER

SERGIO GORINSKI
372 East, 4th Street, #12A
New York, New York, 10009

Email: email@email.com
Phone: (212) 555-2121

STAGE DESIGNER
Set Design/Costume Design/Graphic Art & Design

Master's Degree in Stage Design
Attended Moscow Art Theater School/Worked at Bolshoi Theater in Moscow

---

Born in Tula, Russia, attended the renowned "Moscow Art Theater School," and graduated with a Master's Degree and honors from the gifted program in 1985. Invited to work at the Bolshoi Theater in Moscow as the Assistant Chief Designer, and remained there for two successful years.

A creative and talented painter whose paintings were purchased for exhibition by the "Funds at the Russian Ministry of Culture," and by the Government Bakhrushin's Theater Museum.

HIGHLIGHTS OF EXPERIENCE

- Designed sets and costumes for many Russian, German, and Polish theaters.
- Recipient of highly favorable accolades from Russian and American press.
- Illustrations of creative work have appeared in American newspapers and in Moscow's *Theater* magazine.
- Received outstanding review with illustration by Lee Fleming (*Washington Post*) for exhibition entitled "Four Seasons."
- Presently working with a number of graphic arts agencies combining knowledge of Macintosh and Scitex platforms as well as CD-ROM and multimedia technology.

ADDITIONAL AREAS OF SKILL

Multimedia, concept, and storyboard development
Graphic design
Animation
Video and sound editing

Screen/interface design
Digital photography
3-D design
Digital special effects

EDUCATION

MOSCOW ART THEATER SCHOOL, Russia
Master's Degree: Stage Design (With Honors, 1985)

SCITEX OF AMERICA SCHOOL, Chicago, Illinois
Computer Studies (1993)

PROFESSIONAL EXPERIENCE

Artec Media, Inc., New York, New York, Silicon Valley, California, Moscow, Sosua (DR)   1997 to 1999
ART DIRECTOR

Projects: *SGMA*, The Super Show (Atlanta, GA); *Artofrussia*, Russian Art Mission (*Web Magazine*); *Multimedia Theater*, (in progress); *Multimedia Museum* (in progress); *Multimedia School* (in progress).

ColorBank Digital Sources, Inc., New York, New York   1994 to 1999
CREATIVE DIRECTOR—Multimedia Design

Projects: *ColorBank; Repechage, Artofrussia, Artek Multimedia, Shop Fast, Addison.*

Museum and Theater, Inc., New York, New York   1995 to 1997
DIRECTOR

Projects: *United by Tragedy*, Constantin Stanislavsky's and E. Gordon Craig's Russian Hamlet (Multimedia Exhibit) and "Sonata for Viola and Piano," Dmitri Shostakovich (Multimedia Concert).

STAGE DESIGNER (CONT.)

PROFESSIONAL EXPERIENCE

Theater, Moscow, New York, New York   1985 to 1994
STAGE DESIGNER

Projects:
William Shakespeare, *A Midsummer Nights Dream*
Edisson Denisoff *Edith Paif*, Opera and Ballet Theater of Perm City, Russia
Peter Tchaikovsky, *The Nutcracker*, Children Ballet Theater, Moscow, Russia
Anton Chechov, *Uncle Vanya*, Drama Theater of Tula City, Russia
Mikhail Bulgakov, *Zoyka's Flat*, Drama Theater of Elblong City, Russia
Edmon Rostain, *Sirano de Bergeraq*, Drama Theater of Tilzit City, Russia
Voltair, *Candid*, Drama Theater of Oriol City, Russia
William Shakespeare, *Romeo and Juliet*, Drama Theater of Tilzit City, Russia
John Patrick, *Dear Pamella*, Drama Theater of Tilzit City, Russia

Bolshoi Theater, Moscow, Russia   1985 to 1988
CHIEF STAGE-DESIGNER ASSISTANT
Coordinated all elements of production in the face of deadline pressures and budgetary constraints.

Projects:
R. Schedrin, *The Lady with the Dog*, Bolshoi Theater, Moscow, Russia
M. Mussorgsky, *Boris Godunov*, State Opera and Ballet Theater, Estonia, Tallinn
W.A. Mozart, *Don Giovanni*, Komische Opera, Berlin, Germany
G.F. Handel, *Giustinno*, Komische Opera, Berlin, Germany

References and Supporting Documentation Furnished upon Request

AIRCRAFT DISPATCHER

JAMES S. FRANKLIN

789 Kingston Road
Memphis, Tennessee 38152
Phone: (561) 555-1234/Fax: (305) 555-4321
Email: email@email.com

Seeking Position as...

AIRCRAFT DISPATCHER
Over 30 Years' Experience in Aviation

Perfect Safety Record

**Customer-Service and Quality-Control Management/Problem Solving & Conflict Resolution
Organizational Leadership/Outstanding Technical & Mechanical Aptitude**

CORE STRENGTHS

Communication skills (verbal and written)
Scheduling—flexible and adaptable to changing environments
Time management—solid organizational skills
Quality control—attention to detail

Decision making under pressure
Team player—cooperative style
Enforcing company/FAA policy/procedure
Safety and security coordination

■ Computer Skills: Windows, Word, Excel, PowerPoint, proprietary software, and Internet applications

AVIATION/MILITARY TRAINING & EDUCATION

Graduate: Sheffield School of Aeronautics, Fort Lauderdale, Florida
  - **FAA-Approved Aircraft Dispatcher Training Program, 2/2000**
  - **Sheffield ETOPS and AIFP Seminars**
Graduate: United States Air Force NCO Academy (in residence), Knoxville, Tennessee, 1986
Graduate: United States Air Force Senior NCO Academy, Maxwell AFB, Meridian, Mississippi, 1988 (Leadership)

AVIATION LICENSES

Private Pilot License, 1975   Commercial Pilot License, 1978   Aircraft Dispatcher License, 2000

PROFESSIONAL EXPERIENCE

NORTH CAROLINA AIR NATIONAL GUARD, Memphis, Tennessee   1991 to Current
Aircraft Loadmaster/Loadmaster Instructor/Master Sergeant (E-7)—FULL TIME

  ➢ A full-time member of the ANG—orchestrating training and preparation for recruits.
  ➢ Logged more than 8,300 accident-free flying hours as crewmember on C-130 transport aircraft.
  ➢ Weight and Balance expert—ensuring safe flying conditions.
  ➢ Trained in Crew Resource Management (CRM)—effective communications between crew members.
  ➢ Highly experienced in the area of "hazardous cargo," for shipment by military/civilian transport.
  ➢ Awarded numerous citations, including AF Commendation Medal, Achievement Medal, and Humanitarian Medal.

BELLSOUTH TELECOMMUNICATIONS, West Palm Beach, Florida   1984 to 1991
Testing Technician/Electronic Technician/Switching-Equipment Installation Technician

  ➢ Successfully scheduled five-man team to meet critical work deadlines for multimillion dollar BellSouth project.
  ➢ Made crucial decision in quickly restoring communications for major hospital as a result of facility failure.
  ➢ Adhered to stringent safety and security policies compiling a perfect safety record spanning 30 years.
  ➢ Improved efficiency by developing highly successful tracking reports/spreadsheets (for work in progress).
  ➢ Maintained a consistently high level of quality in all projects performed—and those of team members.

References and Supporting Documentation Furnished upon Request

17

Trades

CERTIFIED ELECTRICIAN

SEAN H. HOPKINS

2578 South Haverhill Road
Rumney, New Hampshire 06222

Email: email@email.com
Telephone: (603) 555-1212

CERTIFIED ELECTRICIAN
12 Years' Professional Experience—Residential, Commercial, & Industrial

Loyal, Dependable & Trustworthy/Outstanding Technical Skills
Customer-Service Specialist/Excellent Training and Supervision Skills

---

A highly qualified, dedicated, technically skilled Electrician recognized as a team player seeking to contribute to and grow with a progressive and innovative company/organization.

AREAS OF STRENGTH

Basic electronics	Interior/exterior lighting	OSHA safety and regulatory compliance
Energy management	Diagnose/troubleshoot problems	Employee supervision
Project management	Communication skills	Customer service/quality control

EDUCATION/TRAINING/CERTIFICATIONS

CERTIFICATIONS:

Red Badge Certification	Thermolag Certification	Fire Watch Certification
"Hazmat" Certification	Respiratory Protection Certification	CPR and First Aid Certification

FORMAL TRAINING:

J.A.T. C., West Palm Beach, Florida
Journeyman Wireman, 1995 (5-Year Joint-Apprenticeship Curriculum, 8,000 on-the-job hours)

❑ Approved for work in nuclear facilities.

PROFESSIONAL EXPERIENCE

RUSSELL-THOMAS, Plymouth, New Hampshire   1995 to Current
Master Electrician

FISK ELECTRIC, Medley, New Hampshire   1993 to 1995
Electrician

NPS ENERGY SERVICES, Harrisburg, Pennsylvania   1997 to 1998
Foreman/Electrician (Seabrook Nuclear Power Plant)
(Temporary Assignment—Requested by NHDE)

- ❑ Recipient of numerous safety awards for safe workmanship.
- ❑ Worked as "Job Steward," acting as a liaison between employees and contractor.
- ❑ Performed the electrical work in an $11 million "smart house" in Plymouth.
- ❑ Worked in the Control Room and in the Containment Building at the Seabrook Nuclear Power Plant.
- ❑ Installed security and data systems for Barnett Banks throughout Northridge County.
- ❑ Worked on the fire alarms, power, and security systems at Manchester International Airport.
- ❑ Installed Emergency Generating System and Fire Suppression System at Logan Airport.
- ❑ Foreman for the Lighting Protection Project at the Southern Bell Central Office.
- ❑ Performed maintenance on more than a dozen Southern Bell buildings/locations.
- ❑ Installed and set up the Halon System at a large Concord Correctional Facility.
- ❑ Directed five separate Barnett Bank projects in Northridge and Becker Counties

References and Supporting Documentation Furnished upon Request

DAVID T. DONAHUE

2230 Water Fall Circle
Palm Beach Gardens, Florida 33410
(561) 555-1212/email@email.com

Seeking Position as…

FIRE CHIEF: CITY OF RIVIERA BEACH
**Critical Leadership Role in Process-Change Management & Operational Improvement
Utilizing Information Technology in Improving Quality of Life in the Community
* Emphasis on Integrity, Quality Management, and Teamwork ***

A dynamic, results-oriented, highly effective Fire Fighting/Administration Professional with 16 years of dedicated service to the city of Riviera Beach—the past four years as Division Chief of EMS. Recognized for outstanding team-spirited leadership qualities accentuating customer service, fiscal responsibility, human-resources management, and strategic-planning/bench-marking expertise.

AREAS OF SPECIFIC SPECIALIZATION

* Visionary leadership; long/short-term goal setting
* Managerial accounting/budgeting
* Public/community relations
* Policy/procedure development and enforcement
* Reorganization/reengineering—change management
* Total-quality management

* Senior-level decision making
* Data analysis/MIS management
* State-of-the-art training and development
* Community and economic development
* Resource utilization/cost management
* Demanding highest ethical standards

CAREER HIGHLIGHTS

CITY OF RIVIERA BEACH FIRE DEPARTMENT, FLORIDA   1981–Present
Division Chief of EMS   6/93–Present

Plan, organize, and direct activities related to emergency medical services, fire suppression, and prevention. Responsible for administration, supervision, and operation of emergency medical services division. Develop and execute $4.6 million budget. Spearhead the planning, coordination, and delivery of cutting-edge departmental training programs. Ensure compliance with governing standards. Review blueprints and building plans for automatic fire-protection systems. Perform fire-scene investigations and coordinate arson investigations with state and local officials. Manage the department's information technology infrastructure and communications system (media/public/police). Continually evaluate and enhance departmental performance and efficiency. Analyze data and benchmark data against accepted norms and internal/external organizations. Work in harmony with directives from the Fire Chief.

Perform preemployment background investigations—active in the recruiting processes and individual/group development. Active participation in labor relations and negotiations. Develop and implement strategic long/short-term goals/objectives and customer-service programs. Review, update, and/or modify standard operating procedures set by governing agencies as required. Participate in maintaining the city's ISO fire insurance rating—review minimum requirements established by rating service. Recommend methods and procedures for maintaining or lowering the city's fire-insurance rating. Review and recommend city codes and ordinances related to fire prevention to ensure compliance with federal, state, and local regulations as well as locally accepted fire-prevention practices.

⇒ Enhanced the community's emergency medical services from a two-unit paramedic first-response system—to a four-unit, advanced-life-support transport system that provides the best possible response times, the most advanced levels of technology, and the highest levels of clinical care in the industry. These enhancements have generated more than $1 million in new revenues for the city since 1995, currently producing $460,000 annually.

⇒ Computerized and automated the city's incident-reporting and dispatch system. Team leader in managing the change from a paper-based incident-reporting system to a computerized multiuser incident-reporting and dispatch system. Wrote a grant that provided for pen-based computer tablets allowing paramedics to capture incident information in the field, print the run report at the hospital, or fax reports to relevant parties.

(Page 1 of 2)

FIRE CHIEF (CONT.)

David T. Donahue
Page two

Notable Achievements – Continued:

⇒ Managed and directed transformation from the department's antiquated VHF radio system to the current state-of-the-art 800 MHz trunked communication system. Team leader in planning, directing, and managing this extensive project.

⇒ Developed city's current fire code and current fire-prevention code—providing for reasonable requirements that take into account the city's limited financial position and available resources for fire-fighting operations.

⇒ Spearheaded the planning/implementation of the department's efforts to lower ISO risk class, thereby reducing casualty-insurance premiums for residents and businesses. Results: Lowered department ISO rating from a Class 5 to a Class 4.

⇒ Developed a comprehensive infection-control plan to adhere to state and federal requirements and to reduce the Worker's Compensation costs to the city.

⇒ Prepare annual budget—$4.6 million. Reengineered the department's budgetary process by implementing spreadsheet technology. Established templates that have been adopted by other departments to achieve similar gains in efficiency.

⇒ Significantly enhanced department training. Established a process whereby department contracts with Palm Beach Community College and North/South Technical Centers to provide on-site training to department members on a regular basis. Member of the Countywide Training Executive Board.

⇒ Selected by the Fire Chief's Association of Palm Beach County to participate in the development of a countywide incident-command system. Cooperative contributor in the development of a regional disaster-response unit. As a Board Member, assisted in the establishment of a Federal Regional Disaster Medical Assistance Team, comprising members of a four-county area for response to state and national disasters.

SUMMARY OF PRIOR POSITIONS HELD:

Fire Lieutenant	10/90–6/93	**Fire Inspector**	2/86–9/86
Driver Engineer	3/88–10/90	**Fire Medic**	8/82–2/86
Fire Medic	9/86–3/88	**Fire Fighter**	6/81–8/82

EDUCATION & TRAINING
(Over 6000 Hours of Continual Training in Every Aspect of Fire/Emergency-Service Delivery & Management)

FLORIDA ATLANTIC UNIVERSITY, Boca Raton, Florida   1993–Present
Bachelor's Degree: Business Administration (Currently enrolled)
PALM BEACH COMMUNITY COLLEGE, Lake Worth, Florida   1980–1988
Associate in Science Degree: Fire Science Technology
PALM BEACH COMMUNITY COLLEGE, Lake Worth, Florida   1981–1982
Paramedic Certificate

STATE OF FLORIDA CERTIFICATIONS:
Certified Paramedic, 1992
Certified Fire Fighter, 1991
Certified EMT, 1991
Certified Municipal Fire Safety Inspector, 1983

NATIONAL FIRE ACADEMY COURSES:
Tactical Operations for Company Officer, 1990
Incident-Command System for Emergency Medical Services, 1997
Advanced Leadership Issues for EMS, 1997

- References, Supporting Documentation, and Affiliations Furnished upon Request -

FORKLIFT OPERATOR/WAREHOUSE SUPERVISOR

COURTNEY GLENDALE
18 Brookshield Drive
Las Vegas, Nevada 70623
(505) 555-1212 / email@email.com

Seeking Position as...

FORKLIFT OPERATOR
WAREHOUSE SUPERVISOR

Recognized for 100% Perfect Safety Record—and Strong, Team-Spirited Work Ethic
11 Years' Experience

More than 11 years' experience as forklift operator, fours years as warehouse supervisor in charge of six warehouse employees. Excellent work experience supported by verifiable letters of reference.

AREAS OF STRENGTH

Forklift and heavy-equipment operations	Shipping & receiving operations
OSHA regulations and code compliance	Traffic management and control
Inventory management—JIT systems	Cycle and perpetual inventory control
Employee training and supervision	Documentation and record keeping
Quality control	Customer service

EMPLOYMENT

Las Vegas Beverage and Distribution Center, Las Vegas, Nevada   1993 to Present
Forklift Operator/Warehouse Supervisor

- In charge of all forklift operations for 55,000 square-foot warehouse distributing beverages to businesses throughout Las Vegas and the neighboring communities.
- Began as stock clerk and worked way up to warehouse supervisor and lead forklift operator in charge of six employees.
- Train all new employees and ensure all new hires are cleared for safe work.
- Maintained a 100% safety record—reducing liability claims/losses by hundreds of thousands of dollars.
- Helped build morale and reduce employee/warehouse turnover.
- Outstanding technical/mechanical aptitude—repair most forklift trucks on premise.

EMPLOYMENT (Prior to 1993)

Bartender:

Sloop John B's	Las Vegas
Happy Harold's	Las Vegas
The Ace in the Hole	Las Vegas

EDUCATION/TRAINING

OBERTON COMMUNITY COLLEGE, Toronto, Ontario
A.A. Degree: Electronics, 1987

Continuing Education
Warehouse Management
Just-in-Time (JIT) Inventory Seminar
Computer Classes: Word, Excel, and Internet

References and Supporting Documentation Furnished upon Request

HEAVY-EQUIPMENT SUPERVISOR/OPERATOR

MICHAEL ROBERT PORTER

Primary Residence (Bahamas)
PSC 112 Box 9
FPO AA 34056-0008
(242) 555-2188 Ext. 6261
(561) 555-5155 Ext. 6261

U.S. Address
212 Junonia Court
Fort Myers, Florida 33908
(941) 555-1212
email@email.com

HEAVY-EQUIPMENT SUPERVISOR/OPERATOR
Specializing in Crane and Rigging Operations
25 Years' International Experience

Over 25 years' successful and verifiable experience in General Crane Operations/Heavy Lifts/Heavy Hauling/Excavation and Grading/Land Clearing and Road Construction/Air and Marine Transportation. A safety-oriented professional supervisor/operator who works well with people at all levels—and with all nationalities in a "team-oriented" environment. A leader who assumes responsibility and delivers results.

PROFESSIONAL OVERVIEW

SUPERVISION

- Planning, supervising, and drawing for dual crane projects and complex lifts
- Crew training and development
- Safety management
- Work scheduling
- Customer relations/service

CRANE & RIGGING OPERATIONS (Hydraulic & Friction)

- Up to and including 100-Ton Hydraulic (Certified—Navy Document NAVFAC P-307)
- 300-Ton American Ring Horse Crane (Certified—Navy Document NAVFAC P-307)
- Use of 150 Metric Ton Barge-Mounted Stiff Leg Derrick Crane
- Offshore from 200 ft vessels
- In remote, mountainous, hard-to-get-to terrain (Africa/Bahamas)
- With fragile cargo (U.S. Navy ASW weapons & electrical materials)
- With large, oversize material (innovative rigging and development methods)

EQUIPMENT (Other)

- Bulldozers (up to and including D-9 Cat)
- Road Graders/Rollers
- 25K-Loader (C-130 Cargo Unloading)
- Backhoe/Excavators

PROFESSIONAL EXPERIENCE

RCA/GE Government Services/Autec Range Services/Raytheon Corporation
Atlantic Undersea Test and Evaluation Center, Andros Island, Bahamas
1982 to Present

SUPERVISOR: BASE SUPPORT OPERATIONS/HEAVY EQUIPMENT CREW (1999–Current)
- Supervise up to 10 crew members for Base Support Operations. Direct loading and off-loading of cargo on Mobile Sea-lift Command barges, as well as on American, British, and Canadian C-130 (military), DC-3, DC-4, and Convair aircraft. Coordinate and supervise all crane and rigging operations. Train all crew members, schedule workflow, and ensure that safety procedures are adhered to/enforced. Work closely with all range users and customers.

(Page 1 of 2)

Michael Robert Porter
Page two

PROFESSIONAL EXPERIENCE

RCA/GE Government Services/Autec Range Services/Raytheon Corporation
(Continued)

CRANE/HEAVY-EQUIPMENT OPERATOR & RIGGER (1982–1999)

- Operate/maintain cranes and heavy equipment. Certified on cranes to 100 tons and on 300-ton American Ring Horse Crane. Recipient of various *Safety Awards* (1987–present). Load and unload C-130 military aircraft and MSC barges. Other job responsibilities included working as Pier Shop Foreman for Marine Operations (18 months) and developing a comprehensive training program/manual to test/certify ship's engineers for the safe operation of cranes. Cross-trained as Relief Engineer.

Morrison-Knudsen Company, Inc.
Six-Year Assignment on 1700-Kilometer Electrical Power Transmission Line in Zaire, Africa
1974 to 1981

GENERAL FOREMAN—TRANSPORTATION, HEAVY AND MARINE

- Supervised the transportation of oversized electrical equipment (transformers—36 pieces, over 100 tons each) from ports to construction sites. Directed up to 20 people. Primary responsibility was operating 150 metric ton, barge-mounted stiff leg derrick crane. Operated five specially made 24-wheel pivot-&-lift-system rail cars for heavy hauling. Successfully controlled special handling, rigging, and transportation of fragile, oversized electrical equipment to construction sites, with no losses.

- Supervised crane and rigging operations, loading of river barges, rail cars, and trucks for transportation of materials to remote and isolated sites. Also involved with land-clearing and road-building operations in addition to camp construction. Began in 1974 as Expeditor and Loadmaster.

EDUCATION & TRAINING

CERTIFICATES OF TRAINING (1986–Current)

Certificate of Training: Occupational Safety Training on NAVFAC P-307 Category 1 & 4 Operator (40-hour course)
Certificate of Training: Basic Instructor Training Course on Mobile Cranes & Rigging Considerations (40-hour course)
Certificate of Training: Safety Training Course for Mobile Crane Operator Evaluation (3-day course)
Certificate of Training: Ordinance and Explosives Handling and Transportation, NAVSEA OP5 (35-hour course)
Certificate of Training: Occupational Safety Training on Applied Rigging Practices (24-hour course)
Certificate of Training: NAVFAC P-307 Crane Safety Course (5-day course)
Certificate of Training: Triennial Forklift safety Training Course (6.5-hour course)

High School Diploma:
Eau Gallie High School, Melbourne, Florida, 1972

Languages: Working knowledge of French and various African Tribal Dialects

PERSONAL

* DOB: 5/8/54
* Health: Excellent
* Current U.S. Government Security Clearance
* Will Travel/Relocate Worldwide

* Marital Status: Single
* U.S. Citizen and Passport
* Computer Literate

- References Furnished upon Request -

RAMP AGENT

RONALD T. MILLER

12390 56th Place North
Lake Charles, Louisiana 70610
(318) 555-1354

Seeking a position as....

RAMP AGENT—SOUTHWEST AIRLINES
Five Years' Ramp Experience with AMR Services

Ramp Loading & Unloading/Cabin Service/Bag-Room Experience
Outstanding Team Player with Good Communications and "People" Skills

---

Seeking a position as Ramp Agent utilizing five years of prior experience with AMR services. A self-motivated, energetic, and hard-working individual seeking to contribute to efficient ramp operations in a team-spirited manner.

WORK EXPERIENCE

AMR SERVICES, INC., New Orleans International Airport, Louisian   1996 to Present
Lead Ramp Service Clerk

- Ramp loading and unloading of aircraft; cabin service; bag room experience
- Loaded and unloaded U.S. mail and commercial cargo
- Worked on "Team On," a 12-person team recognized as the top production team at NOIA
- Promoted to Lead Ramp Service Clerk after eight months on the job for outstanding performance

SAM'S CLUB, New Orleans, Louisiana   1990 to 1996
Freezer Cooler Associate

- Responsible for providing outstanding customer service
- Stocked, loaded, and unloaded merchandise; ordered frozen foods for department
- Ensured customer service and a clean/safe shopping environment

BUDGET RENT-A-CAR, New Orleans, Louisiana   1988 to 1990
Hiker—Auto Transport

- Drove rental vehicles to and from budget locations throughout New Orleans
- Provided valet service and ensured proper cleaning of vehicles
- Received numerous letters of commendation from customers

EDUCATION

Graduate: Two-Year Mechanics Program, Dover Technical School, New Orleans, Louisiana, 1988
Graduate: Lake Worth High School, Lake Worth, Louisiana, 1986

REFERENCES

Furnished upon request

TECHNICIAN/TECHNICAL-SUPPORT PROFESSIONAL

GERRY J. BENTLEY
4715 Pinemore Lane
Westin, Ontario L5P 8B3
(905) 555-1212/email@email.com

Seeking Position as...

TECHNICIAN/TECHNICAL-SUPPORT PROFESSIONAL
Telecommunications & Related Environments

Quality Specialist/Customer-Service Driven
20+ Years' Successful, Verifiable Experience
Bilingual: English & French

A highly creative, technically skilled, and results-focused professional recognized for providing technical solutions and support to maintain and enhance business/residential equipment/infrastructure in a timely and cost-effective manner. Skilled in the following:

- Installing cable/wiring
- Water analysis
- Back flow tech
- Drafting
- Technical sales

- Transmission-equipment erection
- Basic electricity
- Impact-fee coordinator
- Submersible-pump technician
- Customer-service specialist

Professional Experience

LUCENT TECHNOLOGIES, Toronto, Ontario   1999 to Current
ACST Installer
Assembled, erected, aligned, mounted, and removed all framework, equipment, and apparatus; cabling and cable removal—run and secure cable including copper, lightguide, and coaxial cable. Play-station wiring on customer premises; prepare cable tags; butt and strip copper cable; wiring—splicing in straight color code; pair/fiber count, including continuity checking; basic/complex wiring. Basic testing—fusing, timing, and lead and power verification; using test equipment, such as voltmeter and multilead automatic continuity system tester.

- Complex wiring, 310 block Lucent Manufacturer
- Installed transmission equipment, Fujitsu, Teltec, Bellsouth, AT&T, etc.
- Cabling of equipment; Fiber-technology testing and installation

Professional Experience (prior to 1999)

EMS ENVIRONMENTAL, Toronto, Ontario   1995 to 1999
Technician
Responsible for testing and repairing of remediation systems for petrochemical industry.

- Technical specialist for submersible pumps
- Technical repair of electrical equipment for remediation sites
- Installed CBR cables that enhanced superconductive performance by 12%, saving the company thousands of dollars

Education/Training

OBERTON COMMUNITY COLLEGE, Toronto, Ontario
A.A. Degree: Engineering, 1994

Continuing Education
Xerox Sales Training
Water Treatment Specialist
Career Consultant—Microsoft Computer Training

References and Supporting Documentation Furnished upon Request

WELDER/FABRICATOR

BERNARD PARKER
18 Allan Circle
Durham, North Carolina 27707
(919) 555-1212/email@email.com

Seeking Position as...

WELDER/FABRICATOR
Mig/Tig/Gas/Stick/and Plasma for Custom Fixtures and Finished Products

Recognized for 100% QUALITY Work/Perfect Safety Record
Trained in Lathes, Mills, Drills, and Polishers
21 Years' Experience

Twenty-one-plus years' experience as a professional welder/fabricator. Outstanding work ethic with attention to quality, costs, and project scheduling (deadlines).

AREAS OF STRENGTH

Strong technical and mechanical aptitude	Custom fabrication and welding
OSHA regulations and code compliance	Skills in all types of welding
Have own set of tools	Excellent trainer in high-skill work
Communication skills—verbal and written	Quality assurance
Customer service	Project coordination—expense control

EMPLOYMENT

Strong Weld, Inc., Durham, North Carolina   1995 to Present
Welder Fabricator

- Perform for all types of fixture welding, including mig/tig welding of stainless to carbon
- Work within strict tolerances; perform welding of metal .004 to 1/4 inch
- Contributing member in the fabrication of precision cloisters for HVAC applications (exceeding EPA standards)
- Fabricate various products based on customer specifications—work with major clients, including Office Depot
- Welded cooler tanks used in plastic-injection molding—developed technology to reduce welding time by 25%

O'Sullivans Fabrication, Durham, North Carolina   1991 to 1995
Welder

- Performed detailed welding for manufacturing equipment—$1 million and up
- Utilized customer's blueprints and assembled heavy machinery to withstand high-tolerance levels
- Responsible for precision welding on flat-base construction equipment
- Assembled stainless steel equipment using purge/tig, hand-free, and out-of-position welding

EMPLOYMENT (Prior to 1995)

Courier/Driver	UPS	1984 to 1995
Maintenance Supervisor	High-rise Cleaning Service	1981 to 1984

EDUCATION/TRAINING

DURHAM VOCATIONAL AND TECHNICAL COLLEGE, Durham, North Carolina
Welding and Fabrication, 1985 and 1986

EDDIE BRODY HIGH SCHOOL, Durham, North Carolina
Graduate, 1984

References and Supporting Documentation Furnished upon Request

MAINTENANCE AND REPAIR TECHNICIAN/ON-BOARD RIDER

JAMES HOGAN

85 Hunting Trail
Mobile, Alabama 97263
Home: (205) 555-1212/Cell: (205) 555-8787

Seeking position with Amtrak as…

MAINTENANCE & REPAIR TECHNICIAN/ON-BOARD RIDER
Offering Outstanding Customer-Service and Problem-Solving Skills

Painting/Electrical/Plumbing
Carpentry/Cleaning

A loyal, dependable, and trustworthy individual seeks position where solid aptitude in maintenance/repair, combined with excellent interpersonal and relationship-building skills, can contribute to organizational goals and objectives.

STRENGTHS

Problem solving and troubleshooting	Cost-effective preventative maintenance
Customer service and quality assurance	Organization and time management
Employee training and supervision	Landscape and grounds maintenance
Communication skills—verbal and written	Policy and procedure enforcement/compliance

HIGHLIGHTS OF PROFESSIONAL EXPERIENCE

CHARLES EISEN'S PAINTLESS DENT REMOVAL, Mobile, Alabama   1997 to 2002
Technician/Customer Service

- Contributed to the successful start-up for company specializing in working with automobile dealerships—taking out minor car dents without performing any bodywork.
- Promoted business to key dealerships throughout South Florida in addition to performing the technical work.
- Performed work and achieved 100% customer satisfaction ratings on a consistent basis.

PRIME MANAGEMENT, Mobile, Alabama   1990 to 1997
Maintenance Supervisor

- Supervised two people responsible for two association properties—a 700-unit association and a 1,000-unit association.
- Worked with owners/tenants and amicably resolved points of contention and property-related issues.
- Handled emergency/crisis situations with proficiency, in addition to providing preventative-maintenance work.

COUSINS BUILDING SERVICE, Mobile, Alabama   1986 to 1989
Handyman/Small Construction/Repair Technician

- Performed various handyman work—built decks, built additions/extensions, and refinished basements.
- Remodeled bathrooms and kitchens; put down tile flooring.

EDUCATION

Graduate—Two-Year Technical/Vocational Degree: Boces Technical School, Mobile, Alabama, 1985
Graduate—Lindenhurst High School, Porter, Alabama, 1982

References Furnished upon Request

Index

Note: **Boldface** numbers indicate illustrations.

ABOUT THE AUTHOR

Jay A. Block, CPRW (Certified Professional Resume Writer), is the contributing cofounder of the Professional Association of Resume Writers and Career Coaches. He has written four previous books on the subject of resume writing (*101 Best Resumes*, *101 More Best Resumes*, *101 Best Cover Letters*, and *101 Best .Com Resumes*) and has pioneered the strategic, value-based approach to crafting effective resumes. Please visit Jay Block's Web site at www.jayblock.com. He welcomes your comments and/or questions, and you may email him at careerpassion@aol.com.